To John and Mar...
Womens' Weekend
October 18, 1992
Love,
Roger

TIME AND THE TOWN

A Provincetown Chronicle

Also by Mary Heaton Vorse:

A FOOT NOTE TO FOLLY

LABOR'S NEW MILLIONS

THE PRESTONS

THE NINTH MAN

MEN AND STEEL

SECOND CABIN

TIME
AND THE TOWN

A Provincetown Chronicle

by Mary Heaton Vorse

The Cape Cod Pilgrim Memorial Association
Provincetown: 1990

Provincetown Classics in History, Literature,
and Art #4

Copyright 1942 by Mary Heaton Vorse
Reprinted with corrections 1990 by the
Cape Cod Pilgrim Memorial Association
P.O. Box 1125, Provincetown, MA 02657

Case Bound   ISBN # 0-945135-04-1
Perfect Bound   ISBN # 0-945135-03-3
Library of Congress Catalog Number 90-81455

Contents

PART III

WARTIME

[1917–1921]

PART IV

DAYS OF THE LOCUST

[1922–1926]

PART V

DEPRESSION

[1927–1931]

Part VI
NEW DEAL
[1932–1936]

Part VII
A WORLD ENDS
[1937–1941]

CHAPTER ONE

Provincetown

I

CAPE COD is thrust out from the coast of Massachusetts sixty miles into the Atlantic like an arm with a fist on the end. Within the fist's shelter sits Provincetown.

When we saw it first from the deck of a boat making the trip from Boston to the Cape, it seemed to rise out of the sea. It stretched out as we approached it, low-lying and gray, its skyline punctuated with a standpipe and the steeples of churches. Gray wharves ran out into the bay. It was a seafaring place that lived from the sea and by the sea and whose one crop was fish.

When I drove around the town in a horse-drawn accommodation, I knew that here was home, that I wanted to live here always. Nor have I changed my mind in these thirty-five years, nor for one moment wished to live anywhere else, though I have been over half the globe.

The town is three miles long and two streets wide. The front street follows the bay's curve. The two main streets are woven together with a tangle of narrow lanes so numerous no one person knows them all.

Portuguese fishermen made an informal meeting place midtown. Down the narrow streets ran beautiful dark-skinned children. Old women stood in doors of Cape Cod houses, looking as though they had come yesterday from the Western Islands.

The vast harbor can hold the entire Atlantic fleet. The combination of wild and austere country bordered by the Atlantic Ocean, flanked by glittering dunes, holds one forever. You are in a populous, exciting town, yet a five minutes' walk takes you to untamed, back country. You live in a land place and yet all the ships of the sea touch here.

What I experienced when I first drove through Provincetown's long street, when I walked through the low, scrubby woods "in back" through the dunes to the outside shore, was as definite, as acute, as falling in love at first sight. The knowledge that this was to be my home forever did not come as a shock, or with any sense of surprise; it was rather as though I were invaded by the town and surrounded by it, as though the town had literally got into my blood. I had also the sense of completion that a hitherto homeless person has on discovering home.

I am not the only person who came here to spend two weeks and remained a lifetime; I am not the only one who if exiled would feel as though my taproot were cut. I have read letters written back from the Azores by homesick boys. I have seen letters from the Pacific Coast from other children—"Oh, if I could only see Provincetown again!" On holidays by boat, by train, in car, hitchhiking, the young people come streaming back. There are boys and girls who exist only for the times when they can return home.

It is almost as if this devotion to Provincetown were secret or a special sense. People either like it extravagantly or see nothing but a town of small houses built too close together, existing on a barren sandspit, surrounded by scrubby woods and inhospitable dunes, rimmed by a beach covered, more often than not, with broken bottles and dead fish. Many loathe the town on sight and see only that it is crowded, noisy, dirty; they hate the very landscape and long for lush pastures and green trees.

There seems to be no middle ground, unless one excepts those tourists who call Provincetown "quaint." And it is not quaint. It is a serious town; the way it is built has to do with the difficult and dangerous manner in which its living has always been earned. Provincetown lives by skill and daring, by luck and chance, for fishing is an immense gamble —riches on the one hand and death on the other. So tragedy, the imminence of death, and adventure prevent that stagnation which is the usual fate of small towns.

When I try to account for the passion which Provincetown rouses in the hearts of the people who have lived here, it is these elements which determine its quickened, high sense of life. People here have been nourished by beauty and change and danger.

Children who listen to tales of adventure, improbable escapes, heroism, and sudden death, as events which have happened in their front yards, find other places tame. A boy can see living heroes walk the streets, men who have been through hairbreadth rescues or who have made miraculous catches of fish, men who gamble with death to make a quick market.

If Provincetown were wiped out—my house and my town gone—I would be as vulnerable as a hermit crab without its shell. Wherever I go I carry Provincetown around with me invisibly. And as I am, so are most of those who live here.

II

In the face of the perilous business of the sea, Puritanism never took a firm grip on this end of land. People in Provincetown have always danced and sung. The Portuguese came early and brought with them their Latin gaiety and gusto for living. The blight of gentility and pseudo-culture that spread over English-speaking countries in the nineteenth century never crept over us as it did inland. When the blood of inland folks was chilling, Provincetown men were going to the Arctic and the Antarctic after sea elephants and whales, or making voyages to the West Indies and the Caribbean, and touching at the Azores.

Men who fish for a living must have an easy courage. A good seaman cannot spend his time doubting himself. If you have an inferiority complex in the face of a storm you get drowned. Those who stay alive have the habit of measuring themselves with the elements from the time they are babies.

A man who can make his living from the sea, and who has the arrogance caused by having mastered the water from the time he can walk, is of necessity a good animal. Such people have eager senses and warm affections. They take love and the joy of children as their natural right. Today's emptiness stems partly from the loss of this good animal heritage which nourishes a warm, deep, instinctive relation between men and women and a good understanding between parents and children.

People disciplined by the sea enjoy life. Intimate with the seasons, they are aware of every hour of the day. There never was a man with his good animal instincts intact who lacked either playfulness or dignity.

Men in Provincetown are not uncertain and apologetic. A man may be captain of nothing more than a small dory, but he will have that air of authority and command which makes for pride, and a man's lack of pride is an abomination in the eyes of his wife. Better by far the arrogant, proud man who—as so many of our Portuguese captains do—refuses to go to the store even for a package of cigarettes than one who meaches around looking for the bits of a split personality. Men grow well in Provincetown. At the garages, in the business places, on the wharves, and on the street there are men who look as if they owned their world.

III

Provincetown, with a finger of land thrust far out to sea, is as sensitive as a barometer to the weather of change. And yet Provincetown people have always resisted change. They fear the threat of the unknown lest their town become something else. Yet it has remained uniquely itself in the midst of perpetual modification.

Change is part of its essence. Provincetown is not static; it never stands still. Its manner of earning a living from the sea alters with new conditions and as the world outside compels. Provincetown has been changing ever since its first fishermen's huts gave place to houses.

The very conformation of its land is shifting. The dunes walk. I have a map of Provincetown which is over one hundred years old. It shows that clams are now dug where there were once planted fields and that vessels now sail over old pastures. The sea crashes down the sand cliffs to disclose the wrecks of former days. Lighthouses and life-saving stations are moved back against the encroaching sea. Islands are joined to mainland, and sections of mainland become islands.

To record Provincetown's chronicle even in a few brief flashes is like looking through a lens where history's processes are speeded up. The tempo of change is inevitably swift in Provincetown. The span of a few generations has compressed the changes of a thousand years. Land alters before one's eyes, the sea sweeps over islands where once sheep grazed. The primeval forest is hewn down, the Indians vanish, the face of the land is changed from wooded slope to desert.

Empires have been undermined and deserts created in the ancient world by the little nibbling mouths of sheep.

[13]

But in Provincetown a century sufficed to disturb the earth's crust and set the desert sands rolling.

The industry of making salt set the town whirring with windmills. A discovery of salt elsewhere ruined the industry. The time of the great whalers came. Oil gushed in Pennsylvania and drove them from the seas. Within the span of a man's lifetime wharves were built and a hundred sails brought back salt fish. The wharves were alive with their sailmakers, riggers, tryworks, ship chandlers.

Ice was manufactured, and fresh fish supplanted salt fish. The fleets of fresh fishermen adorned the bay for a brief time and these too now are gone. New methods of fishing and freezing have mechanized the sea as they have the land.

It seemed as if the soil and the sea would withstand this march of the machines, but they are being conquered before our eyes. The sea's bottom is being plowed up and the ocean's fertility gutted. Sweatshops of sea and soil are replacing the free owners of land and vessels. Fishing and farming, the last stronghold of the individual, are altering their immemorial ways. The industrial revolution, which at first passed them by, has caught them now.

Our ways of thinking and living have changed far more than the outward aspects of the town. Look back only thirty-five years and you glimpse a different world, where war was supposedly outlawed and progress assured.

An immeasurable arc of time has gone by in these years. There is no clock which can measure these leaping hours. In a few short years the world has shrunk. Thought spans it in seconds and man in a few days. We did not dream that the more placid society of earlier years in which we lived was hatching wars which would challenge the foundation of our beliefs.

The house I live in, Kibbe Cook's house, was built by people whose very approach to existence is so different from ours that it has altered beyond recognition.

CHAPTER TWO

The Cook Saga

I

KIBBE COOK carried in his small person the whole history of the rise and fall of the whaling industry. He had lived and prospered in the great days of whaling. He and his brother, Captain Ephraim Cook, owned a larger fleet of whaling vessels than any other single man on the Cape. The house I live in is said to have been built by his grandfather, and Kibbe Cook was born here and died here at the age of eighty-four.

The house had not been his for some time. It had become the property of Benjamin Lancy, a lawyer who came of a well-known Provincetown family. He was reputed to be a usurer who foreclosed mortgages on widows and orphans. Lancy was gentle-spoken, a man of culture, a strange, slight, sinister figure. While he no longer owned his house, Kibbe Cook was permitted to occupy it during his lifetime.

He lived amid the clutter of his old furniture, with the handsome gilt wallpaper sagging from the walls, bricks from the chimney tumbling down, and the conservatory, which had delighted him in the days of his prosperity, long since fallen in. The logs of his whaling vessels, his rocker, his luster cup with "E. K. Cook" engraved on it, and his sextant are still in the house.

Though he died penniless he still had the aura of wealth and achievement around him. A neighbor of mine says that when he was a little boy he thought Kibbe Cook was the greatest man in Provincetown until one day, coming in to sell blueberries, he saw the old Captain kissing his colored housekeeper who looked after him in his old age.

Kibbe Cook in his prime was reported to have been worth a fortune. They tell stories of his creditors coming to him for payment when he was poor: he would reply that he had no money but would play Mozart for them. Then the little man would take the big cello from its case and play in payment.

At one time there were eight Cooks living in a row. They built their fine houses opposite the sea and all owned shares in their whaling fleet. The Cooks then owned the land from bay to sea. Their wharf must have run as far out as Lewis' wharf, nearly as far as Railroad wharf, for at low tide one can still see its rotted stumps far out from shore.

The Cooks owned a way large enough to bring up their great vessels. They owned Pigeon's three-story building, which was used for stores. They had all the necessities for bringing up and repairing their vessels. What is now Burch's store was then their ship chandler's shop, and they owned the forge which was Clarence Snow's when we came here. My neighbors have photographs of Kibbe Cook's whalers tied up to the wharf in front of my house.

II

Suddenly the great whaling industry that seemed so secure, that had piled up wealth on the Cape, made great fortunes in New Bedford and Nantucket, collapsed, and with it the wealth of the Cooks.

So strong are the tides of change that today not a single Cook lives in the neighborhood or holds land where once the family was so powerful. When we came here, the widow of Captain Alfred Cook lived next door but one.

Next door to me is the house now owned by the Higgins,

[16]

who moved here not long after I did. We are so close together that we cannot help looking into one another's windows. Their house towers over mine. It is built on a tiny pie-shaped piece of land with almost no garden and belonged formerly to Captain Daniel Cross Cook, whose wife had insisted on building on this land.

Her cousins and her brothers-in-law urged against it, but all in vain. This domineering lady insisted that she must be on the front street. She wished, she said, "to see the sun rise over the sea from the eastern chamber."

The building of the house was an offense and an affront to Captain Alfred Cook, who lived next door. Being an old captain, he spent his leisure looking out on the bay and watching the vessels in the harbor. His comfortable house was set a little back from the road, and this pretentious dwelling cut away his harbor view. The big house was built, to the disgust of all the other seven Cooks.

"There," said Daniel Cook, when it was finished. "Now eat it! Ain't nothin' else to eat."

But on his side, Captain Alfred Cook was also building. He built an enormous arbor. It towered up above the first story and topped the second story. When it had blocked the view to the eastward as effectively as the big house blocked his view to the westward, he was seen painting it.

"What you doin'?" asked a neighbor.

"Painting this arbor black as hell, and blacker!"

Upon his own side of the "arbor" he planted flowering vines. So Mrs. Daniel Cross Cook looked out, instead of at the sunrise over the water, at a pitch-black wall. For years the arbor stood there. Only as he lay dying was the Captain persuaded to relinquish his spite.

"I'll take it down anyway after you're gone, Alfred, so you may as well take it down yourself before you go," his wife urged, hating to see him go with animosity still in his heart.

Ebenezer Cook, Kibbe's brother, who lived in the house

to my right, had the prize of the biggest whale ever caught out of Provincetown. It was taken in the south channel, southeast of Chatham, on May 11, 1843, in the little pink-sterned schooner *Cordelia* of Provincetown. The great fish was valued at over $12,000 and could he have handled it all it would have made three hundred barrels of oil and one-half ton of bone. This great whale has gone down in legend.

III

The logs of Kibbe Cook's whaling vessels tell of voyages to the South Seas and the Arctic Circle for "sea elephant and whale." Their brief, succinct, day-by-day accounts give a history of whaling, of boats stove or fluked, of shattering storms and near shipwreck, of mutiny and death. None of these voyages were shorter than ten months, and some lasted two or three years.

A sample of understatement comes from the log of the schooner *E. H. Hatfield*, September 10, 1872:

All these 24 hours fine weather and a gentle breeze from the South west at 9 A.M. saw a Shoal of Sperm whales at 10 A.M. lored both boats the larboard boat went on to a large whale and struck got the boat stove and lost the mate and one man. R. G. Craig Mate and George L. Stone Seaman. Starboard boat took the remainder of the boats crew and looked around for the lost men but saw nothing of them the boat being so badly stove she wasn't worth taking on board saved all the craft William E. Coe Seaman badly hurt got struck on the back when the boat was stove at noon kept off for hom so ends these 24 hours Latt 32.03 Long 43.15.

Not all the entries were so grim. For instance, earlier on the same voyage the mate—the same one who was killed later, incidentally—wrote, ". . . at 7 A.M. rose A Shoule of Spurme whales at 8 A.M. lored the boats *Whales in bad mood* Did not get fast. . . . So ends this day."

From the log of the schooner *Alcyone* one gathers that the crew and the cook were not on the best of terms:

Friday the 13th of Nov. 1868 All this Day fresh gales from the N by W. at one P.M. shiped a See which stove in the Galley and a pease of the bulworks on the port side filled the Gally full of water and put out the fire but the Cook managed to make tea and boil potatoes in the morning when the Cook turned out to make a fire he found that the Coper kettles with all the Cooking utensils were gone the watch was Called mustered all hands but none of them knew anything about the articles that was missing after break fast Called the men into the Cabin one at a time and questioned them the result of the investigation was that some of the men had thrown the Cooking utensiels over board, as fast as they ware examined they ware put in irons and Sent on deck Soends this Day Sor a Ship Stering S. E. Lat 31.39 Longt 40.29 W.

Sat. Nov the 14th Comes in with strong winds from the N. Ship Steering S. E. by S. testimony of all hands during the investigation it was presently demonstrated that the following named men was the gilty parties jay Charles touret, patrick hicks, henery touret, Charles S. mellard these men was tied up and after a while they Confessd that they threw the Cooking utenseels over board it was also Clearly demonstrated that they had had some bad advice from a party or parties who had ought to have none better. . . .

The record goes on to show that the men were forgiven and set to work.

IV

Once when I was in New Bedford I went to the whaling-vessel museum, whose chief exhibit is the *Lagoda* exactly half the size of the real vessel, complete from the small sofa back of the saloon to the little sewing room of the captain's wife, to the great copper kettles for trying out. The custodian was an old whaler who claimed to have been "often upset by whales." He gave a dramatic account of harpooning the whale, cutting it up, and the final trying out of the fat in the copper kettles.

During the talk it came out that he hailed from Province-town. I told him that my home had once belonged to a whaling captain, Kibbe Cook.

"Kibbe Cook!" he cried. "One of my first whaling voyages was in one of his vessels! I sailed in the *Hatfield*, Keene Conwell, master. Ha! that was a voyage!"

It was a wonderful voyage full of dallying in strange ports, touching on beautiful islands. They had not even tried to catch whales. This was a voyage! A swigging, swanking, wassailing voyage!

"Yes," he added, "I set sail in the *Hatfield* on the thirtieth of December, 1873."

When I got back, I found in the logbooks: "The *Hatfield*, out of Provincetown, December 30, 1873. Keene Conwell, master," written in a fine old hand, a circumspect account of this great whaling cruise which never caught a whale.

Whalers were built with a sofa in a tiny saloon at the end where the captain and his wife would sit. There was also a tiny stateroom known as the captain's sewing room. Many an intrepid woman went with her husband over the far seas; many a child was born in the Arctic or around the Horn. I knew such a whaler's wife, who had followed the sea many years with her first husband. She was notable, as women must be who have endured life on board a whaler with courage and patience. She had been above the Arctic Circle and had seen her vessel frozen in; she had sailed below the Arctic Circle, had seen whaleboats fluked and stove, men die and great whales harpooned and killed.

"What was your worst experience?" I asked her once.

"Well," she reflected, "it was when we were coming back after two years in the Arctic. I'd sailed a bride, with a bride's pretty clothes. Dresses were dresses in those days and not a bit of cloth tacked together. We spoke of New Bedford vessels, and I went gamming with the captain's wife and I saw she had on mutton-leg sleeves and me with my sleeves skin-tight and not a yard of cloth anywhere to make them over. *That* was an awful moment. I'll never forget it, when I saw I'd have to land in old-fashioned tight sleeves!"

V

From Nantucket to Martha's Vineyard and from Martha's Vineyard to New Bedford and thence to Provincetown, wherever old fellows gather, great stories are still told of whale and whaling days, stories of courage, of adventure, and of brutality. The life on board a whaler was so brutal that American seamen would no longer ship in them. "Crimps" carried them aboard on the American water front, for no Americans would willingly go whaling. Crews were shanghaied or recruited from the Azores.

But the whaling captains of modern times could rival the toughness of those of an earlier day. In Juan-les-Pins, in 1927, I met a retired revenue cutter captain named Jesse Glover, long in the service in the waters of the Northwest. He had much to say of the Cape Cod captains on the Pacific coast of a not-distant date.

A captain out of New Bedford gave a party to an Eskimo village and when the fumes of the party had cleared, the men found themselves ashore, while the whaler had made off with all the women of the village. The Eskimos promptly complained to the government and for two years Jesse Glover in the revenue cutter chased the New Bedford captain and his kidnaped village of Eskimo women.

"And when we came up with them two years later, I can tell you they had increased and multiplied," said Jesse Glover.

He also told of visiting another of our New England whaling captains and finding an Eskimo woman with her child aboard.

"Whose boy is this?" he asked.

"The little rat's caught in my trap call him mine," said the captain.

The last whaling captain to sail from Provincetown was Captain John Cook whose final cruise was in the *Viola* in 1913 from the Pacific coast. He wrote and lectured on whaling and would stop me on the boardwalk, dressed in his blue suit and bowler hat, a heavy gold chain on his waistcoat, the conventional dress of a captain ashore. He would be at the same time a great sea captain and one author talking to another. His exploits were greater and more tragic than his accounts of them.

Eugene O'Neill's play *Ile* is based on his story and that of his wife, Viola Cook. Mrs. Cook sailed many a voyage with Captain Cook. She made a three-year cruise with him aboard the steam bark *Navarch* from 1893-96. In 1901 she spent a fifty-eight-day spell of unbroken night in the Arctic, the thermometer fifty-seven below zero. She was quoted as saying at that time, "Sewing will help to destroy the monotony which will manifest to assert itself at times."

In 1903 she made her last voyage with her husband. After the first year the vessel was not yet "full," and the crew which had signed on for a year offered to wear the vessel down to San Francisco.

"San Francisco!" said the Captain. "We'll p'int her north till she's full."

The crew mutinied. The mate and Captain Cook stood off the crew, and the story is that one of the mutineers was whipped, in spite of Mrs. Cook's protest, and another kept in the brig for a year's time.

Mrs. Cook went down to her cabin and turned her back to the porthole and "thar she sot." She stayed there for nine months, until the vessel was full of oil and turned southward again. When Viola Cook came ashore her mind had been shaken by the loneliness and perhaps by the cruelty of her husband.

This crew, on landing, sued the Captain. Captain John Cook is one of the few captains, in all the history of the sea, from whom a mutineering crew recovered damages.

What Mrs. Cook may have seen of brutality, she wouldn't admit into her consciousness. She would be seen in her yard, brushing out the Captain's clothes when he was expected back. She would say to herself, "Never better a pair of legs went into any pants than Johnny Cook's legs," or, brushing the derby hat which captains wore ashore, "Never a better head went in any hat than Johnny Cook's head." She would hang up the Captain's drawers, remarking contentedly, "Takes a big rear to fill these drawers!"

Especially disturbed was she at the full of the moon, and one could hear her wailing hymns at such times. The story is, too, that when Captain John Cook came home he pushed heavy furniture beside the door of his room because Mrs. Cook had the habit of honing the kitchen knives razor-sharp, as the knives of a whaling vessel are kept.

Viola Cook's death was in keeping with the stark tragedy of her life. Neighbors noticed that no smoke had come from her chimney for a day or two, and when they broke in they found her on the bathroom floor, where she had died of heart failure.

VI

The early settlers found the waters of Cape Cod Bay teaming with whales. They named Wellfleet Harbor "Grampus Bay," on account of "the abundance of these species which the Indians were cutting up." Burke in Parliament made a speech called "Argumentum Piscatorio" in praise of the whale men of America who sailed from Hudson Bay to the Falkland Islands. Truro six miles away claims the first whale men and the old records of Nantucket tell that Ichabod Paddock went from Cape Cod—that is, from Provincetown—to Nantucket for the purpose of instructing in the art of killing whales from the shore.

In the old days, lookouts for whales were kept on Pond Landing at Truro at all times. When whales were sighted, the cry of "Towner!" was shouted from man to man. This cry could sometimes be heard great distances over the calm water and people came running to man the boats. "Towner" is an Indian word meaning that a whale has been sighted twice.

When the King's officers came to Cape Cod, recruiting men for the French and Indian War, they complained to the governor that all the young and strong men were off whaling.

It was in these days that the question of Sunday whaling was a hot one. One of the best known of the early ministers, the Reverend Edgar F. Clark, was asked, "If you had been out six months and had not seen a whale, and then on Sunday sighted one, what would you do?" Mr. Clark answered, "I think I should call all hands together and ask the Lord to bless us and then I would go and get the whale."

There were tremendous catches of blackfish, a variety of whale, which have also become legend. These fish rush ashore after small fish and are stranded by the receding tide.

Shebnah Rich records in his *History of Truro*:

One Sunday late in the fall of 1834, when the fishermen were quitting, some on their way home in boats from Provincetown, an immense school of blackfish was discovered. It was a time of intense excitement; most all, including Church members, joined in the race. The vast school of sea monsters, maddened by frantic shouts and splashing oars, rushed wildly on the shore, throwing themselves clean on to the beach; others pursuing, piled their massive, slippery carcasses on the first, like cakes of ice pushed up by the tide, till the shore presented a living causeway of over six hundred shining mammals, the largest number at that time ever driven on shore in one school. They landed at Great Hollow. The news reached the church just at the close of the morning service. During the next few days while the stripping was going on, thousands came to the circus. Some who had never seen such an aquatic display were wild with delight, jumping from fish to fish and falling among them as among little mountains of India rubber. The churchmembers who took a part had a formal trial; I think none were expelled.

In 1874 the largest school ever known was driven ashore at Truro. They lined the shore from Great Hollow to Pond Landing, a stretch of a mile, and their number was 1405.

Their stench was terrific while the 27,000 gallons of oil were in the making.

VII

Melville in personifying Moby Dick only followed the custom of the whalers. In story after story of whaling days the whale is endowed with a reasoned ferocity, almost human—a sardonic sense of humor and the tenderness of a human mother.

But for all the notice taken by the whale she might never have been struck [says Bullen in describing an attack upon a mother whale with a calf by her side]. Close to her side was a youngling of not more, certainly, than five days old, which sent its baby spout every now and then about two feet into the air. One long winglike fin embraced its small body holding it close to the massive breast of the tender mother, whose only care seemed to be to protect her young, utterly regardless of her own pain and danger. . . . While the calf continually sought to escape from the enfolding fin, making all sorts of puny struggles in the attempt, the mother scarcely moved from her position, although streaming with blood from a score of wounds. Once, indeed, as a deep-searching thrust entered her very vitals, she raised massy flukes high in the air with an apparently involuntary movement of agony; but even in that dire throe she remembered the possible danger to her young one and laid the tremendous weapon as softly down upon the water as if it were a feather fan. So in the most perfect quiet, with scarcely a writhe, nor any sign of flurry, she died, holding her calf to her side until the last vital spark had fled, and left it to a swift despatch with a single lance thrust.

"Whales in the sea, God's voice obey," says *The New England Primer*. If that be so, it is the only thing that these fierce and yet playful monsters obey. When Melville wrote *Moby Dick*, he crystallized the sense of wonder and terror and adventure that was in seafaring men's minds concerning the great sea mammal. From the time of Jonah to the picture of Pinocchio, when a child's fantasy suddenly turns into an epic of the onrushing fury of Monster, man's imagination has been involved with the insane bravery of hunting leviathan.

VIII

The epic chase of the whale is no more. The whaling of Kibbe Cook's day has vanished. Whaling has passed almost entirely out of American hands. The whaling methods of today are as different from those of Kibbe Cook's day as a small hand loom is from a rayon factory.

Whales today are fished for food and fat substitutes, and to make glycerin, high explosives, and soap. In Kibbe Cook's day the average whaling ship was three hundred tons' burden, the average catch three thousand barrels of oil. To get this amount of oil took from three to four years.

The so-called mother ships of today are in reality great factories. Their average tonnage is thirty thousand, their season averages no more than four months, and they catch five hundred thousand tons a year. These mother ships have every improvement. The crew consists of two hundred and forty men who have a salary and a percentage.

The mother ships have a number of killer boats which use a gun firing a one-hundred-fifty-pound bomb or explosive harpoon. The whale is towed back to the mother ship and is hoisted to the vessel, which opens a vast door torn in its side to admit the entire whale.

Eighty per cent of the whales today are taken in the Antarctic. Today's whalers cannot capture the sperm, right, and bowhead whales, which were the stand-by of the old whalers, because these mammals can hear a power boat twelve miles away.

In 1939 England had ten mother ships, Norway ten, Japan six or more, and Germany from four to six. Argentina and the United States had only one apiece. Between them they caught thirty thousand whales yearly, and the destruction has been so great that the size of the huge monsters is becoming smaller each year, and unless international action is taken the whale will become one of the fabulous monsters of the past.

CHAPTER THREE

Kibbe Cook's House

I

I STILL call my house Kibbe Cook's house, as though it were only lent me. Last summer on the New Beach I got to talking with an old lady, who turned to her husband to say,

"Isaiah, here are the folks who live in Kibbe Cook's house!"

The name of the old owner sticks partly because no one but the Cooks ever lived in this house before us, partly in the unconscious recognition that this house and the Cook family spanned an important part of Provincetown history.

Within this Provincetown, which differs from every other town in the world and which has its own individual shape, aspect, essence, is Kibbe Cook's house, which again is different from all other houses in the world.

The first week we were in Provincetown we saw Kibbe Cook's house sitting under its big willow. The shingles were gray. The big square chimney was tumbling down. A board was nailed across the sagging front door. An unkempt path led to this closed door and grass grew high around it. Bricks had fallen from the underpinnings.

It had that untenanted and miserable air of a house whose people had died and left it abandoned. For this old house was not merely closed. It was a home going begging. The front windows with crooked shutters aswing seemed to peer out into the world, seeking for a family to make it live again. It had been lived in from father to son and had been planned and built by them, and how good were its proportions, how comfortable was its outline.

All the weeks of that first summer, there the house sat; and we in our first excitement about Provincetown, when we were not out on the bay or exploring the back country, did not give it the half-hour which would have made it ours.

II

When we looked at it next year, it had been painted and repaired by David Stull, "the ambergris king," and was for sale. The first time I went through it I knew that this low-lying yellow house was my own house, the place for me to live, forever, as the year before I had known that Provincetown was to be forever my home.

Seen from the street it looks small; in reality it is ample, rambling on room after room. Its wide fireplaces can hold big logs. Its best rooms are wainscoted, and the woodwork has been fitted in with nice workmanship. The rooms have a comfortable dignity for all their low ceilings and their modest size. There are plenty of cupboards and closets. It is so old that the doors are not planed but gouged, with door latches on many of the doors instead of knobs and old H L (Holy Lord) hinges to keep away the witches.

And best of all it is a house comfortable for a woman to work in. I like to live in an old house. I like the careful, leisurely workmanship of a former day, the patina which comes only with time, the golden dimness that the years lay across a well-constructed dwelling. Above all, give me a house whose work I can do myself if need be. In a house of a shape and size where I can do my own work I am insured against fate. No home means home to me that must have paid service, a house where you must necessarily be overworked and uncomfortable if you cannot find some-one to do your work for you.

It is the true Cape Cod house, story and a half, low-crouching. The front rooms and two upper chambers give on the bay. I have looked out of my window through the years while the world changed and while sail gave way to power. Glancing out as I sit writing the bay varies from hour to hour and is never twice the same. This morning the fog was opalescent; the sun shining though dimly behind it, and in the fog swooping, ghostly, a part of the sea's dim iridescence, a faint pattern of sea gulls. There was nothing else but the thick, radiant fog, the sweep and hover of the pale birds. Now the fog has lifted, the whole bay is adazzle, and you cannot look into it any more than at the sun. But out on Long Point the fog bell tolls a warning.

I judge the house is at least one hundred and fifty years old. Its floor boards are wide. Its cedar shingles are made by hand. Its beams are joisted together. The nails are hand wrought. Among the underpinnings of the house are the masts of vessels. It has a round cellar of the kind known as "smuggler's cellar," in the middle of which is a hook. This hook was there for the purpose of rigging a tackle to let down the barrel of Jamaica rum, which Provincetown captains smuggled from the West Indies.

The house was sheltered by a great willow tree. In the middle of the back yard another wide willow tree spread its branches. The one near the house was the biggest on the Cape. People used to drive up in buggies to measure it to see if their tree had yet caught up with ours. A little distance behind the house was a barn in fair repair.

The earth between house and barn was brought as ballast in the holds of vessels that had belonged to Kibbe Cook and his father. When he was a rich man he had made a fine garden and had grown things under glass. The lot is queer-shaped, narrow in front, house crowding close to its neighbor on the front street, land broadening out like a bottle into an acre lot behind.

III

It was on this piece of land and in the house with its windows on the sea that we struck deep roots. I have had as valid and important relation with this house as a woman can possibly have with another human being. I have had it lie obedient under my hand, humming along like a fine, well-running machine. I have had it impersonal, when it was run by some person other than myself. It has got away from me like a runaway horse. I have had it jerk and jump, be cross-grained, as though it resented the lack of my proper care, and tried to thwart me and to come between me and my work.

It has had times of such stillness and quiet enclosure that it seemed an extension of myself. There have been strange and phantasmal times, when all the doors have swung wide open and people have come hurtling through until it had not the privacy of a railway station. It has been sanctuary to me and it has supported me.

I have gone far away from this house, and have seen war and famine and watched history being made, and always in the back of my mind there it was, waiting for me. Away, I can reconstruct every knothole and I remember the malignity of the former back kitchen which was always a glory hole. Through the many side and back doors of my house has poured a stream of youth, a stream of friends, from the first days until now.

IV

You can have a well-run house and not do the work yourself. You may have a perfect establishment and have your center of interest elsewhere. You can let someone else run your house or hire someone to run it, but it will be yours no longer. Your status is that of boarder. It shelters you as does any other roof and four walls. There is no longer between you and it that subtle relation which makes the sum of house plus woman, a living thing—a place called home. You must run it yourself. You must give it time and thought if not your labor.

You yourself must wind your house, and you must wind it every day. Take your mind from it a few days and it gets out of order, things get lost, dust softly mantles furniture and this even with good maids.

A woman may not be indifferent to her house. It is part of her and serves her—or it is her enemy. Your house can destroy you; the very way the doors swing may kill your peace of mind. A house must give you the blessing of peace and privacy. Your room must be a sanctuary against the world. Many a woman has gone stale, has had her family turn upon her the faces of enemies, because her room gave her no defense against them.

Not only is all my life contained here in Kibbe Cook's house, but here lingers the life of other days. I have always felt that the first owners were only around the corner. The dining room has a door which is always opening as if by unseen hands—when this happens there is a silence and someone says: "Kibbe Cook." I have always felt that the people who lived here before me had left something behind them very kind and very good which I inherited and by which I knew how to profit.

This house is a happy house. When I first came here to live many people would tell me stories about Kibbe Cook's wife and Kibbe Cook's mother. These kind and lovely women shed their radiance far beyond the grave. I have a feeling of knowing a great deal about them, though I know little beyond the fact that they were beloved by their neighbors.

Not only the Cooks are very close to me in this house, but so are my mother and my father. There are so many things that were in my own home in New York and Amherst. Pieces of furniture that I knew so early that objects still seemed to me like people with personalities of their own. The whole story of my life and of my family is told by objects in this house. There are here all the touching accumulations of different generations—pieces of china from one grandmother, a tea set from another, a secretary and chair that came from Sandwich and that had belonged to Mason White, the children's great-grandfather. There are samplers embroidered by the women of my family.

As I am the sum of generations, so is my house. In its shape and its furnishing it tells how the people of New England lived many years ago. There are here memories of the children which recur without reference to time. Now sharp and clear comes a memory of one or another of them as a baby. Again a memory of a near-by Christmas.

Our houses are our biographies, the stories of our defeats and victories. To any woman who has not a house I would say, "Go and buy one if it be but two rooms." Not to have a house is to fail to share the history of your race. Women are meant to have houses as they are meant to have children of their own.

V

A new house is a great event. Even a rented house is an adventure, but a house of one's own is an enlargement of life. That summer we were very rich. We had not only a new house; we had a new baby, Mary Ellen. We had a new boat and a new pony named Kite.

We made great plans that summer. A friend surveyed the house and Bert drew an elaborate plan with the points of the compass on it and lettered, THE ESTATE OF ALBERT WHITE VORSE. Here are indicated shrubbery, gardens— vegetables, flowers, and fruit orchard.

We went to work fencing it in. Bert dug the postholes with enthusiasm and abandon. He had zest for living which he expended upon the house. He developed an unexpected ability to use tools. Friends came and worked with us to help us make it our home.

The front room was Bert's room. He arranged the furniture, chose the wallpaper to match the long, old gold curtains that we had brought from an apartment in Paris. He built the bookcases in the corner. He bought the fine heavy homemade cherry table that seemed to belong there and at an auction bought me the homemade pie cupboard that for so many years served me as manuscript cupboard. The desk was his and the big chair. The room has different pictures but its essence has never been changed. It is as Bert planned it.

I can see him dressed in white duck and coast-guard jumper, working over the boat or around the place, Heaton at his heels. He loved the sense of ownership, of building something. I see him always young, full of this new sense of having a place of his own in the world, making friends with our neighbors, with Mr. Stull and Captain Kennedy, with Mr. Atwood and Mr. Pidgeon who were at work in the shipyard opposite, with the Avellars who were to be my friends forever, with the Seavers and young Donald MacMillan, who had then gone north only once and with whom Bert talked about Arctic exploration. He himself had been in the Arctic on a Peary relief expedition and always hoped to go again.

I have a double sense when I think of him, of all this having happened very long ago—in another world, in another existence. At the same time I see him clearly as though only a minute ago I had looked out of the window and seen him at work in his white clothes.

CHAPTER FOUR

Age of Innocence

I

THERE were no movies or radio. Marconi had only sent his first message across the ocean. In the small towns, cars as yet were only for the rich. In many small towns few private houses had bathrooms, electric lights, or telephones. Victrolas were just beginning to be common.

Lincoln Steffens was writing his articles about the boss-ridden cities. S. S. McClure went crusading; and a group of liberals led by John Philips founded the *American Magazine*. It was the day of the muckrakers. Young men spent a year in a settlement after college and girls of good family for the first time picketed in the white-goods workers' strike. Women were agitating about suffrage. There was a wave of liberal thought throughout the country. Young People's Socialist Leagues flourished in little towns in Kansas and Indiana which not twenty years later became hotbeds of the Ku Klux Klan.

In Europe the British Labour party was being born. In England, France, Germany, in Italy, there were strong labor movements. There were great co-operative movements everywhere. The social atmosphere was one of innocent hope. People everywhere naïvely believed that war was outlawed. They thought once the bosses were ousted, a good government was voted in, and the monopolies were curbed, everything would be all right. The President of the United States, Theodore Roosevelt, talked of "malefactors of great wealth." Young people were thinking of socialism. Debs rolled up a vote never equaled by the Socialist party again. The unsuccessful Russian Revolution of 1905-07 had stirred people profoundly.

New England was prosperous. Thirty-five years ago capital had not gone south and west. Foreigners—Polacks and Hunkies—were reclaiming abandoned hill farms. Spindles hummed in New Bedford, in Fall River, in Rhode Island, in Lawrence and Manchester. Small factories run by a single family dotted New England, here a hat shop, there a leather works. Shoe shops were bringing workers to Lynn. New England was still a workshop. It was an age of innocence, a time of hope.

We did not dream that the horseless carriage, the heavier-than-air machines, Hudson's little submarine, Marconi's spark that spanned ether, would burst open the seams of our society, or that our peaceful days were breeding war.

The only guns we ever imagined we would hear were the salutes fired when President Theodore Roosevelt laid the cornerstone of the Provincetown Monument built in the image of Sienna's Torre del Mangia. Why this famous Italian tower was chosen to commemorate the landing of the Pilgrims no one knows. In the Town Hall are some other designs which make one feel grateful that we have our present Monument.

We were hardly through with the great procession which welcomed home Marion Perry after his vessel, the *Rose Dorothea*, won the Lipton cup, when the cornerstone was laid. Roosevelt's coming so soon after our local parade was almost more than Provincetown could bear. The President sailed into the harbor on the *Mayflower* and rode to the ceremony in the same barouche that had carried Presidents Grant and Cleveland when they visited Provincetown.

Twenty-five thousand visitors watched the parade of a thousand white-clad sailors and marines. Seven battleships saluted and shook the little houses almost from their foundations.

Thirty-five years ago the little town was remote from anywhere. Sand roads cut it off from the mainland. It still felt itself an island as it did before the stagecoach lumbered over the sand hills behind the Eastern Harbor and linked it to the rest of the Cape. Truro, a few miles off, seemed far away and people sailed over to Provincetown to buy groceries. Low-swung jiggers with butts of fish crawled down the sandy street. There were already electric lights, but some lanes and most houses still had oil lamps. A boardwalk ran the length of the sandy road, very comfortable to sneakered feet. People walked in the middle of the road, and so ingrained was this habit that, long after cars came, folk continued to walk on the road.

In those days, there was no easy way of running around the Cape. Once one got to Land's End, there one stayed. People didn't go to swim and picnic at Long Nook or Gull Pond or Truro or Wellfleet. They did not go to movies in Orleans or to the theater in Dennis or dine in Chatham and dance in Hyannis.

II

This is how one family lived in Provincetown in those unbelievably remote days. We had spent the winter in Europe, and I came home without my husband because my mother was ill. He stayed behind to finish some articles.

After lunch the pony cart was brought around to the door and we jogged uptown for the mail. At that time, my boat was more important to me than my house. She was a Swampscott dory, twenty-three over all, named the *Molasses II*, and as swift as anything in her class. As soon as I got home that spring I put my boat into the water.

After I had scraped and sandpapered the bottom, I scraped the lofty mast and the bowsprit. In the sun the spars

[37]

were smooth as glass and the new varnish reflected the sun. Now I puttied all the seams. The boat was lapstreak and difficult to calk.

I went to Sy Swift's for a new putty knife. Sy Swift's was an old-fashioned ship chandlery with a touch of general store. The store smelled comfortably of new rope and tar and paint. You could buy ships' lanterns, blocks, anchors, and all the things that belong to fishing boats. You could also buy gardening tools, hardware, leather for harness, buckles, besides all the things that are needed for the house —pots and pans, kettles, brooms.

We were always going back and forth and stopping to talk to Sy Swift, who read largely and was a homespun philosopher. His conversation made his store a neighborhood center. There were always men sitting around on kegs of nails or coils of rope, discussing fishing, the weather, the state of politics, or yarning about the days of whaling and grand banking. Mr. Swift was a stout man and lame with rheumatism. He sat on a high stool before his old-fashioned "pulpit" desk. He would stump around looking deliberately for the rope or the putty or the paint I was purchasing.

He would never make out a bill. "Guess I ain't made up your last bill," he would say, when we were leaving town for the season. " 'Bout fifteen dollars, I should judge, maybe more, maybe less. . . ." He died in 1914; I had been trading with him for seven years and I had never had a complete bill.

His reluctance to make out a bill for small amounts was a relic of the old days when a vessel was fitted for a long voyage and paid off when she got back. The bill finally sent me by his estate was twelve feet, nine inches long, the sales slips pasted one on the other and rolled like a papyrus. I owed, after all these years, seven dollars and some odd cents.

This bill was a record of a careless life. "One wooden rake," it read, "two lbs. nails; one lb. putty; two quarts outside white; one kettle; one whip; one wooden rake. . . ." The rake had been lost and replaced. "One pair of oars," it would relate; "one gallon triple spar varnish; one trowel; paper tacks; one sieve; two quarts outside white; one wooden rake; one whip." And so the whip as well as the rake had been lost! And so it went. And so my life went.

I painted the inside of the boat ocher. Neighbors and strangers lent a hand or gave advice. Fishermen in squidgy rubber boots, a big fish held by the gills, would stop to make remarks and end by taking up a paintbrush. All the fishermen in the neighborhood helped paint the *Molasses II*.

Mr. Pigeon came over from the shipyard and tapped in a little oakum here and there. After Mr. Pigeon had calked my boat—which he did with none-too-good grace, since he hated "puttering jobs" and liked to see some long stretch of work ahead of him and not, as he said, "twitch off from one thing to another"—I painted its decks. While Mr. Pigeon was stepping masts and reeving on the sails, I wet my halyards and coiled and recoiled them so they wouldn't kink.

Now I made my last journey to Sy Swift's for green copper paint and at last painted her bottom. There she was, body white as a gull, bottom glassy green, and her shining yellow-ocher decks and ocher inside only less bright than her mast. I rubbed up all her brasswork, her traveler, her pin, her blocks, the name *Molasses* on her side, and her stern. With pride, Wilbur Steele and I finally launched her—paid out her sheet, saw her sail catch, and floated off on the shining surface of the bay.

Often we raced the *Ginger*, Margery Seaver's boat. "There goes the switchel," Mr. Seaver would say. Switchel is a New England drink composed of ginger and molasses, which used to be brought to the men haying in the fields.

III

The yard was always full of children. Our children were part of that company of young ones always fringing our beaches. I would sit under the tree and, pretending to read, watch the children. They became so used to me that they would go on and talk as though I were not there.

I made notes of their conversations and games and gestures. I made no comments on these notes; I put down what I saw. I wrote page on page of their talk and squabbles. For many years I made these careful notes on how children act, and drew upon them for my book called *Growing Up*, which was first published under the name *Adventures in Childhood*—and also for *The Prestons*.

I knew very little about the affairs of my house in those early days and had as yet formed no intimate relation with the details of the house's running. I loved it, it cheered me, but my task at that moment was to make money to run it and to look after the welfare of the children within it.

All the doors of the house opened outward easily. I stayed in my house just long enough to get work done. No sooner was my work finished than we were out in the boat, or swiftly, sneaker-footed, over small trails across the dunes for a swim on the outside shore; or we would take our supper across and have it on the outside beach with Captain Cook at Peaked Hill Bars.

We would go blueberrying with the children, go on picnics, or sail across to Long Point. We would plunge into the small thick woods to come out on the dunes, which give the illusion of immensity and space. There were a savor to life and a meaning to these explorations. We saw for the first time ponds and trails and desolate, beautiful stretches of the outside shore. There was a cosmic quality to our joyousness which was nourished on sea and woods— the companionship of children, gaiety, and gigantic meals.

I knew that I would never be quite so happy again. For

a moment, a few brief weeks, I had recaptured the happiness I had as a girl, and yet I had the freedom of a woman. I had my house and my children, and yet I had the gaiety that comes only, as a rule, with the irresponsibility of youth.

IV

The feeling that I would never again be so free from care was a premonition. That fall I joined Bert in Morocco. He left there to take a position which had been offered him, while I remained behind a few weeks to finish assignments I had with *Harper's* and *The Outlook* in Italy and Spain.

When I got back from Europe, Bert and my mother both were dead. After these many years, it is still hard to write down these words. My old father came home with me to live. Neither my father nor I gave way to grief. It was rather as if we had been too stunned to feel anything.

My father worked every day in the garden. His garden at home had been his whole life. He had retired from business young, having made a small competency; and in all the months of the year in which one can work outdoors, he had worked like a laboring man. By the time we would come to breakfast at eight, he had done a half day's work. He gave away his flowers, vegetables, and fruit lavishly to anyone who wanted them.

The year before, he had visited us and planted spiraea, phlox, forsythia, golden glow, and bittersweet. Now I was going on with these beginnings, which because of Bert's death could never be as we had planned them. I was lacking some extra ounce of energy to do this. I had not drive enough to earn our living and keep up my boat and the place too.

The surface of life seemed very much as it had been. The routine of the house was the same. It was its inner content which had changed. I knew that I must keep the normal sequence of things going. I must ride along on this momentum of events or the family would be disjointed and fall into its component parts of unrelated individuals going to no destination, just as a home can become chairs and tables and odds and ends.

My father enjoyed company and liked living in a big family, so I kept the house full of young people. Wilbur Daniel Steele, who was a distant cousin of Bert's, was often in Provincetown while my father was with me. Sometimes he stayed with us and sometimes he had a room on the wharf over at the Avellars'. He was beginning to write the stories which were to give him a permanent place in our literature.

Bertha Carter, so long Lillian Wald's right hand, spent her summers with us. There were a great many very tall young men about besides Wilbur and Arthur Hutchins. Lucien Kirtland, who has spent years of his life exploring strange parts of the world, came often. "Red" Lewis came and went. He had written his first book and knew already what road he wanted to take. Both he and Wilbur Steele were trying out their talents, beginning to tap their unknown strength. I have seen a great many people begin writing and have heard some brag they were going to be great writers. Those I have known who later became famous were so busy working they never bragged about what they were going to do.

Howard Brubaker and Paul Wilson would rush down the Cape for a week end of sailing. That was the year we bought a cabin sloop we could cruise in, which we named the *Wilmarato* after Wilbur Steele, Arthur Hutchins, myself, and Tony Avellar, who were the four owners. She was a tublike craft, twenty-eight over all, and could sleep four easily. She was slow in stays and leaked, but we thought her beautiful.

One of our visitors was an older man, Colonel Church, one of the last of the gentlemen adventurers. He had been a colonel in Díaz' army, and when he died without writing his memoirs a section of border history died with him. He was in ill health, thin as a death's-head, with a grace of manner and an elegance that were like something stepped from Bret Harte. He appraised the younger men as to what sort of soldiers they would make. "Now you take that lanky, redheaded boy, Lewis," he would say; "he's the fellow of this lot who'd have staying power in desert warfare."

"Why not Wilbur or Tony Avellar?" I'd ask, for Wilbur had been the outstanding athlete in his class in Denver University and Tony had never known how strong he was. He never had to. Once he and his brother Albert started fighting and it took six men to hold him.

"Oh, they're all right," the Colonel would drawl in his soft, southern voice, rolling a cigarette with one hand, "but that long, redheaded fellow—he'd *never* stop!"

V

I only gradually understood that the whole life of the children and my father rested on my unaccustomed shoulders. I began to realize that my writing was no longer something that helped along someone else, a sort of lucky by-product of our joint lives, but the only way I knew of earning a livelihood.

That summer of adjustment, of learning what it was like to be the only responsible person for a family's welfare, of taking up definitely the household and the house, meant an entire shift, a slow revolving on its axis of my whole approach to existence. For all the rest of my life, there was work to be done first. Working was no longer something I could take up or put down when I wanted.

My attitude toward my house changed at this time. Before this it was an ornament to life and it meant a way of living I wanted and liked. Now my house was the Rock of Ages.

It was then that it became such a part of me that I entered into intimate relationship with it, an intimacy that

[43]

works both ways and often blinds me to defects. As a busy person is not conscious of his own wrinkles as they come, so I am unconscious of the encroaching shabbiness of my house. The fact that it needs paint is an academic question with me, as inevitable as hair graying. When my children bring up these defects I have the same astonished indignation as I would feel were they to reproach me for gray hairs or wrinkles.

Every afternoon when I got through work, about four o'clock, I would walk in the back country with the children or ride Kite. I would jog along by Shank Painter Road, explore distant sand trails, or ride on the Truro moors.

I would see my house, the long ell lit up, sheltered by its two big willow trees, and I would feel affection flowing toward the home that sheltered the people I loved. There they were, all underneath its hospitable roof, and I was outside looking at them, responsible for them. And I would pray to be strong enough and good enough to keep all those in Kibbe Cook's house in health and peace.

CHAPTER FIVE

Old Customs and New

I

THIS was the time when the many-seated "accommodation," which jolted around town, was a social institution. The accommodation got its name by accommodating people. It was our only means of transportation and it stopped everywhere. Mr. Kendrick was my favorite accommodation driver, and it was wonderful to listen to him tell stories of the Cape.

"See that," he'd say, pointing to a thunderhead. "That storm ain't a-goin' to hit us. It's goin' to divide. Part's goin' down the outside, an' part's going down the Bay; they'll join together in Buzzard's Bay." And that, sure enough, is what that thundercloud did.

Mr. Kendrick never did follow the sea any to speak of, he said, "Never did go fishing more'n a matter o' eighteen year." It was hard to see how he made any money. Now he would stop for a crippled woman.

"Can't take money off her," he would say. "She's crippled." Children would get on and off.

"Can't take money off them. Little shavers like that!" Regularly at a certain hour a Portuguese woman and her children would get on. Taking up a whole seat, they would ride solemnly to the end of town and back again.

"Couldn't take their money. Lost their pa last year. Drowned. They got to get a outin' *sometime*." Or perhaps Mrs. Bangs or Mrs. Turner would say politely,

"Could you wait just a minute while I get a spool of thread, or post a letter?" The accommodation would accommodate by drawing up and waiting any reasonable time. Or Mr. Kendrick would say,

"Excuse me, folks, my Aunt Nellie's bakin' blueberry pies this afternoon, and I'm a-goin' to get me a piece." He would come back with blue teeth, remarking genially, "Had a cup o' coffee for me, too!"

There was great indignation in the town when the first motor accommodation charged up the street, no longer stopping for people's errands. If the accommodation didn't come past, ladies frequently "jumped a jigger," the low-swung fish truck.

II

General delivery robbed this town, as many other towns, of the great social event of the day—getting the evening mail. This was the time that boys called for their girls, to go upstreet. All the town was there. Friends met once a day; the east and west ends of town came together.

Another great get-together was the weekly Town Hall dances. Then one saw a cross section of the whole town. Everyone—Portuguese, New Englanders, summer people—danced together. The old people danced and the children danced. The old sea captains came, too. How our young people used to enjoy the turkey trot and the bunny hug, dancing cheek to cheek on a place no larger than a dime!

The winter dances given at Masonic Hall, when the Charmelita was danced by the old Portuguese, were among the gayest and pleasantest of all the dances.

"Refreshments" used to be served under the Town Hall. "Under the Town Hall" is also the euphemistic way of saying "the jail."

The town officer would be on guard as we filed past for our ice cream, crying in a pompous, official voice, "Ladies will please not offer ice cream to the prisoner! Gentlemen will please not offer cigarettes to the prisoner!" while the prisoner would smile back sheepishly at his friends who called to him,

"Hey, Sy! What you ben up to?"

The great costume dances of the Beach Combers and the Art Association were the great affairs of the summer. People spent weeks getting their elaborate costumes ready, while today they are inclined to go in sunburn and a sash. These balls were times of spiring excitement. It was then that explosions occurred. There would be arrests, imbroglios, and scandals. Summer came to its end with a bang. Said one old lady, primly,

"Social Vesuvius, I see, has erupted again."

III

In those days there would be no morning that the town crier did not pass the house, limping and ringing his bell, and crying,

"No-tiz! The Centenary Church will hold a supper tonight at seven-thirty! A—full—at-ten-dance—is—re-quested!" Or, "No-tice! There will be a sale at Duncan Matheson's store Fri-day and Sat-ur-day!" Other things were cried, such as,

"No-tice! An-to-nio Viera's wife has left his bed and bo-ard, and he will no longer be re-spon-sible for her debts!" And yet stranger things would be cried. Public meetings, auctions, entertainments, and personal affairs. When Halloran, a friend of George Cram Cook's, left the *Chicago Tribune* he sent a dollar to have it cried through the streets that he was now going to free-lance. And in wartime, when one of the captains of a big one-hundred-twenty-five-foot schooner was criticized for flying the Portuguese flag, instead of the American flag, at half mast—the signal that he wanted bait—it was cried,

[47]

"No-tice! Manuel Costa wants it known he is as good an American citizen as anybody, having had his citizenship papers thirty years, and three boys to the front. But he will fly the Portugee flag or any other flag he wants at half-mast when he wants bait, bait having nothing to do with patriotism!"

The town crier was an institution with us for many years. There were two criers, one a tiny man with a great voice. When the last crier retired from business, there was no one to take his place, and the custom lapsed, to be resumed as a publicity stunt.

IV

When I first came to Provincetown a front yard that was not ornamented with a few whale's vertebrae or a whale's jaw looked bare. Garden beds were bedecked with large shells, disabled dories were turned into flower beds, and morning glories climbed up the great bleaching jaws of whales. One day Mr. Berry beckoned to me in a friendly way, indicating he had a new treasure to show me. Mr. Berry was our first antique dealer.

"Come inside," said he, "I got somethin' to show you; I got sumpin' you need. Your yard don't look stylish. You ain't got no whale's vertebrees. You ain't got a whale's jawr in your front yard with morning glories twining on it. You ain't got a figurehead. Why, you ain't got nawthin' in your yard. It ain't right for a woman like you. What you need is this ship's bell."

He pointed to a huge bronze bell almost as tall as I. "That'll give tone to your yard, that'll give you style, that'll shut folks' mouths when they start talking how plain your yard is. Why, the other day I see you down on the water front, hollering out to sea like any common woman for your kids to come home to dinner. Now you buy this ship's bell. Come noon, you can ring eight bells stylish and you

[48]

won't have to holler on the end of a wharf no more. Won't be any other house around here that's got a ship's bell. Come noon, you ring eight bells and your kids come right in."

By this kindly advice I saw that I had not lived up to what was expected of me.

V

The arrival of the excursion boat begins the summer. Although we have been joined to the mainland by railway nearly seventy years—until 1940, the year when it stopped crawling twice a day to our land's end—there is still a feeling that with the coming of the excursion boat, we are again joined to the world. It is a reminder of the time when Provincetown was accessible only by vessel. Up and down the water front every siren gives tongue. Cold storages blare, vessels blow their foghorns, and the little fishing boats wind their conchs, to welcome the excursion boat which spills out upon our streets a tide of city folk.

As long as I can remember, the coming of the boat meant a ballyhoo. Barkers stood outside of restaurants, chanting the beauties of their lobster dinners, their chicken dinners, their five-course dinners. Banners with the names of eating places were strung across Commercial Street.

In the old days, a single officer, ununiformed and with but a badge, sat on Long Wharf and directed traffic with a stick, shouting, "Keep to the right," as the boat unloaded its passengers. He sat because he was a paralytic. The town felt that this was a fine job for a disabled man. Then new town fathers were elected; and to the indignation of many, the paralytic was retired and a man with only a lame leg was substituted in his place.

Later Captain Henry Whorf became constable. He would go cranberrying with me and my mother-in-law. Instead of looking for the wild bogs, we stole cranberries from a culti-vated bog.

"What if someone sees us?" I asked him.

"Couldn't do nawthin'," said Captain Whorf. "Couldn't 'rest us 'cause I am the constabule. I'd tell 'em to charge them cranberries to the town pump!"

VI

The old *Dorothy Bradford* had a sign which read, PAS-SENGERS ARE NOT ALLOWED IN OR OUTSIDE THE LIFEBOATS. As you got off the boat you noticed, in the barbershop, one which read, HONEY IN THE COMB. The barber used to say to me,

"See, all city folks cra-zee. They stop, they laugh, 'haw, haw, haw!' I think they ain't seen a bee." And he never found out what the crazy city people were laughing at.

Even today an ambiguous sign near the Atlantic House reads GUESTS HEATED.

Near a house on Bangs Street was a sign which read, HENS TRAVELLING OVER THIS PROPERTY ARE NOTIFIED THAT THEIR OWNERS WILL BE PROSECUTED, while a sign in the cemetery warned, CRUISING OVER GRAVES AND RESTING ON THE STONES STRICTLY PROHIBITED.

In John Francis' general store was a touching sign express-ing the character of one of the kindest men who ever lived.

The sign read, PLEASE LOAF IN THE BACK ROOM.

In the spring everyone went to Truro Maying. Fishermen went, and tough kids came back with fistfuls of exquisite pink-and-white fragrant blossoms. People go Maying now as much as they ever did.

Decoration Day has its own special observances. After the graves have been decorated, the band and a procession with wreaths go down on the wharf, and again the prayers are said for those lost at sea and taps are sounded. There is no year when the sea has not drowned some of our men.

And for those so lost, the children then throw lilac wreaths into the bay.

Christmas to New Year's is our great moment, and the loveliest of all local customs was *Menin Jesu*, the little Jesus, brought by the Portuguese from the Western Islands. The older Portuguese people once kept open house from Christmas to New Year's. Every window in their houses had a candle behind it. A home ablaze with lights meant that everyone was welcome, whether or not he knew the host. Indeed, the most welcome and honored guests were the strangers.

In the front room was a pyramid of graduated shelves. One candle on top, on the next shelf two saucers of sprouted wheat; on the next, two candles; on the next, four saucers of sprouted wheat, and so on. These represented the Resurrection and the Light. At the bottom was a crèche of little figures brought from the Western Islands. To everyone who came was given a tiny cordial glass of homemade wine— beach plum, elderberry, or dandelion—and a tiny cake.

The Avellars and ourselves used to go at Christmas through the western part of town, seeing down a dark lane, under willow trees, houses brilliant with light. In the distance there was the sound of music and singing. The ships' bands of Portuguese instruments, from the great vessels, went from house to house, saluting the *Menin Jesu*. In some houses they would have both the *Menin Jesu* and a Christmas tree—the Christmas tree, with its presents, looking materialistic and Teutonic beside the sprouted wheat and the lights. Little by little the custom of *Menin Jesu* has vanished. Only a few very old people still celebrate it.

The custom of lighting houses remains, and the Christmas holiday joyousness. Children stream home. Friendships are renewed. Our streets are strewn with light. Christmas trees gleam from each house, and lights from each window. People go back and forth visiting. There is a feeling of true gaiety, of kindness throughout the town.

CHAPTER SIX

The Coast Guard

I

THIS town has always been a great recruiting ground for the coast guard. The first ten years I was in Provincetown, from 1910 to 1917, there were 156 wrecks between Monomoy and Race Point. Between 1880 and 1903 there were 540 recorded wrecks; 500 were recorded officially between 1843 and 1859. During the nineteenth century there were far more than 1000 wrecks on the Cape Shoals, and how many thousand people perished I do not know. No wonder this coast is known as the graveyard of the Atlantic.

Yet it was not until a comparatively late date, in 1874, that the Life-Saving Service, as it was then called, was established. Peaked Hill Bars was the station I knew best, though we often went to Race Point and Highhead and even to Wood End. We would sail across the bay and then cross the sandspit to the station.

Of all the stretch of dangerous coast Peaked Hill to Monomoy was the most fatal. This coast got its bad name early. Champlain named it "Mallebarre" in 1602. Men's lives and the treasure of ships' cargoes have been poured on its shores ever since.

It was almost impossible for a sailing vessel to clew off the lee shore from Race Point to Monomoy. A vicious current runs along this elbow of the Cape, making anchorage impossible in a wind. There is no cove or harbor on the shore for sixty miles where a vessel can take refuge.

The process that originally made the Cape is still going on. Off Peaked Hill there is a treacherous outer bar and an inner bar. Charts help not at all, for the bars are constantly shifting and changing their position.

The space between the two bars is a practically sure death-trap, and vessels once caught there are pounded to matchwood. Vessels of all nationality, cargoes of every kind, and countless lives have been shattered on Peaked Hill Bars or the other Cape shoals from Race Point to Monomoy. Fishing vessels were the most unfortunate, for this dangerous coast was in the direct route to the Grand Banks.

The lifesavers' motto is *Semper Paratus* (Always Ready). Their unofficial motto is "You gotta go but you don't have to come back." The stories of the rescues, of the inhuman danger in getting men alive off a wreck going to pieces on the bars, are an epic. In the last quarter of a century a thousand men are said to have been rescued along Peaked Hill Bars alone.

There is masculine monotony in a coast-guard station which reminds one of life aboard ship. Turn and turn about the men cook and clean and scrub and paint. There is a sense of a spacious and leisured life, of time accurately spaced, ample for the specific duties of the station.

All coast guards make wonderful husbands. They are carpenters, painters; they know how to putty a window and how to plumb; how to build a fire, how to keep a cookstove clean, and how to cook.

Come sundown the beach patrol goes out. All night long, from sunset to sunup, the beach is patrolled. Two men go out in opposite directions. At a halfway house they exchange checks with the men coming from the other coast-guard stations. In winter this night patrol is a difficult thing. In some winds the beach lifts itself bodily. The coast-guard windows become ground to a white crust in a few hours. The sand grinds off the skin of a man's face. There are patrols that have to be made on hands and knees.

The patrol carries with him Coston lights and flares with which to signal an answer to a vessel in distress. The calm routine of boat drill, breeches-buoy drill, the lookout, and the patrol, the work of the house, the peaceful monotony, is broken by the paroxysm of storm, of frightful, imminent danger. A pitting of man's puny strength in the work of rescue against the incalculable fury of the sea.

The visitor to these lonely stations sees a peaceful life, men working on an appointed rhythm, spacious, faultlessly clean rooms, men looking out to sea, and, more often than not, whittling gadgets. They seem like ordinary men, some of them already beginning to age. Yet they have to be men of special skill and courage, for the frightful effort of launching a boat through tremendous breakers, or recovering half-drowned or drowned men from the sea, or facing the unpredictable fury of storms, wind, and sand—this part of their work people do not see.

There is no station which has not its authentic stories of incredible valor. It is a dangerous business and there are few years when there is not some fatality among the coast guard.

II

For all time, to me, Captain Ambrose Cook of Peaked Hill Bars will be a picture of a splendid coast-guard captain. He was a tremendous figure of a man—wide-shouldered and deep-chested. He died with his boots on. On his way to a Masonic reunion, he asked for a drink of water, fell forward, and was gone. He would have preferred to go like that, still in the center of life. He was an enemy of all triflingness in man or boy, though in no way a martinet. He had a gift of authority which a man has to have to attain the position of captain of a station.

There was no finer way to spend an evening than to take a few lobsters across to Peaked Hill Bars, in time for supper, for the Captain dearly loved to pick a lobster. We would sit around the campfire, with Mrs. Cook, to hear him spill out tales of wrecks and rescues and of adventure on the sea. His springboard might be a statement like:

"You may call me weak or you may think me womanish, but I'm thutty years cap'n of a station, and I can't yet step on a drownded man in the dark without getting a shiver!"

I went out to Peaked Hills after a wreck had come ashore just over the line of the Race Point territory—for the coast is divided into sections, so much belonging to Peaked Hill, so much to Race Point.

"Well, you almost had another wreck last night, Cap'n Cook."

"Yes," he answered. "But it's time Cap'n Sam Fisher got suthin'. I got nineteen wrecks this year, and seventeen goddam corpses. Cap'n Sam Fisher got only four wrecks and nary corpse. I tell you, you be s'prised how a corpse can bother the cap'n of a station. First there's all your reports. Then there's the permission to be got from the township an' the county for removin' the body; then all his clothes have got to be numbered an' docketed and sent to headquarters. Then, when you're through with all the red tape and finished with him at last, then don't his family write you and ask, 'What was his last words?'—and him whelmed by a thutty-foot wave maybe! . . . No, I don't like truck with corpses."

After he had retired, I asked him, "Do you miss the station, Cap'n?"

"I do an' I don't. I miss it someways, but I'm glad to be shunt of drownded corpses for good."

In the old days at Peaked Hill station there would be always a group of the coast guard whittling, on a bench over by the sand bluff looking out to sea. Glimpsing what to a landsman looked like a speck of white on the horizon would make Mr. Silva turn to Mr. Higgins and say,

"Seems like the *Harvester's* got a new tops'l."

[55]

The coast guard naturally despise summer visitors who get themselves nearly drowned.

"Come a summer man one time last week," said Captain Cook, "and we was sittin' here whittlin'. Sez, 'Think you'd take a dip sometime.' We didn't say nothin'. Sez he, 'Think I'll go and take a dip myself, it's a fine day for swimmin'.' We sat whittlin' and didn't say nothin'. He goes and swims. Putty soon he comes back and sez, 'Well, I had a dip.'

"I sez, 'I seen ye dippin'.' Comes on to blow that night, gets to be an undertow. Next day he goes in again. He don't heed our warning. Sez I, as I brung him to,

" 'I seen ye dippin' today, too. Lucky for you!' "

III

Captain and Mrs. Cook were at the station from sundown to sunup for July and August. We would see Daisy, the life-saving horse, clumping past on her big sand-splayed feet— for even horses get sand-footed on the dunes—taking Captain and Mrs. Cook to the station. Daisy wandered at will around the dunes, but when the dinner bell rang she'd come with her tail up in a smother of flying sand. If she got to the door before the men got to table, she got fed. Otherwise she would have to wait till they were through. And wait she would, snuffling and puffing at the window and peering in. She would wander up behind some stranger when a group of visitors were looking at the lifeboats and affectionately nuzzle a shoulder. If a woman screamed at this, Daisy would look at her with soft, reproachful eyes and walk off with dignity. She had a passion, too, for drinking out of fire buckets.

"That ding-dong hoss don't give a goddam if the hull station was to burn," Captain Cook would grumble.

In the early morning I would find a bunch of roses inside my fence, thrown over by the Cooks on their way home at sunup. These roses are Japanese roses, the sort that never grow wild, and yet there is a bank of these flowers growing out near Peaked Hill, in a tangle of bayberry. Cap'n Cook was "cruising around in back" when he "smelled a sweet scent." It was a bank of these roses growing where no rose had ever been seen. "You lay a course nor' nor'east from the hen coop and you'll come on 'em." The coast guard slipped these roses and transplanted them to their own gardens. How they came here no one knows. Captain Cook said that a bark from China had been wrecked upon the bars some years before; but how this exotic rose had managed to grow as far inland is a mystery, but here it is today in half the yards in town.

IV

Captain Cook would tell stories of wrecks and rescues and legends. One was the story of the coast guard who, when on his rounds, saw a girl "loomin' out of the fog." He was surprised to see anyone so far from the town. The next night he was on patrol he met her once again. This time she seemed so beautiful he realized that he had fallen in love with her and begged her to meet him again. She smiled at him in a dubious fashion and answered,

"I'll meet you again, soon," and vanished in the fog.

Within a few nights there was a wreck of a Portuguese vessel from the Western Islands. There, on the deck, a child in her arms, was the girl whom he had met in the fog. She recognized him and waved to him.

As the surfboat came alongside "on the heave of the wave," she threw the child to him. Then she jumped, but missed the boat and was swirled away in the churning sea. Then he realized that it had been her spirit he had seen and that she had given him the child in trust. The child proved to be an orphan and he adopted the little girl and brought her up.

Another story of his was about the captain of Chatham

Bars who saw a vessel in distress and recognized it to be that of his own sons. The storm was so fierce, the risk so great, that he refused to let the surfboat be launched and to risk eight lives against those of four.

"I don't hold with mutiny," said Captain Cook, "but them men woulda been justified, yes, sir, by gee, they'da been justified, if they'da took out that lifeboat against their captain's orders."

With the flames of the fire reddening his face, Captain Cook would tell stories of his predecessor, Captain Isaac Fisher.

"They don't make cap'ns like him any more. Not a cap'n on the coast could have made a rescue like he did in '95, when the four-masted *Job H. Jackson* struck on the inside bar. Like many another before her she was tryin' to make Provincetown Habbor. It was January and ice made as soon as the spray struck. She'd blown out her sails. Waves had stove her deckhouse, her canvas was snappin' so you could hear it like gunfire above the waves.

"Her men had climbed the jury mast and there was six of 'em covered with ice and a-freezin' to death in sight of Peaked Hill. He tried firin' lines to her. The surfboat stood by. They reared the breeches buoy. It waren't no good. If the men were to be rescued 'twould have to be with the surfboat. It was a sea you couldn't lainch a boat in. The men stood by, for the sea to moderate.

"Wasn't no other human bein' could have lainched a boat. Wasn't no other human bein' had the skill to lainch the boat nor to clear it. Cap'n Fisher he stood there. He watched them ice-covered men a-hangin' on to the jury rig.

" 'Goddam it to hell,' says he, 'I can't stand this no more. I am a-goin' to resk it.' And he did, by gee.

"No one had never seen steerin' like what he done with his oar. There wasn't ever no man ever pulled better. The lifeboat was swirled clear around. She stood straight up on her starn, but Cap'n Isaac Fisher he whipped his oar around and headed her straight again. A wave fell away from her so swift she was hangin' in the air and you could see sky between the wave and her bottom, but he held her head on, he held her firm. She come up to stabbad of the wreck and he steered her in amidships alongside and rescued every one of them dang men who would have froze to death."

Among the most tragic wrecks of Peaked Hill Bars was that of an Italian vessel whose captain and mate were found, by the rescuing coast guard, with their throats cut.

All the crew were arrested and taken to jail. They spoke no word of English and in all the town there was only one person, Mrs. Seaver, who could talk Italian. To her the crew protested their innocence. The captain had mistaken Highland Light for Race Point. So great was his shame at having wrecked his vessel and, as he thought, lost the lives of his crew that he and the mate committed suicide. It was his first command and he wore around his neck the Saint Christopher medal his bride had given him to keep him safe from harm.

V

For many years wrecks added to the income of all the Cape towns. During the Revolutionary War a vessel from England came ashore between Peaked Hill and Race Point with every imaginable necessity. "A providential wreck," the people called it, as they garnered merchandise of every kind.

The *Provincetown Banner* of 1857 remarks coyly, "Our village has presented quite a cottonish aspect during the present week, the cargo of the *Jenny Lind* which came ashore at the back side of the town being conveyed across to our port to be reshipped to Barnstable," the *Jenny Lind* being a cotton ship.

There was the wreck of the *Coriolanus* in 1863. This vessel was full of dress goods and sewing materials of every

[59]

kind. When I first came here, ladies were still sewing with *Coriolanus* thread; some even had *Coriolanus* dresses.

In the early days here, all lifesaving was a voluntary matter often done by the wreckers. With so many accidents along the coast, wrecking was then a profitable industry. Good livelihoods were made in dragging for anchors that had been slipped. So profitable was wrecking, the stripping of ships, the beachcombing of wreckage on the back side, that the popular sentiment of the Cape was against making this coast safer.

On September 5, 1854, Emerson recorded: "Went to Yarmouth Sunday 5th, to Orleans Monday 6th; to Nauset Light on the back side of Cape Cod. Collins, the keeper, told us he found obstinate resistance on Cape Cod to the project of building a lighthouse on this coast, as it would injure the wrecking business. He had to go to Boston and obtain the strong recommendation of the Society."

Kittredge, in his history of Cape Cod, excuses the Cape Codders by reminding us that in 1854 almost all of the Cape's outstanding men were shipmasters or otherwise engaged at sea, so that this opposition was not representative. He speaks of the valor of the wreckers and maintains, "The only flaw in the character of these amateur lifesavers is that they seem to forget their humanitarianism in their zeal for a profitable job. In this respect indeed they furnished the last echo of the triumphant yells which in earlier and robuster years had accompanied the plunderer of wrecks in their pell mell rush to the beach."

The Massachusetts Humane Society preceded the coast guard and in the early part of the nineteenth century established shelters at intervals along the coast. The Reverend James Freeman, one of its founders, wrote a pamphlet giving detailed instructions to shipwrecked seamen how to find their way through the hollows to some farmhouse or where the huts were located. These shelters were supposed to be provided with firewood stove and water. Thoreau in 1849, coming down the Cape, chanced upon one of these inhospitable shelters. Sand had sifted in, water there was none, nor fuel. It was a frightful coast to be wrecked upon on a dark night, with no way of finding a town.

In spite of opposition of early days, one by one the lights which guard our coast were established. Bell buoys warned of reefs. The type of lifeboats was improved. The men at sea are now perpetually watched over. Within sight of Provincetown are four lights. The great first-class light, Cape Cod light, known to us as Highland Light; Race Point light, which is not seen from the harbor side. Wood End has a red eye and a slow, thirty-second flash; and Long Point, a fixed white light.

Drastic changes have been made in the coast-guard service.* Vessels are so much safer that Highhead, Peaked Hill Bars, and Pamet stations have been closed. With the passing of Peaked Bars station an epoch ended. It is as though some security has gone, as though the ships at sea and our own vessels were not so safe with the watchtower at Peaked Hills empty.

* Recently the status of the coast guard has been changed. It has become part of the navy.

CHAPTER SEVEN

History

I

THE history of the coast guard is the core of Provincetown's history. For Provincetown's history is the story of men against the sea. Dates by which this town reckons time are those of great storms. Here stories are not of battles, but of the long-sustained fight for safety at sea. This has been true from the time when Leif Ericson, son of Eric the Red, first discovered Cape Cod in 1003, hundreds of years before Columbus ever thought to span the ocean. Other Norsemen followed and even attempted to colonize. An Icelandic manuscript states they found *"Strand-ir lang-ar ok sand-ar"* (long and sandy strands) as they sailed along the back side of the Cape.

There is in Provincetown a mysterious wall in the cellar of a house, called the Norse wall. It is made of stone the like of which is not found in these parts and it was so deeply overlaid with sand that it is evidently of ancient date. The Norsemen came on rock ballast, but no one has yet traced the origin of these stones.

Before the Norsemen were the Indians. By Dr. Hammett's laboratory in Truro there is a great kitchen midden where Indians came to feast on shellfish and left behind them vast mounds to tell of their feasting, together with bits of broken pottery, arrowheads, and other vestiges of their merrymaking. Indeed, you cannot scratch the Highland anywhere without coming on Indian relics.

The notion that the Pilgrims came to a wilderness is far from the truth. Within the deep forests were organized communities of peaceful Indians. The dozen or more of Indian villages and tribes were connected with one another by well-worn footpaths. Later these footpaths became our roads, the King's Highway followed the old Indian way, the transverse road from Hyannis to Yarmouth was a famous Indian trail.

An Indian culture underlies our lives from one end of the country to the other. Indians have named our mountains and rivers. We borrow their designs. They spun over the entire country a frail web of names and legends which keep them forever in our memory.

II

Basque, Breton, and Norman fishermen touched here, as did French and Dutch explorers. Long before its settlement as a town it was the meeting place of adventurous fishermen who drank rum with the Indians. The definitive discovery of the Cape is given to Captain Bartholomew Gosnold who, on the twenty-sixth of March, 1602, set sail from Falmouth, England.

As they cast anchor off what seems to have been the coast of Maine or Cape Ann, they were visited by eight Indians who amazingly came to them "in a Biscay shallop, with sail and oars, an iron grapple and a kettle of copper." One of them was "apparelled with a waistcoat and breeches of black serge, made after our sea fashion, hose and shoes on his feet; all the rest (saving one that had a pair of breeches of blue cloth) were naked." Gabriel Archer, one of the chroniclers of Gosnold's vessel, reports,

"We had again sight of the land, which made ahead, being as we thought an island, by reason of a large sound that appeared westward between it and the main, for coming to the west and thereof, we did perceive a large opening, we called it Shoal Hope. Near this cape we came to anchor in fifteen fathoms, where we took great store of codfish, for which we altered the name and called it Cape Cod."

A half-dozen nations named and renamed Provincetown. On one map, Provincetown Harbor is called "Fuic Bay." It has been called "Niew Hollant" and "Staten Hoeck"; Barnstable Bay "Staten Bay," and the sea north of it "Mare del Noort." The shore between Race Point and Woodend was called on one map "Bevechier."

On Captain John Smith's map of New England, Provincetown Harbor is known as Milford Haven, while Massachusetts Bay appears as "Stuart's Bay." Prince Charles tried to change the name of Cape Cod to Cape James; no name stuck but Cape Cod. Cotton Mather was right when he said, "Cape Cod is a name which I suppose it will never lose till shoals of codfish be seen swimming on its highest hills."

III

The Pilgrims made their first landing in Provincetown Harbor. They looked out upon a thickly wooded shore of virgin forest. *Mourt's Relation* records, "After many difficulties in boisterous storms, at length, by God's providence, upon the 9th of November, we espied land, which we deemed to be Cape Cod, and so afterward it proved." That winter was a bitter one. The ice in the harbor was said to be eighteen feet deep. In the ebb tide the ice floes sank to the harbor bottom and strong winds and incoming tides piled them high on the beach in icy ramparts.

The Pilgrims landing found here fresh water and a cache of corn which they took, as well as a copper pot. This valuable utensil they threw into the Eastern Harbor. The white explorers and settlers, as they landed, were well treated, aided, and helped by the Indians, without whose kindness the colony would not have survived the winter.

Here in this harbor the Compact was signed. I have heard Edward Everett Hale say as he later stated in writing, "The Compact which was written and signed in your harbor is more important than the Declaration of Independence and was its father."

These are its words:

In the Name of God, Amen. We whose names are underwritten, the loyal subjects of our dread sovereign, Lord King James, by the grace of God, of Great Britain, France and Ireland, King, Defender of the Faith, etc., having undertaken for the glory of God, and the advancement of the Christian faith and the honor of our King and country, a voyage to plant the first colony in the northern part of Virginia, do by these presents, solemnly and mutually, in the presence of God, and one another, covenant and combine ourselves together into a civil body politic, for the better ordering and preservation and furtherance of the ends aforesaid; and by virtue hereof do enact, constitute and frame such just and equal laws, ordinances, acts, constitutions, and offices from time to time, as shall be thought most meet and convenient for the general good of the Colony; unto which we promise all due submission and obedience. In witness whereof we have hereunto subscribed our names at Cape Cod, the 11th of November, in the year of the reign of our sovereign Lord King James of England, France and Ireland, the eighteenth, and of Scotland, the fifty-fourth, Anno Domini 1620.

Birth and death attended the Pilgrims' landing. Peregrine White, the first white child born in the colony, was born in Provincetown Harbor. Part of the White family settled in Sandwich and there are descendants of his living in Provincetown to this day.

Governor William Bradford's wife, Dorothy, was drowned in the harbor and three others of the little company lost their lives during the Pilgrims' brief stay. There is a tablet in their memory in the old Winthrop Street cemetery. The women brought their washing ashore on a Monday, so washday has been Monday since then, and America's first washday is commemorated by a tablet in the West End of town.

[65]

For years after the Pilgrims' arrival this land's end was the meeting place of fishermen, of freebooters, and beachcombers. Tradition has it that the first settlement, a huddle of fishing shacks, was made here in 1680. But so roisterous were these first settlers that pernickety Truro petitioned "to know if the Cape Cod was in their jurisdiction or not, so they could deal with some persons." The precinct of Cape Cod was incorporated into a town named Provincetown in 1727, but the title to all lands still rested in the Commonwealth.

The end of the Cape, the fist beyond Eastern Harbor, was named the Province Land. On the Province Land anybody could squat. Even when the town became prosperous and good houses were built to replace the meager fishermen's huts of the early days, there was still a portion of it called Province Land where anyone might put up a house. There were no deeds beyond that of quitclaim deeds until late in the last century, when an act of the legislature had to be passed to invalidate the titles of the land.

There is still a Province Land. Large tracts of sand and woods belong to the "Province" of Massachusetts. Even today people may put up buildings upon it with the consent of the government. A State Forester lives here who looks after the Province Land and plants trees and beach grass to keep the dunes from shifting.

It has always seemed to me that there has remained in Provincetown something of that communal feeling that in the early days decreed that land belonged to anyone who used it.

Fishing drew more and more people to settle here, but for a few years Provincetown was a tiny though prosperous community with ten dwelling houses besides some store buildings. The first meeting house was built in 1717 near the Old Cemetery. But the war and the privateers discouraged the inhabitants. After the Revolutionary War, only three families remained of what had been a thriving village, though Provincetown and the rest of the Cape either privateered or mustered out their men to fight the British.

The rich fishing grounds tempted people back, and twenty-five years after the Revolution the town had grown to a settlement of more than two thousand people. A contemporary newspaper account describes Provincetown thus: "Houses, saltworks, and curiously built hovels, for uses unknown, are mixed up together. It would seem that the God of the infidels, which they call chance, had a hand in this mysterious jumble."

Saltworks lined the beach. These were turtle-back contrivances of wood, and the water to fill them was pumped up by many windmills which dotted the shore. The discovery of cheaper salt elsewhere ruined the salt industry.

Shebnah Rich, in his history of Truro, gives a lively description of the town of those days:

The quaint village hugging the crescent shore for three miles, hundreds of windmills from the shore, wharves and hilltops all in lively motion and commotion, the tall spars of the vessels in port, the steep hills rising like huge earth-works of defense, and the low sandy point half-coiled around the harbor, anchored at the tip by the lighthouse of old Darby fame, was a sight that could be seen nowhere else in this land, and was more like the old Dutch and Flemish pictures of Hobbema and Van Ostade than anything I have seen.

V

War always meant ruin to Provincetown. Sixty miles out to sea it is vulnerable to enemy attack; its handsome harbor tempts the enemy ships. If one were to chart Provincetown's prosperity, in each war there is a profound dip. The War of 1812 set the town back once more. Few names of Provincetown men appear on the rosters of the navy because the Provincetown fishermen were all privateering.

Provincetown was blockaded in the War of 1812 and a British frigate lay at anchor in the harbor. The little vessel *The Golden Hind*, Captain Small, Master, ran the blockade and kept Provincetown revictualed. At that time the Eastern Harbor was already silting up and vessels of any draft could only go in at high tide. There was, however, a hidden channel through the willows, so at "low tide in the dark of the moon" *The Golden Hind* would slip into the Eastern Harbor. By the time the frigate nosed in the next morning there would be no sign of *The Golden Hind*. It had been sunk in the deep waters. They would ballast her up and pump her out and calk her good and out she would go again, under the very nose of the British.

As yet there was no road in the town, and people used the beach. In 1829 the Provincetown minister, Mr. Stone, wrote to a friend, "Would you believe that there is a town in the United States with 1800 inhabitants, and only one horse, with one eye? Well, that town is Provincetown, and I am the only man in it that owns a horse, and he is an old white one with only one eye."

It was at this time that a Provincetown boy cried, at seeing a horse drive along, "Hey, Pa, how does that craft steer without a rudder?"

The town began to take on its present aspect after the first quarter of the last century. In 1838 the first wharf was built, and in the next ten years thirty wharves sprouted "Up Along" and "Down Along." Sixty years ago there were fifty-five wharves. It was about this time that the front street was laid out.

The cutting of the road made a commotion that all changes have caused in Provincetown, and passionate was the conflict over the sidewalk. So bitter was the feeling that many refused ever to use the sidewalk and walked on the sand of the road all their days. The debate in town meeting lasted a week, and it is interesting to note that Mr. Abraham Chapman, who was for sidewalks, was challenged as not being an American citizen. This handy missile was thrown early.

VI

The church history of Provincetown is full of drama and movement. The little community of fishermen were not Calvinists, and the General Court at Plymouth served notice on them "to show cause why they did not entertain a learned orthodox minister of the gospel to dispense the word of God to them as required by law." The General Court also donated one hundred fifty pounds for the pious purpose of building a church, which was erected on Meeting House Plain. It was near North Meadow Gut, now called Gosnold Street, and Shankpainter Pond, which extended close to it in those days. It was not far from what is now Saint Peter's, the present Catholic church.

In November, 1793, they voted to build the new church on the same site which was called the Old White Oak because of the oaken timber cut from Provincetown hills. They sold stock in the meeting house at forty shares and auctioned the pews to the highest bidder. After the Revolutionary War there was a revolt against the severe Calvinist doctrine and the strict domination of the church. Methodism was strong on the Cape in early days. Its slogan was "Salvation is free," and it stressed Christian living rather than the orthodox opinion, the spirit in place of the dogma. The Orthodox tried to kill the rising Methodism.

The town meeting led by the elders voted no Methodist church might be built in Provincetown. The Methodists brought a lumber schooner from Maine with timber for building their church. The Orthodox seized the lumber, hacked it to bits, and crowned Town Hill with a blaze of it, and tarred and burned a Methodist minister in effigy.

The Methodists brought another vessel of timber and guarded their building while it was constructed. Soon they

[69]

built the Methodist church with spire and bell which stands
to this day. One of the Methodist ministers, Epaphras
Kibbe, was well beloved and from him came the name
Kibbe Cook, former owner of my house.

VII

From 1830 until after the Civil War was the greatest
heyday of the Cape. Prosperity in Provincetown reached
its high point in the eighties. Vessels crowded beside the
wharves. Truro alone built forty-nine one winter. Her
shipyard had three vessels at a time in the stocks. Packets
plied from the Cape towns to Boston, carrying fish and
coming back with supplies. Other packets made New York
their port.

Fleets of whaling vessels went to the Arctic and Antarctic
after sea elephant and whale. Riches flowed from whale
oil and bone and ambergris. A fleet of bankers sailed to the
Newfoundland Banks after codfish. Provincetown grew and
prospered, put out more and more wharves, and finally became the richest town per capita in Massachusetts.

The seventies were a great time of building. In 1873 the
railway first connected Provincetown with the mainland.
Amid rejoicing it had crawled slowly and carefully down
the Cape. Wood End light was built, and the Life-Saving
Service after all this time was first established. New schools
were erected. St. Peter's Roman Catholic Church was established, fulfilling the dream of the Portuguese population.
When the town house on Town Hill was burned a new
High School was at once put up. A fine library was built,
remarkable for those days in a town of this size.

In 1885 the fishing industry was worth nearly a million.
After that there was a slow decline. Fresh fishing superseded
salt fishing. The activity on the wharves lessened. Summer
people from Boston began to come, forerunners of a mighty
horde. The wharves began to fall into disrepair. The coop-

ers and riggers, the ship-chandler stores, folded up. People wanted to eat fresh fish instead of salt.

The great fishing towns on the Cape had lost their harbors. The sixties saw their decline. Truro, which so long had outstripped Provincetown, became a quiet village. Her houses were abandoned when no more fish came to her wharves. Wellfleet had ceased sending vessels for whale or to the Newfoundland banks. Provincetown remained a great fishing port and built cold storages and increased the number of her weirs to bait the fishing fleet. The whaling days brought the Portuguese to Provincetown, and these island people have taken root here. They were by nature great seamen and great fishermen. By 1896 there were two thousand Portuguese in Provincetown and the fishing was already largely in their hands.

In the ten years which preceded the beginning of this chronicle, the Provincetown fishermen began experimenting with gasoline. The fleet of the fresh fishermen, the one-hundred-foot schooners, which fished George's Banks was increased, but the wharves declined and the population was dropping slowly but steadily.

Each year a few people made what they thought was "a discovery" of this unique fishing village.

VIII

Provincetown still fought great storms and gales. One might almost say that Provincetown's written history begins and ends with a hurricane and is punctuated by great gales.

In 1635 a hurricane like that of 1938 swept through New England and the lower Cape. "The wrecks," says Governor Bradford in his record, "will remain a hundred years, and the fury of it will frighten men from the seas forever." It mowed the forest like a scythe and its twenty-foot tide flooded thousands of acres.

In 1728 the Cape at Orleans was torn apart. The sea

[71]

swept through to the bay and whaleboats rowed in the channel. A line gale came bellowing from the South and piled wreckage on the edge of the lower Cape in 1815. The gale of 1841 stands out, when the graveyard of Truro was filled with the men who perished in that single storm. A white squall struck in 1853, so suddenly that twenty-one vessels between Highland Light and Race Point went down. The tidal wave which rolled up Provincetown Harbor in 1871 carried the ship *Nina* bang into the post office. Disasters of former days still brood over the town. A hundred years ago the thirteen Cape towns had 914 widows. Truro alone lost between six and seven hundred men at sea between 1780 and 1880. With a population of less than two thousand there were one hundred and five widows in 1837. Storms still mean danger and death to Provincetown.

People in Provincetown still date happenings from the November Gale of 1898. That night the wind blew over one hundred miles an hour. It is very hard for a person who has never been in a gale like this to understand the force of wind. A sixty-mile gale will lift a beach bodily. In the face of a much less violent gale it is impossible for an ordinary person to walk across the sand dunes. During the Portland gale the wind blew with such force that all the windows on the seaside of Highland Light and the Marine Observatory were shattered as though by gunfire. It blew so hard that men were lifted off their feet.

That night the *Portland* foundered somewhere off Highland Light. There were one hundred and seventy-five aboard her and everyone was lost. By ten o'clock at night the bodies and wreckage were coming ashore. By next day the coast guard was swamped by the terrible work of salvaging the dead. Five hundred persons were drowned at sea in this frightful storm. For days drowned creatures were cast up all along the coast, especially between Highland Light and Race Point. Maybe it was at that time that

[72]

Captain Cook got his aversion to stepping on drowned men in the dark.

In the town itself, not a chimney was left along the water front. Vessels were lifted up from their moorings like cockleshells and tossed across the beach. A heavy dory was picked up and rolled like a hoop by the wind, over and over, along the length of the water front. It was found at the other end of town from which it started.

More than twenty boats perished within the harbor's shelter. The sea rose until the front street was covered with water, until the water went to the back street and people were taken from houses in boats. It is high tide and an easterly gale that mean peril for Provincetown.

It seemed as though the entire town might go—as though the sea would whelm houses, vessels, and town together. While the hurricane of 1938 was less severe for Provincetown than the Portland gale, had there been high tide and a slight change of wind when the hurricane struck, the town might have been washed from its moorings.

Men fought this loss of life with lights, buoys, foghorn, and bell. Steam lessened the frightening loss of life. Canals cut the danger down. Radio beams guide the fishing fleet today. Yet the battle is not won. Unpredictable hurricanes can yet tear the vulnerable Cape apart and overwhelm its towns.

CHAPTER EIGHT

The Onion

I

PROVINCETOWN is like an onion. There is here layer on layer, whorl on whorl. Three civilizations have met here and formed a unique strain. The old New Englanders, the Portuguese, and the summer folk have made a town individual in the world.

Layers of different cultures are superimposed one upon the other, yet each layer exists as part and parcel of the whole. There is the world that is represented by the Women's Club, the Research Society, and the Library Association. There are summer people owning houses, who yet are counted as summer folk. There are art students, actors, and writers who come to do serious work. Transient summer visitors, the vacationers, people off on a good time, who come to Provincetown with an idea that here anything goes, make up yet another world.

The town ranges from austere beauty to garbage and tin cans on the beach. Endurance and heroism are commonplace and it relaxes from these high virtues to bawdy moments.

How can one give the whole content of a town so complex? More, I think, by telling its stories than any other way. You can't tell all the stories. There are some that would lead to libel. I would like to say of a local man, maybe, that he was a life-loving man, full of gusto. He had fun when he stepped over the line and got mixed up with women. Getting mixed up with other women was mixed up with music and drinking and church. So he lived and had a good time and his sins didn't trouble him much. I would like to make a picture of such a life-loving, sinful, and likable man, but you cannot say in our times that such a man liked women and liked to drink sometimes without making him mad and his wife madder.

There are other stories which would be so rich, so full of an earthy stink, you would not be telling the truth because you would detract attention from the greater truth, men's minds being what they are. Yet I imagine that it is only because I am afraid of public opinion that I do not write everything.

It is the kind of town where men time out of mind have risked their lives unhesitatingly to save others, where few grow to manhood without courageously having faced danger; while on Town Wharf you may hear a gusty joke shouted from one vessel to another.

The town is alive, moving in a deep stream which sometimes overflows. The mixture of summer people and town gets too strong and goes off in a roar. People get a disease called Augustitis when the mixture gets too rich. There comes a time when the combination of sea and the sweeping color of the dunes—the exciting and excited people who get together on the beach and the heady salt air of Provincetown—all combine to give one a special sort of intoxication.

The hot roar that some Provincetown drinkings have let off are part of its life. Great wassailings are not isolated or meaningless. They are the explosions of society. They are the signs and symptoms of a vital civilization. Here they are sporadic, for Provincetown is not a drunken town. It works too hard and too dangerously in earning its living.

Provincetown from its earliest days has been freer, richer in life than its neighbors. Back in 1727 Truro asked to be severed from Provincetown because of the goings-on there. Provincetown gloried in this separation and laughed to itself. Truro sitting discreetly in the folds of her moors looked down her nose at Provincetown and still does. The Cape early wrote, in legend, its opinion of the folk on Land's End.

Captain Jeremiah Snaggs lived up the Cape and he did not die in the odor of sanctity. The story is he tried to escape the devil by various devices. He dodged the devil in Barnstable, he eluded him in a hollow tree in Orleans, he escaped from him in Wellfleet by putting a jack-o'-lantern which looked like him in a tree, but in Provincetown the devil caught up with him.

"Well," said Captain Jeremiah, "you caught me fair and squar'. Whar do we go from here?"

"Go?" said the devil. "Nowhar. Ain't we to Provincetown?"

II

The Portuguese brought here their Latin warmth and gaiety. "The southern rose has been grafted on the sturdy oak of New England neatness and thrift." They are woven into the fabric of the town whose discreet white houses shelter a south-European population. Dark faces on the streets, beautiful dark-eyed girls who love color and who make the streets gay with their bright dresses and their laughter. The daring of Portuguese fishermen is part of Provincetown's legend. The silver Lipton cup, trophy of the fishermen's race, was won by a Portuguese captain. Less hard-bitten than the Spanish, harder than the Italians, great storytellers, great jokers, are the Portuguese. The interwoven strand of the Portuguese and New England culture is so close you cannot tell where one begins and the other ends. The meticulous neatness of New England, the passion for perpetual painting and papering, has been adopted by the Portuguese but they don't "fight it day and night" as do some New England housekeepers. This valuable virtue has been softened by their zest for living.

Their customs have been intermingled with ours. Deep Portuguese speech is everywhere on the wharves, in the streets. The same boy who shouted to his father in Portuguese will talk in the most unadulterated New England accent about the "habbor" the next minute. They are so much a part of the town that today one could not imagine Provincetown without them. Good looks, gaiety and daring are their inheritance, yet they have the conservatism of the Latin. In many houses girls are brought up strictly, boys must be in early, but at home they have a good time.

III

At one end of the incredible gamut of character in Provincetown one might place Captain Cook of Peaked Hill Bars, a great lusty, life-loving man with the quality of command that any captain must have. He was a rock of a man, a landmark of the old days, salty, humorous, just, impatient, a man of stature.

Mrs. Cook was one of the many older women I got to know who had suffered too much from the sea. She had lost at sea father, brothers, cousins. It had taken toll of one generation in her family after another, so she never looked at the sea if she could help it.

Every sunup she drove in from Peaked Hill Bars. Every sunset she drove back again, through the dunes' splendid desolation, but she turned her eyes away from the blue line of ocean. She had never seen the breeches-buoy drill or the boat drill. She had watched that horizon too often from the time she was a girl for the return of menfolk who were not to come. She was a lovely woman and a notable one, but permanently saddened by tragedy.

The story of Mrs. Mary Mooncusser was also an emanation of Provincetown, but she seems to me to stand for the revenge of all the frustrations of New England and of small towns. I can tell her story because she is dead and if she had any relatives in this town I never knew it. This all happened a quarter of a century ago or more.

One summer I needed a cook, and a gray-haired, neat, elderly woman applied for the place. She dressed in gray percale with spotless white aprons, and the respectability of her appearance and speech could not be exaggerated. There was never such a tidy body, the lamp chimneys shone, the kitchen was scrubbed, she was a good cook. One day one of my neighbors came to me in embarrassment and said,

"I think you ought to know about Mrs. Mooncusser, with a young girl taking care of Mary Ellen and all. Poor thing, it's not her fault, her husband got her into drinking ways, but once in a while, not often, well, she drinks, and then she doesn't know what she does and she lets in anybody—fishermen, old men, little boys, she don't know." It was like finding a sewer where you thought there was a brook.

So one day when Mrs. Mooncusser didn't come, I went to her house with a lame excuse that I couldn't afford two girls any more. I knocked on the front door and no one answered, and I went to the back door and it gave under my knock. I went through a spotless kitchen into a spotless living room. There was an antimacassar on the padded back of a rocker. A tortoise-shell cat sat purring in the sun. Geraniums bloomed at the windows. You could have "et from the floor," as the saying goes. Everything was order and peace in the bright morning, and I called,

"Oo-hoo, Mrs. Mooncusser!" And out from the bedroom off the sitting room came Mrs. Mooncusser.

Her neat hair was drawn back from her face and done in the accustomed gray knot. She was so old that already she had the gray look of age. There was nothing whatever the matter with Mrs. Mooncusser except that she was stark naked, and she said,

"Good morning, Mrs. Vorse, sit down," and she herself sat down and rocked gently, with the morning sun streaming in on her bareness.

And I said, "Good morning, Mrs. Mooncusser," and then told her what I had come to say.

"I was expecting this but I'm sorry to leave you, Mrs. Vorse, because you've been very nice to me," said she, rocking gently, her bare feet padding the floor.

And I said, "I am sorry to have you go, Mrs. Mooncusser, as you have been very nice to me too." Then she got up and I got up.

And she said, "Let me let you out the front door, Mrs. Vorse."

So standing there, naked, and apparently unconscious of it, she opened the front door, and I went down the neat path bordered with zinnias. She watched me go. The personification of the dark things hidden in all small towns.

Captain and Mrs. Cook are one pole and tragic Mary Mooncusser is the other pole of Provincetown contrasts. The arc described between the two is vast. The Cooks were characteristic of many Provincetown men and women of their day. There was a high level of character, breadth, and integrity among them—men and women who had nothing mean and nothing narrow in their natures. There were men of wide culture like Mr. Gifford and Mr. Atwood the ichthyologist. The Cape had a long tradition of broadmindedness. Provincetown early broke away from the narrow Calvinistic doctrines. Methodists and Universalists here found an early foothold. These men and women were liberal without laxness. They had an interesting society that one may find reflected again and again in the writers of that period. This readiness to listen to science, the ability to suffer the pain of a new idea without flinching, was a characteristic of the Cape.

IV

The pull and haul between those who wish to keep the cake of custom intact, the conflict between the conservatives and the progressives, can be studied in detail in Provincetown. Changes always came and every innovation was resisted fiercely.

There is a dominant note of liberality which shows itself in the public-spirited policy of the Nautilus Club, the tone of *The Provincetown Advocate*, and in many church societies.

Yet the showing of a Spanish Loyalist film was forbidden, and a beloved pastor found it best to resign because he sponsored a lecture by Granville Hicks. Films which have been passed by the Hays office have been forbidden here. The laxness of certain groups of summer visitors has stirred up reaction.

"You see an awful lot of queer people here," said a summer visitor to an old resident, looking toward two fishermen in oilskins, tramping down the street, each with a big cod by the gills.

"Sure do," replied the ancient, looking toward a crowd of robust summer girls, shorts over their fat hams, "but come Labor Day they'll all be gone."

I heard two fishermen say, as they watched two ladies in pajamas with big magenta designs that resembled eggplants wandering up their sterns, "What queer birds you see when you ain't got your gun!"

Sometimes this mixture of summer pleasure seeker and the delicate New England culture of old ladies forms a strange picture. I remember one year during the Art Association Ball when the refreshments were in the Unitarian

Church. It was at a time when people went to great pains for their costumes. It was the time too of the greatest license in manners and morals of the prohibition, flaming-youth era. Hula dancers and Indians and young men dressed as the seasons, with bunches of grapes around their middles and vine leaves in their hair, all tripped across to the Christopher Wren church where the ladies served ice cream and cake to the revelers—two different worlds meeting in the assembly room of the church.

The town itself is split into the East End and the West End. Way-up-along is to the westward, Down-along to the eastward. The road Up-along has two sharp turns caused by Lancy, who when the front road was laid out declared they'd have to saw right through him before they could saw through his saltworks.

"Well," said one of the selectmen, "get your saw," but Lancy stood firm and so the road has two perilous turns.

East End and West End used to fight each other in mighty battles. Boys from the East End used to come in bands to rescue a lone East End boy beaten up by the West End gang. Up in the honeycomb of back streets to the westward there is an almost unbroken Portuguese colony, where many an old man and woman speak but little English, and dark-skinned beautiful children line the streets.

The miles that separate east from west are long miles. My next-door neighbors had living with them an aged relative whom I knew only as Miss Philomena and whom I saw as a delicate, aged profile against a window. When she died, Mrs. Higgins said,

"Poor thing, she was lonely here. She didn't get to see her friends often, so far from them."

"Where did she live?"

"Oh, she was from the westward," Mrs. Higgins said. It was as though she spoke of a prairie woman planted in the Eastern seaboard.

Today, with cars, "the westward" is more accessible to

us, but the East End and the West still have each its own specific flavor and the old rivalries are not yet dead.

V

The town is built on a fabric of societies and clubs. The Board of Trade, looking out over the water, is the businessmen's club, just as the Sandbar to the westward is the fishermen's club, but each talks fish and each talks politics. The Eastern Star has a strong chapter, and the wife of the captain of Wood End Light has never missed a meeting for years. She has come over the breakwater through blizzards and gales which churned the harbor into foam and into which no boat could venture.

There are the Anchor and the Ark, the Odd Fellows and the Lions, the Companions of the Forest and the Daughters of Rebecca. There are the Art Association and the Beachcombers, the artists' clubs, Visiting Nurses Association, Red Cross units, Taxpayers Association, Library Club, the social clubs like the Friday Club and the East End Club, one for town dwellers and one for summer folks. The Nautilus Club is the women's club, the Research Society where descent from a *Mayflower* ancestor is required for membership. The military societies, the Legion, Veterans of Foreign Wars, Women's Auxiliary and Women's Relief Corps. Church societies, Catholic Daughters, Knights of Columbus, Sisters of St. Joseph, the Guild of St. Mary's. Get Together and Willing Workers. Now to these are added a dozen relief and defense societies. There's no person in the town who doesn't belong to one or another of the church societies or the Masonic orders or the social clubs.

These many societies, spread throughout the country as well as in Provincetown, are but an attempt to substitute something for the communal life and worship which so short a time ago were the basis of society. Getting together is one of life's necessities. The need to work and play and worship together is as fundamental as to rush together to the defense of one's country. Every civilization has had its communal dances and songs. Here in the western world we have fallen apart. There is nothing to satisfy this elementary need which gives strength to the lonely, isolated spirit of man.

This is our weakness. Our strength does not multiply in our daily lives. There is a creative force in people doing things together. The great creative power of the multiple spirit is almost cut away from us.

The vitality of Fascism has been the recapture of this need, so unfulfilled in the isolated modern world. Fascism has perverted to its uses one of the most generous and powerful instincts of mankind. In the western world we reach out for pathetic substitutes. We prance around in trappings and insignia, while we wait for a master voice or war to bring us together again, thinking and working together, for a common creative purpose.

VI

In the welter of summer and winter, town and off islander, Portuguese and New Englander, there are certain consoling, sober constants; the fishermen in sea boots, a fish by the gills. The troops of hard-faced, brown-bodied, sea-going little boys who haunt the beaches in droves, following the same pursuits year after year. There is always a new intent band of them and they give the effect of never having changed. There is another constant, the old ladies, who emerge from invisibility come Labor Day. They wear hats that do not change with the years and look more like a stern, rockbound coast than a head covering. The old ladies must die and the gnome-like boys grow up, but there is an everlasting new crop of them, acting alike, dressing the same, though the years change.

Notable old ladies have made part of Provincetown's

history. When I came here, people still talked about Kibbe Cook's wife and mother. Mrs. Paine, who helped me with Ellen once, was a woman no one could forget. Stately and dignified, yet salty and liking a joke, she was the product of a worth-while civilization. Many of the older women when I first came here had traveled far seas with their husbands, like Mrs. Lavender who, when her husband fell ill, navigated his packet to Havre, France. The children traveled with her and she taught them about the stars of heaven and the wonders of the deep. She informed their minds with great literature, and when the time came to go ashore to school they were far ahead of other children in their knowledge. There were other women who remained at home and learned to master anxiety and wait with serene hope long months of uncertainty until they became tempered as brave women do in war. In these softer days, they have passed down to their children many of their virtues learned in this difficult school. They had the good manners which come from faith, dignity, and kindness, and the meeting of disaster with courage. No wonder so many of the older women's fame is part of Provincetown's heritage.

VII

It's a wide swing of the pendulum between this hard core of Provincetown's character and the summer explosion which explains why Provincetown is conservative and unconventional at one and the same time.

When you try to tell of the moral climate of a town you think in terms of people first and events next, though maybe it should be the other way around. Given a certain sort of society with its institutions, its organization, you get certain results in character. The civilization which is just ending was punctuated by cycles of panic and depression. It swung a desperate pendulum between great fortunes and destitution. The corner of land, Provincetown, has reflected each depression. It went down like a sounding lead in each war. It bred people resistant to disaster. It has been invaded by a noisy company of summer visitors.

Yet the carousers are as May flies dancing over a fruit paring, in contrast to the growth and fruiting of an orchard. The May flies dance and die, the trees follow the august march of the seasons. So Provincetown follows the seasons' march, living austerely by the weather, for weather here has meant life and death, prosperity or poverty.

Listen in to any knot of men talking together on the wharves or loafing on the steps of the bank or congregating to the westward in the Sandbar Club. They talk about one thing—fish. They talk about fish and the prices of fish. They talk about their recent catches, the disasters that are the fate of fishermen. The older men talk of the days of fabulous catches. There are a few among the old men who have been whaling. They are getting as rare as Civil War veterans. There are plenty who've been banking. Many of them who are now dragging or seining or dory fishing have known the glorious days of the fresh fishermen, the hundred-foot, two-masted schooners. But whatever form of fishing these men have known, or what vessels they go out in today, they've all gambled their lives for fish and they've all known the adventure of danger.

"Fish are queer people. Don't let anyone tell you different," Captain Kendrick told me. "No one but God can fathom their ways. Take bluefish. Up to 1890 bluefish was a big catch hereabouts. Ain't been none but a sprinklin' sence." Nor to this day have the bluefish ever returned. Some essential food they sought has vanished. Why? No one knows. We are surrounded by mystery when it comes to fish.

So men talk less trivially than elsewhere, if not less bawdily. For when they talk of fish they talk also of life and death and danger and heroism and mystery.

Analyze the social structure of a town with its component

[85]

parts of artists, fishermen, scientists, explorers, businessmen, writers; give its physical aspects, a fist-shaped sandspit thrust out to sea; tell of the roar of its summer crowd, and yet there you have nothing to explain this piece of land called Provincetown.

Craftsmen come here to work in wood and in silver and glass and in an almost infinite variety of materials. Two schools of art have fought desperate battles among themselves, and pictures that have been painted here are scattered among the museums of America. No town of its size has so many names in *Who's Who.*

Tell its stories both heroic and shameful, observe its contrasts, analyze its complexities, and still one has not the answer as to why Provincetown has been so fruitful a spot or why it has bred great sea captains and explorers, writers and painters. For out of its gurry and out of its courage and its surrounding beauty has been made a town that is quick with creation.

CHAPTER NINE

Provincetown Houses

THE very houses are subject to change and move about as though not anchored to the land. In most places when a man builds a house he builds it and there it stands, practically unchanged, keeping the same form in which it began, and almost invariably in the same place. This is not true in Provincetown. Houses there do not remain upon their foundations. Formerly, every summer one saw houses cumbrously moving down the front street.

People in Provincetown do not regard houses as stationary objects. A man will buy a piece of dune land above the town and a cottage on the front shore, and presently up the hill toils the little house. Or he buys a piece of shore front and a cottage on the back street, and presently the house is wambling along to take its place on the water.

It has always been so since the old days. Provincetown people got a habit of moving their houses long ago when there was a settlement of forty-eight houses over by Long Point. This sickle of sand which encloses one of the finest harbors on the North Atlantic was so narrow that encroaching storms played havoc with it and threatened at one time to sweep the narrow point away. It was too valuable a harbor to be destroyed and the government took it over. But the thrifty Provincetowners asked the government:

"What are you going to do with these houses?"

"Nothing," responded the government.

"Well, can we take them?"

"If you take them away," answered the government. The

Provincetown fathers consulted together. And next, houses supported on wrecking barrels bobbed solemnly across the bay. They "figgered" it this way.

If wrecking barrels can support and bring up from the sea's bottom a vessel of many tons' burden, why can't a raft of wrecking barrels support a house on the surface of the water? It could and did. Arnold's Radio Shop, formerly Matheson's Department Store, then our principal store in town, was once the schoolhouse, and though a large building it went to sea and became an amphibious animal. They say that so gently were these houses eased off that the moving didn't interfere with the housewife cooking her dinner.

It is not only from Long Point that houses have moved. The old records show that there was once a considerable village on Beach Point. Long ago all these houses were hauled away. Some were moved to Provincetown and others to Truro.

There was also a settlement known as Hell Town, between Wood End and Race Point; of this not a vestige remained. When people no longer needed to fish on the outside shore because of the coming of motors, these houses were moved into town. I asked Captain Kennedy, a neighbor of mine, why they called this settlement Hell Town.

"Because of the helling that went on there," he answered, simply.

One of the things that made me take to the town the first day I came was that the houses in Provincetown one and all were built for the convenience and comfort of the people who lived in them. They were built, too, for a generation which knew nothing of paid service. There was no "servant problem" in Provincetown when its comfortable houses were put up. The first houses faced the sea. The kitchens looked out upon the encroaching dunes.

In spring and fall a prodigious carpentry goes on in Provincetown. As soon as the summer people go, houses cut bay windows and dormers with the regularity of a baby cutting teeth. Other houses sprout ells and porches, still other houses build them a Cape Cod cellar, for our cellars are mostly above ground, it being difficult to build one in the sand.

In many of the yards there are little flocks of houses, of "shops," of two-room dwellings. Houses shrink and diminish as people's folk come home or go away. The mother of a neighbor of mine came to live with him in her old age and he moved down a two-room cottage which he attached to the main house, as Kibbe Cook did to my house, so his mother needn't be bothered with the children and could have her own privacy.

After a time the old lady died, and he moved the house away again because he said it made him feel lonely. Next his sister's husband died and home she came with her children. Well and good. He moved down the cottage from the back lot. So the progress of a house can be marked by the additions in the family. As the family grows, the ells sprout. When a mother comes home to live, the west addition with the bay window is put on. When the girls grow big the porch makes its appearance and the ell is raised so that the twins will have rooms of their own.

Provincetown men are not landsmen. Almost without exception they have at one time or another "followed the sea." Certainly their forebears have. Provincetowners have spent so much of their time on the sea in ships that they look upon houses as a sort of land ship or a species of houseboat and therefore not subject to the laws of houses.

Every man who owns a boat or a vessel overhauls it, alters it, tinkers with it. That is why all Provincetown people tinker with their houses and keep adding to them perpetually. The people here are seafaring folk and that is why carpentry on houses is never done and why the houses do not stay upon their foundations after the fashion of those in other towns but go wandering up roadways or sandy dunes.

Many a ship's timber has gone into Provincetown houses. Some have been partly constructed from the fine knees of old vessels and the magnificent timbers of dead ships. Frederick Waugh's studio was made that way and the interesting Flagship owes much of its uniqueness to Pat's beachcombing. This likeness of Provincetown houses to ships explains some of their architectural peculiarities. In many an old house the door opens on a narrow entry. The stairs mount sheer. They are not really stairs but a companionway. There are upper chambers where the small windows are like portholes, as though built for security against the weather rather than for light.

When the Winslows bought a piece of property near us and went to build a new house there, the question was what to do with the old house. The carpenter was a Provincetown man and he was not for a moment perplexed. He rolled the old house out into the bay and there he anchored it. A storm came up and for two days the distracted house rocked and curtsied. Its shutters and doors blew open and the blank windows and the yawning door looked like a doleful screaming mouth.

One day Tony Avellar shouted to me, "Want to come and tow a house over to Beach Point?"

He hitched his gas boat to the house and slowly we chugged and bobbed across the Bay, where men rolled the house across the beach, and there it became a garage.

George O'Neill, the poet, and his mother were looking for a house to buy and found one in Wellfleet. It was a lovely house, remote behind a hedge of lilacs. Yet this house, in some ghostly fashion, resisted their buying. Keys, when they wished to go in, would be lost. Furniture moved so they stumbled over it. They had a curious sense of being unwanted as they walked through the house they coveted. After a number of disquieting episodes they left the house alone awhile. But they could not stop wanting the old Cape Cod house behind the lilacs. I drove with them to look at it again.

We got to the lilac hedge, but there was no house at all. They were sure this was the place where the house was, but there were only scattered plaster and a few bricks, and the place where the house once had been was overgrown with summer weeds.

We thought we had taken a wrong road. We searched until some old neighbors told us the house had been bought back by relatives of its former owners, and, as the old people said, "had gone to Chatham." It was as though this house had slyly evaded intruders until its own family had come for it.

It would not be fair to Provincetown not to speak of what you might call the "barn and fishhouse architecture." For most of these little unpretentious dwellings have been done over with so much ingenuity and love that they fit into Provincetown's old-time charm far more closely than some of the new houses which have been built "Down-along." Back of my own house is now one of the pleasantest dwellings in town—a long white house with blue shutters and pleasant bricked paths leading to a studio. A few years ago this was an ugly barn.

In the fishhouses on the shore the big room that was used for storing tackle and mending nets is transformed into a living room of ample size. Dormer windows make pleasant bedrooms of the loft formerly used for storing sails and gear and nets. Add a picket fence with a bright flower garden on each side, and you find what was formerly a mere "store" transformed into a pleasant habitation.

One could write a book about the stories of Provincetown houses. There was the Lancy house, for instance. This house now belongs to the Research Society and Museum. It stands out like a sore thumb from all other Provincetown houses. It is a three-story house and has what seems to be a brownstone front, and looks as though it might have been a house in a small-town city block. But it is not made of stone, it is made of wood, and it is covered with some composite mixture that gives it a look not quite like brownstone but a horrible ersatz brownstone. This was a discovery of Lancy's father and he jealously guarded his secret, for he expected to make a fortune from it. People everywhere would buy this horrid mixture and plaster it on their houses, and all New England would be covered with a pseudo-brownstone blight.

But God was merciful. This horror was not to be. When the old man died, the formula could be found nowhere. His own house was a living testimony to his invention. It not only worked but it has endured through the years.

Lancy ransacked the house from attic to cellar. He pried bricks from the hearth. He looked in the chimneys for a hidden repository. He tore up boards. Nowhere was the formula to be found. The fortune that he thought was in his hand eluded him forever. This permanently soured his disposition. The house with its pretentious furniture and its Nottingham curtains was shut up, while he and his sister lived with miserly frugality in the basement, impoverished forever in their minds by the fortune that had escaped them. Now it has been bought by the Research Society and houses Commander MacMillan's Arctic collection.

There was once a house to the westward whose front path was divided in two by a fence. So long had it been divided that a large tree had grown in what had been the front path. Two brothers lived here who had not spoken for a generation. Each brother, and his family, went in their own side door. Neither one had trespassed the invisible line drawn through the front entry, and when one brother died he left his share of the house so the other brother could not buy it. I never knew the cause of this lifelong quarrel, whether it was of some deep-seated and terrible wrong, or a clashing of personalities over some trivial pretext. The fence has been cleared away now. Strangers have bought both sides of the house, but I should not like to live in it.

Houses in Provincetown are still restless and movable. One of the latest houses to wander around is the old Pamet Coast Guard Station which was bought by the Marx', cut into sections, and moved from its niche on the shore to the hills above where there is a magnificent view. And only the other day Mr. Chipman, the house mover, died while he was moving five cottages from inland to the shore.

CHAPTER TEN

Our House Grows

I

IT WAS natural in a town where houses were almost as easily moved as boats that as soon as Joe O'Brien and I were married, we should think about changing our house. One of the first things we did when we first came to Kibbe Cook's house was to rearrange the hallway. David Stull had closed the sagging front door, put a window where the door had been, and made the main entrance through what had been a small bedroom. It was an untidy entryway which gave upon a narrow hall. Joe knocked down these walls, giving us space and light, and built bookcases on either side.

Knocking down walls and letting in light were symbolic of Joe, for more than anyone I have known well, he wanted light and truth and looked at the world with a long view.

Joe O'Brien had been a newspaperman a great many years, for he began writing when he was only fifteen. He had left newspaper work to free-lance and was getting into his stride when together we went to the Lawrence Strike of 1912.

This strike was a peculiar one because it influenced the lives of a great many people. It seemed to be the point of intersection for writers as different as Lincoln Steffens, William Allen White, George Stannard Baker, who is our cousin; Fremont Older, the famous editor of the *San Francisco Chronicle*, saw this strike. There was something about these striking textile workers which moved deeply everyone who saw them. For Joe and myself it was decisive and he threw himself into the labor movement, working in it until he died, and I followed him.

It is hard for me to write about Joe O'Brien, not because he has been dead for over a quarter of a century, but because he is as vivid and alive as if he had just walked out of the room. Having once lived with his clear mind, I have turned to it for counsel through the years. It is a habit for me to try and see events through his intelligence, which so quickly pierced sham and subterfuge in his incessant search for truth.

It is somewhat terrifying to think of all the writing going on in Kibbe Cook's house that summer. Joe was writing what was to have been a book, Wilbur Steele was writing his subtle and intricate stories. He was never a story ahead. He was always sure every story was going to be his last, which plunged him into a deep gloom, so at variance with his roughhouse gaiety. He and Joe O'Brien were a wonderful pair, both with a seeing eye, an awareness for what was going on, almost frightening.

The nucleus of what was to be the Provincetown Players was forming that summer. Susan Glaspell and Lucy Huffaker had taken Miss Roseboro's house. Hutchins Hapgood and Neith had come to Provincetown.

Sinclair Lewis was back, living at the Avellars' wharf. He was prodigious. He would come into the house, roaring that "he had a girl and her name was Daisy, when she sang the cat went crazy, with delirium and epilepsy and all sort of cataleptics." A stream of fantasies, of stories, of ideas streamed from him. He never stopped. He ate almost as much blueberry pie as Wilbur Steele. He wrote a whole boy's book in three weeks, seventy thousand words, called: *Nick and the Aeroplane,* probably the first airplane book for boys. He wrote it to make money to begin his first novel, *Our Mr. Wrenn.* He raced through the first twenty thousand words of that in the next three weeks and when Joe and I read it, we knew here was an author.

He was never still, his hair flamed, his blue eyes blazed, his long, sensitive hands gesticulated. He got himself sunburned to dull plum color over and over again and peeled. He galloped over the dunes barefoot. He shook sand into the picnic basket. He came in shouting he had an idea, and a flood of nonsense to float Noah's Ark would resound through Kibbe Cook's house.

I would chase him out with a broom. The children would join in. The dog would bark. We would go slamming in and out Kibbe Cook's house doors, with Red leading all of us, looking like one of the earlier Sennett films. Joe O'Brien, Wilbur Steele, and Art Hutchins joined in these cosmic roughhouses and it was as if a herd of buffalo pounded through the little house.

II

The house had run down during 1910 and 1911, when I could do little more than hold my head above water, nor had I the feeling for the house which I left to others to run. I was, indeed, a glory-holer. I kept a superficial order and got rid of things by stowing them away in drawers and in closets. Since I had had to be both father and mother and make the money for the house, I had let the house get out of hand.

Automatically, Joe straightened out the house as he straightened out my life. The affairs of the house hummed along well under his hand. The house began to shine.

When he went through a room it looked better for his having been there; the book he put in place or the picture he straightened or the garment he picked up, he did unconsciously, as if he weren't really thinking about it at all. All Joe's life, order followed him around like a dog.

He brought many things with him to the house: Japanese

prints and brass candlesticks and books. His workroom was the second front room and he made a carpenter's bench in the barn loft, for he was a good workman and liked to make things. Soon we had a garden and chickens, a group of individualists, several of whom, especially the Rhode Island Reds, refused to take motherhood seriously and were always getting out, leaving their young to the more balanced Plymouth Rock, Zarathusa.

We had a garden again and Joe had old Captain Bickers repair the *Molasses II*, badly strained by last year's sailing. The house was rich in children. There was a sense of living and growth.

All the Avellar children, our other family, lived here most of their daylight hours. Joe made a children's playroom out of the back kitchen. It had a blackboard with colored crayons, stone blocks, and mechano for building, an elaborate soap-bubble outfit, beads for stringing, and all kinds of games. This and the swings and Timmy, our bulldog, and Kite the pony made the place a lodestone for the children around there.

III

We had great festivals in those days. The time all twelve Avellars came for Thanksgiving dinner will never be forgotten. It was a great sight seeing Joe O'Brien carving one of the turkeys at one end of the table and Pa Avellar carving another turkey at the other end, while a Virginia ham stood ready on the side table. These and jellies and preserves of all kinds had been sent from the farm in Virginia where Joe's mother lived. That day we sat down eighteen to table. That was a real Thanksgiving.

Halloween was on even a more ample scale—with every neighborhood child bobbing for apples and real jack-o'-lanterns everywhere. While Christmas, with Tony Avellar for Santa Claus, was a Christmas to remember forever.

Mother sent not only turkey, but holly and mistletoe from Virginia. The farm that had belonged so long to Joe's family, the Granthams, poured its riches into our house. There was a bond between the two distant places. The farm house on the pike leading to West Virginia and Kibbe Cook's house became neighbors. Our big salt codfish, cranberries, and beach plums went to the farm, seeming but meager exchange for the farm's bounty.

It was that time Kite developed the habit of coming into the house. She would watch the maid setting the table and would then lift the latch with her nose, tip over the sugar bowl, and eat the sugar and the bread while Katie del Ponte, our Italian girl, screamed. There was no knot Kite could not untie and she would let herself out of her stall and careen off to eat Prince Freeman's lettuce, while Captain Kennedy would call to me from over the fence,

"Jibe her, Mis' Vorse, jibe her!"

I remember him calling to Heaton who was letting the reins drag as he drove the pony cart uptown,

"Look to your sheet to port, son, and haul in the slack!"

Always an opinionated animal, Kite's inflexibility of character made us part with her, since she refused to recognize motorcars. When she felt like turning, she would whirl the cart around, motorcar or no motorcar. Twice she almost wrecked us.

We stayed until after Christmas before we went to Europe. Just before we went, we gave Kite away to a child to the westward, off the main streets, who had infantile paralysis. Kite passed her declining years doing exactly what she felt like, with a red ribbon braided into her forelock.

IV

When we came back to Provincetown, in 1913, we started a Montessori School among our neighbors. I had had an assignment for the *Woman's Home Companion* to do a series on the Montessori Method, which could only be studied in Rome.

War and Fascism killed the Montessori system in Italy. Mme. Montessori had been a teacher of deficient children and had searched for the lowest threshold by which such children could be developed and taught reading and writing. She discovered that young children see with their hands and that a child desires to handle things as a part of its natural way of learning about the world he lives in. Much of her training was the development of the senses. In teaching children to write, for instance, large sandpaper letters were given the children, and the child traced these letters with its fingers as it read them. After a time, the phenomenon occurred called "bursting into writing." The child would take a piece of chalk and write in good script the words which his muscles had memorized.

In our Provincetown school we were trying out the method under laboratory conditions. There were Ellen and another little girl from New York, three of the Avellars, two Portuguese, and two Yankees, so our group of nine children had been brought up in three different ways. Our teacher, Mildred Jenkinson, had studied in the Montessori School in Rome, but had no other experience of teaching.

It was an extraordinary and fascinating thing to see the system work—to see these children of different strains, self-disciplined, learning the elementary things about numbers and reading and writing through the system of sense training. One day Janet Lewis burst into writing. She went to the blackboard and with a piece of chalk wrote her name, unfalteringly. I think she was close to five years old.

We spent the fall evenings making plans about raising the ell of the house. It was a very full house now and needed more rooms. Heaton and Ellen were growing big. Soon, when Ellen had a room of her own, there would be no guest room. At that time there was a long hallway upstairs at the head of an enclosed stairway. If we changed the stairway around, the downstairs hall would be larger and we could cut a good-sized bedroom from the hall, put in another dormer window and, when the roof over the ell was raised, have an upstairs bathroom.

We stayed late in Provincetown and from the children's stone blocks we built a working model of the house as we wanted it. There sat Kibbe Cook's house in red blocks with a gray slate roof and with its ell raised. We left the little model there all winter and it was from it that the carpenters rebuilt the house.

V

The next summer when we came back we had little Joe with us. That summer we intended to make Kibbe Cook's house bigger, but before we were there long, Joe fell ill. By July he was in the Presbyterian Hospital and the baby and I were staying with Frances Perkins, so we could be near him. Joe put off the operation until fall.

While he was in the hospital in Boston, the World War crashed down on us. Looking back on it, it seems impossible that we should not have realized more clearly that war was upon us. But we had shut our eyes to it. All of a sudden our whole outlook had changed—the rosy certainties we had had that the civilized world was beyond war, and if the good sense of the international bankers did not stop war, why then international labor would. All of us in Provincetown were profoundly shaken and there occurred then a curious upheaval.

That summer there were several I.W.W. boys staying in town. Fred Boyd, a gifted but unstable young Englishman, was recuperating from a jail sentence which he had incurred, as many of the workers had during the Patterson strike. Fred, who never could drink, got tight and telegraphed Jack Reed, Lloyd George, the Kaiser, and other celebrities to stop the war. The more sensitive and least stable of the group reacted to the world eruption by going on a strange binge, during which time two people tried to commit suicide.

The normal and tougher-minded people merely looked on the world with unbelieving eyes. It meant a complete read-justment for those of us who were brought up to believe that peace was now a permanent thing.

Joe came back from his operation and made what we thought was a good recovery. Great discussion went on among us; whether we should enter the war or not, discus-sions about preparedness. We still believed that one could vote down a world conflagration, and make motions about hurricanes. We believed that then, and twenty-five years later many people again believed, that it was in the power of individuals and nations to decide whether to take part in a world upheaval or not.

It was good to turn from these discussions to the chil-dren, to young Joe who was growing so fast, the children's friends, and the simple things that have to do with running a house.

VI

In March, 1915, I went abroad for four months as war correspondent. When I came home, my whole conception of life had changed. I had seen war, and I could not talk about what I had seen to anyone but Joe. I do not mean I couldn't talk, but I couldn't make anyone understand what I had seen. I had gone to Europe with pacifist leanings and came back sure that we would ultimately be in the war.

I was cut off from the people around me who had theories about keeping out of war and who wanted their lives to go on undisturbed. That summer there was an intangible bar-rier between me and everyone but Joe. He understood what I tried to say. It was a comfort to be building our house together.

All the summer of '15, Joe O'Brien worked on his house and had the joy of seeing his baby grow big and strong. We saw all our plans come true. We arranged the halls as we had planned and built four more bedrooms where the low ell had been, with a porch over the back of the house. Joe worked like a carpenter all summer. We had all the excitement of building our own house, one of the everlasting satisfactions of mankind, together with the pleasure of keeping our old one. Now we had built ourselves into Kibbe Cook's house and made it really ours. The house had grown. Then one day when we were driving around town in the accommodation we saw a sign FOR SALE on the Lewis wharf. We said together: let's buy it.

In the fall, Joe acted in the first play of what was to become the Provincetown Players and helped clear out the wharf for the first series of plays.

But the illness which he had had the year before came on him again. He went to New York to the hospital, never to come back to his new house. Joe O'Brien died young. He had lived over a crucial time in history. He had lived intensely and had packed into his years more living than most do into a long lifetime, and he had attained a curious wisdom before he died.

Susan Glaspell wrote this about him:

JOE

(Joseph O'Brien died October 27th, 1915)

It's strange without you. I do not like it.
I want to see you coming down the street in the gay woolly stockings
    and that bright-green sweater.
I want you to open the door of my house and brightly call "Hello!"
We used to rage about the way you kept us waiting—
Honest now, were you ever on time anywhere?
But I'd wait—oh, I can't say how long I wouldn't wait if there
    was any chance of your finally swinging along and charming
    away my exasperation.
That was a mean advantage—
Letting us wait and then spoiling our grievance with a smile.

I want to sit over a drink with you and talk about the I.W.W.
and the damned magazines and the Germans; I want to argue
with you about building bookshelves and planting bulbs.
I want awfully to tell you a joke I heard yesterday.
And now that you are gone I want intensely to find you.
What were you, Joe? I don't think any of us really know.
Many are talking about your warmth, but there was something
diamond hard in you.
Something unyielding and inexorable to all not you.
Many are talking about your gaiety; none of them loved it more
than I did,
But I want to know about those reservations; I want to know the
you that brooded and lived alone.
They say you were so sunny; but ah, you were so subtle.
Much I do not know, but this I know—
You saw things straight; nobody put it over very hard on you.
The thing in you that thought was like a knife blade,
Muddling and messing made you sick.
Your scorn put the crimp in a lot of twaddle that goes on among our
kind of folks—
How I'd like to hear you cuss some of them out again!
Graceful levity—fiery dissatisfactions.
Debonair and passionate.
Much I do not know and never shall, but this I know;
I feel the sway of beauty when I think of you.
A fresh breeze; a shining point;
Pure warmth; pure hardness.
Much given and something withheld;
A jest—a caress—an outrageous little song. A gift. A halt in speech—
a keen grave look of understanding.
Undependable and yet deeply there;
Vivid and unforgettable.
Is that at all you? Would you laugh if you saw this?
Well, laugh, but I say again,
Unforgettable.
Strong clear violet; the flash of steel;
The life of the party—a tree way off by itself.
Oh, what's the use? I can't.
I only know my throat's all tight with the longing to have you open
the door of my house and brightly call "Hello!"

CHAPTER ELEVEN

Clan Avellar

I

BESIDES my own family I had another, the Avellars. Our two families were so close we scarcely knew where the Vorse-O'Briens left off and the Avellars began. Vorses and Avellars ate interchangeably in either home. They often slept in each other's houses.

All the Avellar children called me "Mother Vorse" and mine called Mrs. Avellar "Ma." Joe, who is a contemporary of Tony's children, calls her "Grandma." Perpetual quarrels used to go on between Raphael and Ellen and Walter and Heaton as to who had the best mother.

"Look, Heaton," Raphael would say, resorting to reason and logic, "my mother is the best mother because there isn't any mother anywhere as good as my mother. 'Tisn't that Mother Vorse isn't a good mother, but my mother is the best mother in all the world." And he was probably right. There was never a home with so much life and so much happiness in it.

What evenings full of friendship and gaiety all of our family have had in their house. Mother Avellar, besides being the best mother in the world, or perhaps because she is the best mother in the world, is also a famous teller of tales. I would rather hear Mother Avellar tell the daily doings around her house than read a book of short stories by any famous author.

The story of what happened to the fish that Isabel did

not give to her *madringa*, her godmother; the story of how Papa almost chopped up the new kitchen cabinet because it wouldn't fit together.

But one of the best of the stories that Mother Avellar told was of the time when they had signed a note to help a relative set up in business, but the concern failed, and when the day came to pay it looked as if their savings would be swept away, when Justin came in saying,

"Ma, I've done pretty good trapping this month." Justin was trapping on shares with Manuel James and fishing had been poor all summer.

"You have? Fifty dollars, my boy?"

"More'n that, Ma."

"Not a hundred dollars, Justin?"

"A little more, Ma."

"It can't be two hundred dollars, my boy."

And Ma tells this with a mounting climax, until almost tearfully she says in a low, awe-stricken tone,

"Not, not *five hundred*, Justin?"

"Here 'tis, Ma," says Justin, still nonchalant, and puts the five hundred in her lap.

II

The four younger children, Justin, Raphael, Walter, and Isabel, were the ones who were at my house when my children weren't at the Avellars'.

Next in order of the ten Avellars were the twins, Gerald and Arthur, who couldn't be told apart. Then one of them broke a bit of his front tooth.

"Thank heavens," said Mother Avellar, "now I won't have to spank both of them." But within a week the other twin broke an identical piece. God was with them.

Formerly it was the custom to have a hired boy to sweep sand out and bring drinking water and do other chores.

Arthur was my hired boy and Gerald the hired boy of my next-door neighbor, Mrs. Atkins. She would call out to sea,

"Gerald, Gerald, come in, I want you."

A brown figure would jump out of the bay and call out smoothly, "I ain't Gerald, Mis' Atkins, I'm Arthur."

Presently I'd call out, "Arthur, I need some water."

"I ain't Arthur, Mis' Vorse, I'm Gerald." The same boy would call.

Arthur and Gerald both enlisted in the First World War. Arthur was in aircraft down in San Antonio. Gerald was in the navy. Both became petty officers in short order, though they were very young, because they had the character and command that were common to the family. Arthur was so eager to get to the front that by pulling various wires he got transferred to a regiment said to be about to sail. His heart almost broke when his new regiment was ordered to Florida and his old regiment sailed instead. It was Gerald who went overseas.

III

Mother Avellar baked all her own bread and on baking days my children couldn't be got home. Indeed all the food that came out of her capacious oven made other food taste like sawdust. I remember going in there one day and the room seethed with children. The bread was just out of the oven. The twins were bawling,

"I want brown sugar on mine, Ma."

Isabel was crawling over her mother, crying aloud for another piece. Mother Avellar was besieged with children. She sliced away at the bread mechanically. My daughter Ellen was saying loudly she wanted more. Mother Avellar's eyes, usually so sparkling, had a lackluster look.

"What's the matter, Mother Avellar?" I cried. "What's happened?"

"Well, Mother Vorse," she said, in a despairing tone, clapping together two big pieces of bread spread amply with butter and sugar, "I'm so lonely. Only eight of the children are home!"

But there were days when Pa Avellar had no such homesickness. I remember him taking up a piece of scantling that was lying on the bulkhead and chasing all his children off. He told them categorically and emphatically just where they would not have a single piece of skin left if he saw one of them before suppertime. He sat down heavily on the bench beside me.

"God, Mother Vorse!" he sighed, "takes patience!"

Father Avellar's impatient, choleric nature was like a motor power which drove all the family and kept them on their toes. The boys were proud of Captain Joe's prowess. They had a fearsome delight in the swiftness of their father's wrath. His anger had neither meanness nor cruelty. It had the swift flow of a life force. You could not imagine Pa without the power of his vital indignation. There is a divinity in such impatience that makes a patient man seem tame.

There are stories of Captain Joe that have become legend. In the days of the gasoliners, the little boats would cluster around an incoming weir boat to get their bait with the avidity of sharks. With frightful rapacity each captain of a gasoliner would try to board the weir boat first. Captain Joe would stand there, a fish fork like a trident in his hand. He would defy the captain of any boat to set foot on his vessel before his name was called.

"Gorramighty," he would cry, "you try to get on my vessel before I tell you and I won't leave enough of you to make bait," and he would follow that up with such artistry of invective in English and Portuguese that men listened to him as though to a mighty orchestra, proud that they belonged to the same species.

IV

I wanted to go out with Pa to the weir; but he felt that a woman around might cramp his style as Mother Avellar had when he got so worried about Wilbur he almost used bad language. Once when our boat the *Wilmarato* was far out by the Point a white squall struck. Wilbur was sailing her.

"Poor Papa was so worried," Mother Avellar said, "that he yelled right out to sea, yelled a mile and a half out to sea, Mother Vorse, just as if Wilbur could hear him,

" 'You so-and-so, cut your halyards!' Poor Papa, he was so worried! He yelled right out to Wilbur, 'Cut your halyards, you goddam fool, cut 'em or I'll kick you . . .' You know men, Mother Vorse, you know where father said he'd kick him!

"And I said, 'Papa, pretty soon you will be using bad language and I shall have to go into the house!' "

That was long ago. Father Avellar is now retired but his righteous indignation has not. Father Avellar does not miss a war broadcast and when the King of Belgium capitulated, Mother Avellar heard him cry into the radio,

"You can't do that, King or no King, you so-and-so. You can't do it, I tell you, you —— ——."

Mother Avellar hastened in from the kitchen.

"Papa! Papa!" she admonished, "the King can't hear you but the neighbors can!"

V

Once I went with Tony, who was the oldest son and who gasses the fleet, to take a boat down to Onset where he was met by his brother Albert and one of his cousins. A family talk like that of the Avellars took in all the world: the cousin in the embassy in Paris, the cousin engineering on the Pacific Coast, the brother-in-law who was a professor in South Africa. The clan Avellar spanned the world and took in almost every profession.

On weekends and holidays a long line of cars stretches in front of the Avellars' house. Ma's children coming home by their devotion proving Raphael's contention that his mother is the best mother in the world. I often wonder if Mother Avellar doesn't burst with pride at the sight of her children and grandchildren. I know there is nothing makes me prouder than when one of my other family calls me Mother Vorse.

CHAPTER TWELVE

Old Wharves

THE Lewis Wharf, which Joe and I bought, pushed out to sea almost as far as Railroad Wharf. On the end was a fishhouse and so wide was the wharf that there was another sizable little building aside from the fishhouse, which was a large building. Farther down the wharf was another shed. The wharf and the buildings were gray and the door and the end of the smaller house were painted red, which time had mellowed and weathered.

On land there was a house whose downstairs was arranged as a store with many shelves around. This house bore the name of the Arequipa. In the old days it had been a ship chandler's and smelled of tar and oakum, and great blocks of tackle of all kinds hung from the ceiling. One could have bought anything here from a fishhook to a great ship's anchor—twine for netting and cable as big as your ankle for the mooring ropes of great vessels, kegs of nails, scoops and oars and all the paraphernalia a man would need for outfitting his vessel. There were clothes and groceries and household goods too, for which credit was given to the wives of the fishermen off on a long trip.

Near at hand there was a small house that had been a fish market. An oyster-shell road led down to the wharf between the two buildings, where carts had driven along its length, loaded with fish or with nets. Here in the days of the old bankers flakes had been laid out, covered with codfish which had embalmed the air for blocks around. Indeed, in the great days of banking the smell of drying codfish hung over Provincetown like a fog.

In his *History of Truro*, Shebnah Rich observes:

What with the salt ocean rolling on the back side, the salt bay washing the front, the thousands of hogsheads of pure salt crystallizing in shallow vats or high piled in storehouses, waiting market, and miles of salt codfish curing in the autumnal sun, Provincetown could lay good claim to being a well-preserved community.

When we bought the wharf the lower story was still full of boats and gear which were only moved out when the Provincetown Players opened there.

The Bangs A. Lewis Wharf had belonged to the Lewis family from father to son, since it had been built seventy-five years before. A little more than a quarter century before we bought it in 1913, the wharf had presented a lively scene. Its history was part of Provincetown's history. For years great vessels had laid up along its side, four large bankers, their salt wet back from the Grand Banks. It was not only a fishing wharf, but it was the lumber, coal, and ice wharf for the East End. Now the last banker had made its last trip from Provincetown the year before. No more fares of salt fish came back from the Banks. By 1912 the fish flakes had gone. Only a few people continued to salt the fine big fish, mostly for their own use, though scullyjos were still hung out to dry to the hardness of a pine knot.

Power and ice had made it possible to send fresh fish everywhere over the United States. In a brief time a great industry had dwindled and what was left of it was in Gloucester. It had taken ninety big sheds to store the fish in the heyday of the salt fishermen. Children and old men found work in spreading out the fish in the flakes to dry and taking them in in wet weather.

Thoreau's description of the town in those days is:

A great many of the houses here were surrounded by fish-flakes close up to the sills on all sides, with only a narrow passage two or three feet wide, to the front door; so that instead of looking out into a flower or grass plot, you looked on to so many square rods of cod turned wrong side outwards. . . . The principal employment of the inhabitants at this time seemed to be to trundle out their fish

[111]

and spread them in the morning, and bring them in at night. . . .
They were everywhere lying on their backs, their collarbones standing
out like the lapels of a man-o'-war-man's jacket, and inviting all
things to come and rest in their bosoms; and all things, with a few
exceptions, accepted the invitation. I think, by the way, that if you
should wrap a large salt fish round a small boy, he would have a coat
of such a fashion as I have seen many a one wear to muster. Salt fish
were stacked up on the wharves, looking like corded wood, maple and
yellow birch with the bark left on. I mistook them for this at first,
and such in one sense they were—fuel to maintain our vital fires—an
eastern wood which grew on the Grand Banks.

Salt fish was part of the wealth of nations for salt fish
was the fare of the poor people, that is, the great majority.
They say Amsterdam was built on herring bones. The fishing grounds off the Grand Banks were a magnet which
pulled to them the fishing boats of four nations. The salt-
fishing fleets from Brittany and those from Portugal were
blessed by their priests before they set sail on their long
voyage. Before ever Bartholomew Gosnold attempted that
first settlement on these shores, thousands of fishermen had
ventured across the Atlantic in search of cod. Their rivalry
was intense. It has been said that "nothing in the annals
of crime could surpass the cruelty of the Newfoundland fisheries who for three centuries were a law unto themselves."

The life of the town centered around the wharves and
the vessels that laid up alongside them. Those who didn't
go to sea saved up money and bought shares in vessels, went
into business furnishing them, or learned a craft for their
upkeep.

Provincetown grew rich on salt codfish. In 1885 sixty
bankers sailed from Provincetown and by that time most of
the captains were Portuguese, though less than ten years before of the Provincetown fleet of nearly fifty there were
only nine Portuguese. The other captains were either "Bluenoses" from Nova Scotia or of old Provincetown stock.

Each wharf had a dozen different crafts working on it—
sparyards, lathrooms, blacksmith shops, block-makers' sail

lofts. Lath workers, calkers, riggers, and painters were all there servicing the fleets of fishing vessels. Coopers making their big casks were never done. Along the sea front by the wharves were shipyards and marine railways for taking out great vessels. There were many sheds where fish were packed and smoked.

There had to be much storage space besides. Some of these wharves specialized in packing and buying and selling to out-of-town markets. Others were used principally for unloading fish. On others were housed storage places for nets and all sorts of fishing gear, or ice or coal to be sold.

Several of the wharves were a thousand feet long, like Union Wharf where Manuel Furtado now has his shipyard where he makes and rents boats. The Central Wharf thrust its thousand feet into the bay near the building now occupied by the Nautilus Club. This wharf had a marine railway for hauling out vessels of great size, and its sheds for various crafts and trades. It had four large ballast rooms loaded with rocks. These spilled upon the beach when the wharf was demolished and are still there.

At the end of the nineteenth century, Provincetown still had a fleet of two hundred and sixty-one vessels which included bankers, coasters, and whalers. At that time there were still thirty-four wharves.

The big vessels in the old days went on a triangular course. Starting out from their home ports they fished their codfish, salted them down, traded them in the Barbados, and came home with cargoes of rum and molasses.

Provincetown had a few vessels of this sort but most of the vessels fished the nearer Newfoundland Banks and spent from two to five months away, "wetting their salt" of which they carried about one hundred and fifty barrels. When a vessel had wet her salt she would come breezing home, Old Glory flying, the sign of a full fare. Crews were paid by the trip, between $150 and $300, and a vessel made from $6000 to $9000 a fare.

When the vessels left, the wives assembled on the wharves to say good-by, and it was a convention that everyone keep a stiff upper lip.

"We Provincetown women," one banker's wife told me, "would watch an off-Cape bride sharp to see she didn't show a tear. That's no way to see a man off when he's going to be away for months maybe."

"How many children have you, Captain Davis?" I asked an old-timer.

"Wife," he said, "how many times have I been bankin' since we was married?"

In a generation all this activity went by. Two bankers only were left when we came and soon they too were "fishing fresh." In a generation all the activity of the big wharves had stopped and the wharves had already fallen into disuse.

For a time the Lewises and Mayos used the old wharf for their fresh fishing. Hauls of fresh fish were unloaded there. Then the Mayos unloaded down by Railroad Wharf and the last Lewis fishing boat and the wharf had been sold. Our fishhouse was scrubbed out and artists lived in it. The Provincetown Players used the downstairs of the big fishhouse for two seasons.

The wharf had many interesting people living there in its day. Lucy L'Engle, whose interesting canvases have long been part of the Art Association's exhibits, had her studio there many years. Viletta Hawthorne Bissell, Hawthorne's sister, who was a notable artist in her own right and a great woman, had her class of sculpture on the second floor.

As long as it stood the old fishhouse was a center of life. We all felt the need of a central, impersonal meeting place. To fill this need a club called "The Sixes and Sevens" was founded. A group of young artists ran it, almost all of whom are today nationally known painters. It functioned gaily, for its clientèle was formed largely of writers, artists, musicians, poets, and playwrights, together with the many townspeople who were interested in the various art movements and who had enjoyed the plays of "The Provincetown."

Now that fishermen no longer tramped down the wharf in their rubber boots and loads of fish no longer came over the side, the old fish wharf could not go on living. The first year that we owned it a fire from an artist's oil stove burned down the smaller house. A carelessly dropped cigarette smoldered between the planking of the old wharf, full of dried seaweed, and the second fire, some years later, burned the big fishhouse at the end. In the winter of 1921 the ice crushed the wharf, leaving only Lucy L'Engle's studio tottering precariously on a few piles.

The story of our wharf was that of other diminished wharves. Like ours they became studios for summer people or homes of restaurants or night clubs. The three theaters, the Provincetown Players, the Wharf Theater, and the present Artists' Theater, all used wharves for their foundations.

Only five wharves are left today. Railroad Wharf, now Town Wharf, was the mightiest of all the wharves. In its day it even had a plank walk for foot passengers, and a railway. The big excursion boats landed there until recently. It is still a place of lively activity. Jokes and songs lighten the work of girls and men filleting fish in one of the sheds. Here the draggers unload their thousands of pounds of fish. The fish are weighed, iced, boxed, and loaded on trucks with lightning speed, and still the old bankers' phrase is used. When a truck is loaded, the cry goes up, "O.K., Boy. Your salt's wet! Haul anchor and break out sail!"

CHAPTER THIRTEEN

The Provincetown Players

I

No GROUP of people ever had less sense of having a mission than did the Provincetown Players. This theater which began so modestly with no aim except the amusement of its own members altered the course of the history of the theater in America. Why it should have had such a success and had such far-reaching results was more than the happy chance which brought plays, actors, and theater together with a leader like George Cram Cook.

The success of the Provincetown Players was, in a small degree, one of those explosions of talent which from time to time transform art and science. Such explosions come only in times when a creative breath is blowing through all of society. The Provincetown Players were part of the wave of creation to which the war put an end. Remarkable things were happening in the world at that time. Bell and Steinmetz and Marconi were making their discoveries. The Wrights and the other men were experimenting with heavier-than-air machines.

The A.T. & T. took telegraph and telephone and webbed the world. Ford had got hold of his idea for mass production. We were changing the aspects of cities. Architects were struggling with the still-unsolved problem of the skyscraper, and Frank Lloyd Wright, unrecognized at home, was revolutionizing architecture and adapting it to modern life.

The government was making far-reaching, though unfruitful, investigations into monopoly. Thinking people throughout the country were concerned with social justice. There was an underlying spirit of creation in the web of events, and we were part of it. Moving pictures were making their first larger experiments. Freud had appeared over the horizon, woman's suffrage was in full swing, the old relations of man and woman were being challenged. The first experiments in radio over KDKA were being made. In the arts there was the same stir of creation which was remaking the fabric of modern life.

II

Living in Provincetown the summer of 1915 among others were Susan Glaspell and George Cram Cook, Hutchins Hapgood and Neith Boyce, the Steeles, the Zorachs, the Henry Marion Halls, Edward and Stella Ballantine, Robert Edmond Jones, and Joe O'Brien and myself.

From the first the leadership was with Jig Cook, without whom there could never have been any Provincetown Players. The plays touched off a fire in him since for years he had been thinking of the theater as a community expression —the old dream of people working together and creating together.

The first plays were given at the Hapgoods' house, with settings improvised by Robert Edmond Jones. One of the plays was given on the porch with the sea for a background. The audience then went on the porch to look into the house for the second play.

Neith Hapgood had written a play called *Constancy*, which was a witty take-off on the stormy loves of Jack Reed and Mabel Dodge. Joe O'Brien and Neith were the actors.

Jig and Susan's play, *Suppressed Desires,* had been written in a moment of gaiety the year before. This famous play was a satire on the Freudian fad of the moment. No one would buy it; theatrical producers called it too special. This "special" play has had thousands of performances. It has been played all over the country by every kind of theatrical group. Through twenty-five years and more, *Suppressed Desires* has sold and still sells.

These two plays were so amusing, there was such a breath of life in the performance, that we wanted to do more. Our wharf, with the fishhouse on the end, was conveniently at hand to serve as a theater. The fishhouse was a hundred feet long and fifty feet wide. It had a dark, weathered look, and around the piles the waves always lapped except at extreme low tide. There was a huge door on rollers at the side and another at the end which made it possible to use the bay as a backdrop. The planks were wide and one could look through the cracks at the water. The color of the big beams and planks was rich with age.

We dragged out the boats and nets which still stood there. We all made contributions to buy lumber for seats and fittings. We made the seats of planks put on sawhorses and kegs. We ransacked our houses for costumes and painted our own scenery. Our first curtain was a green rep curtain my mother had made for me for "theatricals" in our attic in Amherst. Out of these odds and ends we made a theater, which was to have such unsuspected and far-reaching effects beyond the borders of Provincetown.

The night for the first performance came. Four people stood in the wings with lamps in their hands to light the stage. Lanterns with tin reflectors were placed before the stage like old footlights. Four people stood beside the lamp bearers with shovels and sand in case of fire, and with these lights the fishhouse took on depth and mystery.

Two more plays had been written for the new bill in the fishhouse. Jig Cook had written a play called *Change Your Style*. It was a hilarious play about the fight between the two schools of art that was then arising in all its fury and which has never abated since. The character of the beneficent landlord who took his pay in paintings was easily recognized as the beloved John Francis, the friend of writers and artists.

The other new play, written by Wilbur Daniel Steel, was called *Contemporaries*, an episode of the Church Raids. The time was late at night, following a church raid, the place a single small room in a congested quarter of the city.

In the winter of 1914 there had been a great deal of unemployment, and homeless men had sought refuge in churches. In Wilbur's play a mother is worrying about her boy who has got into bad company and is going around with an evil character who has led the boy into the churches. The action took place in darkness.

When the lights went on slowly one saw the cast dressed in the costume of late Rome. The single small room was a room in Palestine where the mother was grinding corn with a pestle. The officer was a Roman centurion and they were talking about a man called Jesus, a bad character who had invaded the temple.

These first pieces were more than little plays to be put on in a summer theater. They were imaginatively related to the things happening in our time, either seriously as in Wilbur Steele's moving and effective play or by satire like *Suppressed Desires*, which I have never seen better played than it was by Susan Glaspell, Jig Cook, and Lucy Huffaker.

I sat in the audience on the hard bench, watching the performance, hardly believing what we had done. The theater was full of enthusiastic people—a creative audience. In spite of its raining in torrents, everyone had come down the dark wharf lighted here and there by a lantern. People had leaned their umbrellas against one of the big timbers which supported the roof. I noticed an umbrella stirred, then slowly slid down an enormous knothole to the sand thirty feet below. With the stealth of eels, other umbrellas went down the knothole to join their fellows under the wharf.

The dark interior, the laughing audience, the little stage with its spirited performance, and the absconding umbrellas are all part of the memory of the first night of the Provincetown Players.

III

All the next winter Jig Cook was thinking in terms of a community theater. The play and the response of the group were stimulating to his imagination. Susan Glaspell wrote of this time in *The Road to the Temple*:

It might have ended there—people giving plays in the summer, if it hadn't been—Do you remember Jig's dream city, how there was to be a theater, and "why not write our own plays and put them on ourselves, giving writer, actor, designer, a chance to work together without the commercial thing imposed from without? A whole community working together, developing unsuspected talents. The city ought to furnish the kind of audience that will cause new plays to be written."

The summer people had gone. Jig would go out on the old wharf and "step" the fish-house. Wasn't there two feet more than he had thought? He would open the sliding-door that was the back wall, through which fish, nets, oars, anchors, boats, used to be dragged, and stand looking across the harbor to the Truro hills, hearing the waves lap the piles below him. He would walk back slowly, head a little bent, twisting his forelock.

"One man cannot produce drama. True drama is born only of one feeling animating all the members of a clan—a spirit shared by all and expressed by the few for the all. If there is nothing to take the place of the common religious purpose and passion of the primitive group, out of which the Dionysian dance was born, no new vital drama can arise in any people." He and Neith Boyce said it together. He came home and wrote it down as an affirmation of faith.

The original group had new members the next summer—Frederick Burt, the B. J. O. Nordfeldts, Jack Reed and Louise Bryant, Harry Kemp and Mary Pyne and Hutch Collins. Terry Carlin, an old anarchist whom all of us knew, took a shack on the water with a young fellow named

Eugene O'Neill. Terry was a tall, beautiful old man, with gay blue eyes and a shock of iron-gray hair. He had fine, muscular workman's hands. I remember meeting him, looming out of the fog, in the back country, with him beautiful Mary Pyne, Harry Kemp's wife. Mary had on a gray cape and her red hair shone through the fog. Together they looked like a symbolic picture of Ireland.

Terry's young friend, Gene O'Neill, was dark and good-looking. He told us shyly that he had written some plays.

When Frederick Burt read *Bound East for Cardiff* at the Cooks', Gene went into the next room while the reading was going on, for his tough, hard-boiled pose covered extreme sensitiveness. There was no one there during that reading who did not recognize the quality of this play. Here was something new, the true feeling of the sea. O'Neill had spent a couple of years as a seaman in his young, turbulent days and he had brought back from the experience the Glencairn cycle. Nothing that O'Neill did later had more truth than his early plays. From that moment he took his place as an important writer.

No one of us who heard that play reading will ever forget it, nor the reading of *Trifles* by Susan Glaspell, which took place at my house. Listening to the plays and giving them the instant recognition they deserved was a company of young people whom destiny had touched. Strange fates awaited them. Gene was to be America's greatest playwright and to withdraw completely from the world. Jack Reed was to be buried under the Kremlin in Moscow, and Jig Cook was to die in Greece and be laid in his grave by the women of the village, a stone from the Parthenon for his head given by the Greek government.

Jack Reed was one of the best reporters this country has produced. He had an immense gusto for living. He was a poet and he hated cant. He could make you see and hear and smell the things he wrote about. He was gay, sanguine, adventurous, lavish in his friendship and his talent, and he was a revolutionist. Lincoln Steffens took him in hand and he went on from there. In one of his magnificent flashes of genius he wrote *Ten Days That Shook the World.*

Gene O'Neill, dark, handsome, silent, had no pose at all. He was himself at all times. You knew more about him when you saw him swim. He swam like a South Sea Islander. Yet this recluse who shunned people was afraid to be alone. The unfriendly universe pressed down on him in the dark and filled him with the forebodings of naked primitive man. He could write the epic of fear, *Emperor Jones,* because no one knew more of cosmic fear than Gene, fear of the unknown, fear of the dark and the universe. There was no such darkness as Gene's after a hang-over. He would sit silent and suffering and in darkness. You could have taken the air he breathed and carved a statue of despair of it. No one has written a story of his life or his unending struggle with an empty universe.

And there was something else he knew—the cry of agony of the human spirit. The surrounding mystery and terror of life were always with him. Much of his best work came from the time when he was bumming around—when he was the companion of sailors and when he sat in the Hellhole with a bunch of bums. When he was young, he liked girls and drinking. He liked the people from the lower depths. While he was with the Provincetown Players, one play followed another. The Glencairn cycle, *Different, Beyond the Horizon, Anna Christie.*

Wilbur Daniel Steele had been the outstanding athlete in his class in Denver University, and when with the Provincetown Players still had the gay high spirits of a kid in college, which hid a subtle, intricate mind, intensely aware of all that was going on around him, and a gift for words and for situation of the first order. At that time, he couldn't give himself up to the theater and the opportunity the Provincetown Players gave others to see their work come alive on the stage as did Susan and Jig.

The intensity and beauty of life flowed through Jig Cook. He lived in the thought of mankind's possibilities. In his poetry and his writings and talk there were flashes of vision which made one live for a moment in eternity. He had a dark brooding quality of the tragic sense as authentic as his illuminations.

These different personalities all touched with greatness formed the center of the group who so quickly recognized the talent of Eugene O'Neill and who gave *Bound East for Cardiff*.

It has never been more authentically played than it was by our group of amateurs, on the old wharf, with the sound of the sea beneath it. Susan Glaspell describes it this way:

The sea has been good to Eugene O'Neill. It was there for his opening. There was a fog, just as the script demanded, fog bell in the harbor. The tide was in, and it washed under us and around, spraying through the holes in the floor, giving us the rhythm and the flavor of the sea while the big dying sailor talked to his friend Dris of the life he had always wanted deep in the land, where you'd never see a ship or smell the sea.

IV

This season was a time of excitement. Jig Cook's vision, the intensity of his approach to the theater, the outstanding talent of Eugene O'Neill and Susan Glaspell, were the core around which the lesser talents revolved. This group which had come together by chance found themselves embarked on something that was bigger than any of them. That summer on the old wharf nineteen plays were put on, six by Gene O'Neill. Wilbur Steele wrote a witty play called *Not S'ma't*.

The two high points in the summer for those who were the working members of the group were Gene's plays and *Trifles* by Susan Glaspell. This play has been used as the model of a one-act play in schools and colleges all over America and has been translated into all the languages of

Europe. There is no country of the civilized world where it has not been played. It, like *Suppressed Desires,* continues to be played by theatrical groups everywhere.

As a playwright Susan Glaspell was a natural. She had written successful novels and short stories of distinction. She had attended no courses in playwriting but she had what was better, a stage at hand on which she could see how a play worked out.

A great deal of emphasis has always been put, and rightly, on George Cram Cook as the moving power which gave the impetus to the group and which made "The Provincetown" the remarkable theater it was.

Not enough has been said about Susan Glaspell and her quality of enthusiasm when a new idea absorbed her. Long after the Provincetown Players I remember when the idea of *Alison's House*, a story based on Emily Dickinson's life, first possessed her. Seeing Susan in those days when she was first plunging her mind into Emily Dickinson's story was seeing a creative force at work.

The plays she contributed were all based upon an understanding of the life of the country—some witty, some ironical, and some tragic. Nor without her would George Cram Cook's intensive work in the theater have been possible. Her constant encouragement and her humor as well as her irony were the things which nourished him and made his never-ending tasks possible.

The Players took in our whole community. Provincetown boys like Frank Henderson acted the plays alongside such an experienced actor as Freddy Burt—who with his wife, Helen Ware, were so beloved and so regretted when they left.

Even the children shared the excitement of the theater. Henry Marion Hall wrote a play for them called *Mother Carey's Chickens*, for which the big door was opened, using the bay for our backdrop. I have never seen so good a children's play, as impersonating Mother Carey's birds they swooped around the stage, crying like gulls. Heaton was Captain Kid and Dave Ericson, Smee, and they quickly transferred the pirate gang from the stage to reality and were a scourge to the shore for summers on end.

Those days were a golden age for all of us who had part in the Provincetown Players. Almost we came near to Jig's vision of the creative community which was to be interchangeable creative audience and creative artist.

The greatest day of the Provincetown Players was between 1919 and 1922. A great contribution was made then to the American stage. But the early days on the old fish wharf stand out with a special clarity and beauty of people working together and creating together.

V

When fall came it was impossible to drop the theater. It was Jack Reed and Jig Cook, I think, who first suggested that the theater move to New York. We went in September and gave ourselves the name of the Provincetown Players. We called our new theater The Playwright's Theater. A little money was collected from the group. The constitution was written by Jack Reed, George Cram Cook, and Frederick Burt.

This was the announcement of the first New York season:

The present organization is the outcome of a group of people interested in the theater, who gathered spontaneously during two summers at Provincetown, Mass., for the purpose of writing, producing and acting their own plays. The impelling desire of the group was to establish a stage where playwrights of sincere, poetic, literary and dramatic purpose could see their plays in action and superintend their production without submitting to the commercial manager's interpretation of public taste. Equally, it was to afford an opportunity for actors, producers, scenic and costume-designers to experiment with a stage of extremely simple resources—it being the idea of the Players that elaborate settings are unnecessary to bring out the essential qualities of a good play.

The rest of the story of the Provincetown Players is history. It was a revivifying force in American drama. William Archer wrote of it:

In the region of Washington Square or Greenwich Village, or . . . among the sand dunes of Cape Cod—we must look for the real birthplace of the American drama.

The Provincetown Players drew to them all that was most talented in America. The list of names of players and poets and playwrights and stage designers is so long that here one cannot even attempt a catalogue.

If they did nothing else they gave immediate recognition to a major talent, that of Eugene O'Neill, which was singularly unsuited to buffeting the commercial theatrical world. It was Jig Cook's work with the Provincetown Players that cracked the hard shell of custom of the theater of that day. It was the Provincetown Players that formed the channel through which the new inspiration and the new ink could flow. We were bound by no conventions. We didn't have to think of box-office or what the public wanted and so we knew what the public wanted better than did the hard-boiled producers who were bound by a thousand conventions and a thousand fears.

I shall never forget the excitement there was in listening to a rehearsal of *The Emperor Jones*. The stark fear in Gilpin's voice. The creative quality of George Cram Cook's suggestions.

It was fitting that on the old stable door of 133 MacDougal Street which had a ring burned into the wood, there was the motto which Jack Reed made for it: "Here Pegasus was hitched."

CHAPTER FOURTEEN

Wartime in Provincetown

I

THE town rocked into the World War, keeping time with the rest of the country but keeping a step ahead. As one looks back to the last war and the stages by which we went in, there is a violent contrast between the temper of the country in 1917 and that which prevailed up to the moment of the Japanese attack.

All the young people who grew up before 1914 thought that war was outlawed. They felt secure in their isolation. In the last war no plane had bridged the Atlantic. Then, as the war was prolonged and the incidents of the German U-boats became more acute, the country walked toward war.

When in April, 1917, in spite of the long debate in Congress, war was declared, the nation had taken a long travail of spirit to reach the final, terrifying conclusion. But after war was actually declared, the country closed itself together like a fist. There was a swing and a rhythm of people walking to victory.

In this present war the cleavage in opinion was so deep

that it has had in it the elements of civil war. Youth has not been brought up on a sentimental song like "I Did Not Raise My Boy to Be a Soldier," but brought up to believe the last war was a phony war and until Pearl Harbor that this war was phony, too. They believed that British propaganda, the big banking interests and munition makers took us into war in 1917. Fishermen's sons in Provincetown, who hardly know the difference between isolationist and interventionist, gave reasons against America's foreign policy that sounded as though inspired by Charles Lindbergh.

The people who were the spearhead to the opposition to war in 1917 were largely idealists, sincere people who could not believe that it was impossible for us to stay outside a world conflict. They were the people who had nominated Wilson on a non-war platform.

In the present conflict, besides the sincere isolationists, there have been sinister Fascist forces who have disputed every step of this country's entry into war. They have ceaselessly, over radio and in the press and using the privileges of Congress, confused the issue and have prevented a clear understanding of the menace before us. The enemy himself shocked the country into a tardy realization of our perilous position. It took Pearl Harbor to convince us that we were vulnerable.

II

Provincetown made a very little noise about the First World War. It had few parades or flag waving. It didn't need them. The quota from Provincetown was thirty-eight, and the number of those who enlisted was three hundred.

Soon after the declaration of war, Provincetown became a naval base. When the fleet came in, there would be a flotsam and jetsam of gobs in white ashore, casting about for something to do, looking vainly for a drink.

Provincetown had always distrusted sailors. Girls of good

character weren't seen with them. I remember Dr. Fitz watching a magnificent procession of battleships leaving the harbor.

"Nine months from now," he said delicately, but gloomily, "I'll be having an awful lot of work I hadn't ought to have."

Now sailors were heroes. We were at war. These boys were going out to fight. They were facing death. From being pests and unwanted, the sailors had become our country's defenders and Provincetown treated them tenderly and gave dances for them in Town Hall, which were attended by the most fastidious young ladies in town. When people are going to die for you, you can afford to dance with them.

It's the thin red line of 'eroes
When the band begins to play.

The boys were all crazy to get "Over There." They were fed up with the tedium of life in barracks. Desire for adventure fed their eagerness, but what animated them was the belief that they were serving a great cause.

We went into war in a crusading spirit. No one who saw much of the armed forces either here or in France could doubt that. The men of the A.E.F. had gone to war for something in which they believed. When they got over there and found war a messy, dirty business, nine-tenths boredom and one-tenth slaughter, it didn't alter the fact that they were fighting for something great. We have begun this war on the defensive.

Provincetown in war days walked soberly. The boys had gone and presently there came back news of those who had died. Friends like Norman Cook were gone, to whom we had spoken nearly every day in the drugstore, and Louis Young, who used to come down to take Heaton fishing when Heaton was little and Louis a big boy. In all there were twelve dead. Their names are on the pedestal of the monument in front of Town Hall.

[129]

III

At that time, of course, we had no radio. We were dependent on newspapers and magazines. The war wasn't as near as it is today. No voices came from England, Russia, Germany, or France. Today, the war steps within one's four walls at the turn of a button. Now, the war demands the energies of the whole people; in the last war it was still true that men must fight and women wait; all that people in Provincetown could do was to sew and knit. The Red Cross headquarters was full of whirring machines. It was strange and touching that Provincetown should be making little black school aprons for French children.

The things that we made in the little towns of America penetrated to the farthest quarters of impoverished Europe. Refugees in the Balkans or in Greece had for their only garments things made in just such sewing rooms as ours in Provincetown. Afghans knitted by some farm woman of the Middle West became a luxurious overcoat for some European peasant who had lost everything.

These Red Cross meetings were sociable. They mixed the people of the town and broke through their cliques. I remember a beautiful old lady whom I had never seen before, who resembled George Washington. She had a fine aquiline profile and a white pompadour rolling back from her face, pink as a country squire's. She might have posed for a sister of our first President. I heard her say, surprisingly:

"Mrs. Foster, if I did believe in hell, it wouldn't have the least terror for me. I've never known a disagreeable thing in this world that I couldn't get used to in two weeks." And buzz-buzz-buzz went her machine.

In 1918 came the flu epidemic. Then Provincetown put on a strange face. Everyone went around masked with an antiseptic cloth. It made one feel that the days of pestilence in the Middle Ages had returned. People were stricken so fast that hospitals couldn't care for them. A hospital was improvised in the Universalist Church. The schools and movies closed. Queer-looking people we were, as in our small corner of the world we fought the flu which was killing the armies on both sides, and killing the boys in camps, as well as those outside. In Provincetown twenty-five died and about eight hundred and twenty-nine were sick with flu.

IV

Provincetown did its share of witch-hunting at that time. Every stranger was under suspicion. Henry J. James in his fine book, *German Submarines in Yankee Waters,* tells of walking on the shore with his father carrying a lantern. They themselves belonged to the Shore Patrol, yet a patrol boat hurried in to find out to whom they were signaling. A sheet hung out of a window to dry would be considered a signal to the enemy and looked into.

Eugene O'Neill and a friend came down in the very early spring of 1918 to write a play. Eugene was exempt from the draft because of tuberculosis. They would go out daily to walk on the dunes. Soon word spread through town that there were two men watching the coast defenses. O'Neill was arrested and it took him quite a while to prove his exemption and that he was the son of the great actor, James O'Neill, who lived in New London. He was then released, but a sleuth was kept upon his trail for weeks. He and the detective both lived at the Atlantic House and it was the detective's duty to read all of Gene's mail. They became great friends.

"Well," he would say cheerily at breakfast, "you got a letter from your mother, Gene, but your girl's forgot you today, but someone's sent you a knitted tie just the same."

Much worse is the incident of an artist called Seabury. He was a tall blond. With a stretch of the imagination, one might think him a German. He had been educated abroad and spoke a different English than that of the Cape people. The artists of the Beachcombers began to suspect him of being a spy. The poor man was persecuted. There was talk of running him out of town, of arresting him, when Max Bohm, the famous painter, came furiously to his assistance and shamed the witch-hunters into silence and sanity. Max Bohm was not only a great painter, but a great man with a burning hatred for injustice.

V

In 1918 the war came to Provincetown. On Sunday morning, July 21, there was a sound of gunfire and a siren sounded, which meant submarine attack. Most of the people here did not recognize it. The sailors who manned the fleet of submarine chasers were hurrying to their stations, and after a while, people realized that three miles off Chatham, the German submarine *U-156* was shelling American shipping.

The steel tug *Perth Amboy*, towing a string of barges, had left Gloucester shortly after midnight. The submarine attacked at a place but a few miles from the U. S. Naval Air Station at Chatham, on one hand, and a naval base at Provincetown, on the other. The first the *Perth Amboy* knew of danger was a deck hand shouting a warning. There was a slight fog from which the submarine fired. The deck hand recognized the wake of a torpedo passing astern and one forward of the tug. As he gave the warning, a shell crashed through the wheelhouse, carrying away the hand of the helmsman, John Vitz. It also set the engine room afire. Then the submarine turned its fire on the barges who had aboard forty-one persons including three women and five children.

The German submarine stayed on the surface of the water for an hour and a half and fired 147 rounds without interference from the naval base or from the aviation forces.

Aid came from the coast-guard station at Chatham. The captain of the second barge had an eleven-year-old son aboard who, when he saw the submarine, waved a small American flag defiantly and got a toy gun with which to attack the enemy. The captain of the last barge was Joseph Perry of Provincetown. This is the official account of what happened:

We were just abreast Coast Guard Station No. 40 at Orleans when the German submarine appeared out of the haze one half mile away, firing at us with both guns. She attacked the tug first, and then the four barges, beginning with the stone-laden *Lansford*, and ending with my vessel, the *No. 740*. The shells fired at the tug struck with deadly accuracy, but the deep-laden stone barge was hard to hit, most of the shells flying high overhead straight for the beach. We received in turn a hail of shot. Shells struck my craft in the bow. Each one just seemed to lift the deck clear. All hands lost but little time getting away from the vicinity in our boats. I saw two flying machines flying high over the submarine. After a while they straightened out and sped toward Chatham. They returned later in the afternoon after the submarine had disappeared.

The coast guard lookout notified the captain of the station off Chatham, Robert F. Pierce, ordered out his surfboat and also notified the naval station ten miles away. The official report of Captain Pierce records:

When about two-thirds of the way off to the sinking tug and four barges we met the boat from the *Perth Amboy* with all of her crew which had escaped. The crews of the barges had left and were pulling for Nauset Harbor in their lifeboats. They landed three miles from our station to the north. On meeting the lifeboat from the burning tug, Captain Tapley of the *Perth Amboy* said: "Do not go any further; we have all our crew here and all have left the barges." No. 1 surfman, W. D. Moore, was put into the lifeboat of the *Perth Amboy* at the request of Captain Tapley to treat the injured man and to render first aid to the seaman who had been so badly injured in the pilothouse. He was lying in the stern of the boat with a badly shattered arm and unconscious from the loss of blood. Mr. Moore at once put a tourniquet on the arm to stop the flow of blood from an arterial hemorrhage and treated the wound of another man who was near him, and assisted in landing the lifeboat through the surf.

After landing, the services of a doctor were obtained and the crew of the *Perth Amboy* were removed to the station. The doctor treated the remaining injured men, and complimented Mr. Moore, surfman No. 1, on his work with the tourniquet, saying: "Whoever put this tourniquet on this man saved him from bleeding to death."

His report ends with the laconic statement, "This was all done under the fire of the enemy submarine."

Where was the fleet of submarine chasers in Provincetown, and where were the planes from the U. S. Naval Air Station? The Provincetown populace and people from all over the Cape had already arrived. The moment people in Provincetown realized that there was an enemy attack at Chatham they jumped into every sort of conveyance and even started on foot. Captain Kendrick stood beside his accommodation, shouting:

"A dollar a round trip to go an' see the German submarine! But I don't promise nawthin'!" Someone asked him:

"What do you mean, Captain Kendrick? Do you mean you won't promise we'll be safe?"

"Safety, shucks no!" said Mr. Kendrick. "I won't promise that the submarine won't 'a' submerged, and you won't waste your dollar. . . . One dollar a round trip to see the submarine! See the enemy craft! Go and see the German submarine!"

Hundreds of people gathered on the shore to see the enemy craft. But she had submerged for good, and we never had a glimpse of her.

Though a crowd of spectators was there, no sub chasers from Provincetown ever appeared on the scene of action. The sailors had jumped to their stations, but the boats failed to arrive. For an hour the fifty-one sub chasers put themselves in battle formation and the flotilla steamed forth out of the harbor full speed to give battle to the German marauders. What happened now seems incredible but it is in the records of the United States navy.

[134]

The commander with his considerable armed force of boats steamed boldly around Highland Light. At that point orders were given to return to port. Apparently the commander did not feel justified in exposing his fleet of small vessels to submarine fire. The boys, full of excitement and eager for action, were amazed. A disgruntled lot of sailors and young officers returned to the safety of the harbor.

Feeling ran high in Provincetown. What were the sub chasers there for if not to chase subs? There were a large number of them and they were armed. The average citizens did not understand much about the science of warfare but they did understand with startling clearness that an enemy submarine could buzz up to our coast, set a tug afire, cause loss of life, loll around the surface of the water for an hour and a half, fire torpedoes and shell American vessels, within easy reach of a large shore patrol and an air base.

The poor boys in the Shore Patrol had a hard time in Provincetown after that. Schoolboys snickered when they passed; their nickname for the "S.P." on their caps was changed by the fishermen to "Slacker Patrol."

Why the submarine was not attacked from the air has never been explained satisfactorily. Many different and complicated reasons were given. That evening up in front of Town Hall where the town was abuzz, an aviator from the base talked to the crowd. He said that there were no bombs in the station. Two seaplanes were observed above the scene, but no one saw a bomb dropped. Captain P. B. Eaton of the U. S. Coast Guard, in charge of the Chatham Naval Air Station, stated that he flew over and dropped a bomb which did not explode. There were various stories emanating from the naval base of acts of heroism, but they always ended with the statement that the bomb failed to go off. There was another story that, being Sunday, men were away on leave playing baseball and that there were only two planes at the air base at the time because the rest were looking for a missing dirigible which was later found off Nova Scotia.

VI

Forty-eight hours before the barges at Orleans were shelled the 13,680-ton armored cruiser, *San Diego,* with a crew of 375 officers and men was sunk by a mine laid by the *U-156* near Fire Island. Three of these men were killed by the explosion and three others disappeared. From Chatham the German U-boat went north. Her object was the sinking of the fishing fleet off the Banks, to deplete the American supply of an essential food. She next sunk the *Robert and Richard* out of Gloucester.

Captain Wharton of the Gloucesterman was taken aboard the U-boat. Americans received courteous treatment. The second officer, who spoke perfect English, told him that he had a home in Maine where he had lived many years. This statement was corroborated by many other victims who were taken aboard German U-boats. The crew of seventy-seven men to a large extent spoke English. The *U-156* was officered by men who knew the intricate Atlantic coast as one may know one's own back yard.

No one who did not know these waters would have ventured into the complex and dangerous shoals outside of Chatham or into the difficult approaches to the Bay of Fundy.

Provincetown was to hear more of the *U-156.* It was she who destroyed the *Annie Perry,* once the queen of the fleet of the fresh fishermen. The *Rose Dorothea,* carrying cargo to Halifax, and the *Jessie Costa* were other vessels from Provincetown sunk by German submarines.

The blackened victims of the *Pennistone,* an English vessel, four badly scalded engineers together with other victims, came ashore on the back side of Provincetown. They had been in open boats for several days and had finally drifted to our shores. The *Pennistone* was one of a convoy which had set out to England from New York and had lagged behind and become a victim of the *U-156*.

In all, eight U-boats ravaged our shores without serious difficulty. They operated during six months, 3400 miles from their base. The score at armistice time was ninety-one ships lost, a total loss of 197,761 tons and 435 lives. These submarines went up the Chesapeake, tried their skill at cable cutting, were within sight of the lights of New York, raided the fishing fleets successfully, and, with thorough German system, destroyed the George's Banks fleet; and they drew upon citizens long residing in America for officers and seamen. We have since learned to call such—Fifth Columnists.

CHAPTER FIFTEEN

Other Ports and Other Harbors

I

DURING wartime the casualties of the Provincetown boys overseas were not our only disaster. There was a frightful loss of life among our fishermen in 1917. A sudden gale came up, one of those murderous freak storms that kill more people than a great tempest. Three Provincetown schooners were lost, and with them thirty-five men, the fathers of families. Provincetown and Gloucester vessels were later found in ports as far north as Maine. All New England came to the help of Provincetown. The *Boston Post* collected a fund of $25,000 for the use of the Province-town widows and orphans.

Before the storm I had hired a fishing boat, the *Kathie C*, to make a long-planned cruise to the Vineyard Islands. Since the Cape Cod Canal had been opened New Bedford had become a neighbor, Nantucket and Martha's Vineyard accessible.

Louise and Tony Avellar, Heaton and a friend of mine and I set out together, the shadows of the storm still over us. The Bay was pale and intense as polished metal. One couldn't believe in yesterday's storm.

We pounded past the silent fishing fleet and rounded Long Point. Once past the lighthouse Provincetown vanishes and there is nothing but a low-lying and desolate sand dune, the remote resting place of gulls. The harbor tongued with gray wharves, the houses trooping into the sea, are gone.

Near Wood End Light a seiner appeared under our lee. In the early-morning sun the men's faces shone like bronze and their red boots, the brown swirl of their nets, and their black boats made a violent contrast against the intense pallor of the sea. They seemed unchanged from those men of ancient days who went to put out their nets for fish.

We dropped them astern, two of them sitting in the crosstree of their sloop, spots of black against the sky's pallor, watching for the ripple of schooling fish to flush the water a darker blue.

II

The sun climbed up among the architectural high clouds and we passed the desolate sandspit which marks the entrance to the Cape Cod Canal, where the hull of a vessel, like the vertebrae of some sea monster, lay bleaching.

All canals, from our hyphen to the Panama, smell offensively of engineering, and though time may soften the newness of their edges, they never fail to give you a sense of their self-importance. At the end of this canal, however, you have your own moment of victory, when the great bridges docilely lift themselves to let you into Buzzards Bay.

Cape Cod Bay and Buzzards Bay are only a short distance apart, but they belong to different worlds. Buzzards Bay is like inland water. On the left hand its harbors are small, the shore bordered with what to us, accustomed to our low-lying houses, looked like the infant progeny of summer hotels. What with its yacht clubs and its summer people it reminded one of Long Island Sound. Some working vessels made their way to Wareham, but until the canal went through, most vessels having a business in the world stopped at New Bedford.

Yachts sped down the sun-soaked bay. We passed slow-going tugs. A satin-smooth, black steam yacht left a wake on which we teetered.

Suddenly we were snatched back from the impersonal aloofness of the sea by a little dark-gray boat of the Scout Patrol which hailed us through a megaphone and asked us our business. This was not to be the last time. All through our cruise we were being perpetually held up by these busy little boats. Finally our captain said,

"Hey, what's the matter with you? Do you go around holding up every fishin' boat you see?"

This boat of the Scout Patrol, like most of them, was manned by youngsters, and one of them answered a little shamefacedly,

"Gets awful monotonous out here. We saw girls aboard."

Poor creatures! They'd hoped for girls instead of two sedate matrons.

III

New Bedford loomed out of the sea, the towers of its mills forming a high rampart, a pall of smoke like a cloud above them. Along the water front were concrete piers. The past and present met in New Bedford. The lofty masts of square-rigged whaling vessels were still there, a scant dozen where formerly two hundred whalers left the port each year.

We made our berth at the fish wharf on which men were hoisting the cadavers of swordfish shocking in their bulk, their fleshy and rather awful corpses sewn up in burlap. A big Gloucester seiner lay next us, her cockpit an eddying pool of nets. To one side a power catboat was loading provisions; and beyond was a Nantucket sloop closed and deserted, her cabin locked, her men ashore. Like all docks everywhere, we were in an impromptu village composed of boats instead of houses.

Fishing boats have no anonymity. As we drew up along the New Bedford dock a dark man was sitting on a keg,

[140]

picking his teeth. He did not glance our way, absorbed in his own reflections, but he threw to our captain:

"Your uncle wants you on the telephone." He had never seen us before, but he knew the *Kathie C.*

Ashore fishermen, chance-met, were exchanging news about the recent gale. New Bedford had lost three vessels, but no lives; Edgartown had a vessel unaccounted for. No one knew where *Nova Scotia Jawn* from Provincetown was. News of wrecked boats drifted through the talk, as the men stood in the shadow of the great square-rigged whalers, the *Viola* and the *Wanderer*; the *Viola* loud with the noise of carpentry, the *Wanderer* receiving the finishing touches, the eagle of her figurehead shining with yellow paint.

Our vessel was part of the fishermen's club where you can hear the coastwise gossip from Maine to Long Island Sound. The master of the lofty *Wanderer* was the brother-in-law of the owner of my boat; they knew our captain, who followed the flounder draggers winters in Hyannis with his gas boat.

They stood under the shadow of the aspiring masts and talked of the gale, which with sudden fury had plunged every seaport town into mourning.

In this fisherman's world, people were chart-minded. To the man on shore the world is composed of land surrounded by bodies of water. To the man at sea the world is a body of water surrounded by land. Mountains interest him merely as landmarks. Shoals, rocks, and bars are his enemies; buoys, bells, and lights his protectors; the hidden currents of the sea and the tides and the winds are alternately friend and enemy. The weather no longer means comfort or discomfort, when a dropping barometer has to do with life and death.

"Boy, we were out in it!" one man kept repeating. "The waves run sixty foot high!" One had a vision of furious seas, a sudden screaming wind, vessels flying toward death like frightened winged creatures; and afterward upturned dories floating helpless. . . . The group changed, shifted, altered, each man contributing his detail of the storm's fury.

As we went up the wharf, we paused before a lofty, square-rigged vessel which seemed to be the home of a flock of goats. They skipped over the rail of the *Clarendon Belle* with the assurance of old habit. We never found out for what port the *Clarendon Belle*, alive as it was with goats, was bound. Its decks were piled high with red and green tin trunks, whose counterparts we presently saw in a shoe store—"At the Sign of the Whale." Provisions, barrels of flour, kegs of salt meat, littered the deck; cargo cluttered the gangway. To judge by the familiar airs of the swarming goats this vessel must have made her berth here for some time and by her looks she would not be sailing for weeks, and yet, incredibly, she was sailing today with her trunks and cargo stacked uncomfortably about her mast. There was something unnatural in her silence broken only by the pattering of goats and the swirl of baggage on her decks.

IV

New Bedford had a fantastic water front, a down-at-the-heel look foreign to New England. There was a measured slowness in the way the people worked. The air was full of golden dust. The paint scaled from the fine old houses, once the homes of whaling captains. They were inhabited by Bravas, Portuguese Negroes. With the soft, guttural, honeyed syllables of Portuguese dripping from their tongues, the Bravas form a town as alien as anything you might find in the mysterious islands to which the *Clarendon Belle* was bound.

So foreign was this part of the town that the children in the streets turned to stare at us, and a splendid Negress with thin Arab features, the yellow handkerchief on her head like a spurt of flame against the faded pallor of the street, checked her stride to wonder about us.

The illusion of the South was deepened at the wharves where cotton bales were being unloaded in leisurely fashion and where bobbins taller than a man were piled in carts.

In the very midst of wharf traffic was a small and flashing garden gay with cannas and dahlias, a garden kept with care and tenderness. It had an air of having strayed in by mistake; one expected to see a whaler's wife weeding it.

The pier opposite us was loaded with channel buoys, up for painting. They lay there in all their huge tonnage, grotesque and lobster red in the evening light. There was something unseemly in thus exposing them to view.

The *Greyhound*, the largest of the shrunken whaling fleet, her sails ready to break out, her masts very tall and stately beside the little busy tug which conveyed her, went downstream to the lower harbor, "bound after a whale."

Each fishing place has its own smell; fish for Provincetown, clams for Nantucket and Edgartown; and New Bedford in 1917 still smelled of whale oil. The docks and the yards behind the piers were piled high with barrels of oil, each one with the initials of its vessel, while in the cavernous shops of neighboring streets there went on an eternal caskmaking and coopering.

The memory of whale and whaling was everywhere, even to the frieze on the corner drugstore—done in a week by a sign painter—which portrayed the various stages of capturing a whale, from the classic "Thar she blows!" to the harpooning of the monster. The traditions of whaling days saturated the water front as inescapably as the whale smell.

V

We made the harbor of Edgartown next day. A bright fleet of little boats, their sails the color of cream, winged their way toward us. We had come from the world that works to the world that plays. The islands of Vineyard Sound had already become pleasure islands; and as the days went by they ceased more and more to live a life of their own. In the end the modern cottages of Vineyard Haven will cover the Vineyard coast and the summer hotels of Naushon and Cuttyhunk will spread until they meet midway at Pasque. They were a prophecy of what was to happen to Provincetown.

Boys in white flannels were helping two fifteen-year-old girls into a boat as spotless as their white skirts. We were in the land where the yachtman's and the fisherman's world go on side by side.

But the memory of the old days was everywhere; even the butcher had been a whaling captain. I suppose there must have been elderly and middle-aged men around the Vineyard Islands then who were not whalers in their youth, but we saw none.

I walked down our dock and a dark shape loomed out of the black and a soft Portuguese voice asked me:

"How's Maria?"

I was on the *Kathie C*, Carlos' boat, and Maria was Carlos' wife, and we "belonged" while I sailed in a Provincetown fishing vessel.

When, because of the weather, we took the steamboat to Nantucket we no longer "belonged." We had become landsmen. The signposts of the sea had no meaning. Tide and wind were unimportant. The fog might blanket thickly but we were as safe and comfortable and as uninterested as in a railway train. The intimate joy of finding the Channel to Quick's Hole was gone; it was nothing to us that Robinson's Hole was a treacherous place and Wood's Hole almost as bad.

We were far from the world of reality and the people who had created these towns and marked and named the shoals and rips and currents and holes and bights.

In Nantucket Harbor one of our fishing vessels lay at

[144]

anchor, beside her a handsome Gloucesterman. The men from the vessels were talking together on the pier. We knew by the very hunch of their shoulders and the large sweep of their gestures that they talked of the storm. They had more news; perhaps the *Annie Perry* had been heard from, or they might be telling each other what had become of *Nova Scotia Jawn*. But we were now outsiders. The fisherman's club was closed to us. We had lost our place in the world. It was like becoming suddenly invisible. We were there and our friends were there, yet we could not talk to them.

Of all the towns on our coast the prize for high perfection belongs to Nantucket. This town is like some beautiful old woman sitting dreaming in a garden. There were no motors then. Its lovely old houses—built in the days when Nantucket was second only to New Bedford—are surrounded by flowers. Nantucket sits back amid her old-fashioned gardens among her lanes edged with Queen Anne's lace and smiles and folds her hands, a little too aware that she is the aristocrat of the coast towns; proud of her faded and excellent beauty which does not lack even the attribute of strangeness. When whale oil and not flowers perfumed the air and Nantucket was young and lusty, she was not so conscious.

Nantucket does not earn her living any more and summer people, off islanders, keep her alive. Already in 1917 two thousand people lived there in winter and thirteen thousand in summer. The summer people cherished Nantucket tenderly; no immigrants swarmed through the wide houses of the old whaling captains, as in New Bedford. The bookstores had an array of new books, telling of the old characters of Nantucket. There was even a glossary of old whaling terms.

A place, like a person, which does not earn its own living lacks moral stamina, and where the minority of the population lives on the majority there is an atmosphere partaking of a flinthearted, grasping step-parent and a grasping board-inghousekeeper.

VI

It seemed good to leave the steamer and pick up the *Kathie C* at Vineyard Haven. On the way home we tied up at the cold storage in the Canal, the dark bulk of a mine sower alongside us.

"Well," said our captain, "it'll seem good to see a real harbor again where there's room to move in—choked up, those Vineyard Sound harbors—bad country, too, full o' rocks and foggy."

"Provincetown," cried a reproving voice in the dark, "that's a sour harbor in a sou'east gale. Boy! Can't tie up to the wharf with the wind from that quarter! I was tied up there alongside a fisherman last week—and he kep' a-jumping up and down."

It was the engineer of a tugboat lying alongside us. Outside of him was a lobster boat from Rockport, Maine. The captain's wife, an ample woman in bloomers, called to us:

"Have you heard *Nova Scotia Jawn* got in?"

We were home again in the fisherman's club, accounted-for people with our place in the world at any wharf on the coast, and glad to be on our way back to our own spacious harbor.

CHAPTER SIXTEEN

Provincetown Harbor

I

THE description of Provincetown Harbor made by Governor Bradford is as good as any which has been made since. It also marks the great difference in fish, fowl, and forest that has occurred since the Pilgrims landed.

It is [he said] a good harbor and pleasant bay, circled round, except at the entrance, which is about four miles over from land to land, compassed about from sea to sea with oaks, pines, juniper, sassafras, and other sweet woods; it is a harbor where a thousand ships may safely ride. There we relieved ourselves with wood and water and refreshed our people while our shallop was fitting to coast the bay in search of an habitation. There was the greatest store of fowl we ever saw. And every day we saw whole flocks playing hard by us, of which in that place, if we had instruments and means to take them, we might have made a very rich return which to our great grief we wanted.

Our master and his mate, and other experienced in fishing, professed we might have made three or four thousand pounds' worth of oil. For cod we assayed, but found none: there is good store, no doubt, in other season. The bay is so round and circling, that before we could come to anchor we went round all the points of the compass.

This deep, commodious harbor made Provincetown the principal fishing port of the Cape and kept it alive when the rest of the Cape harbors were silted up. If it were not for its broad and beautiful expanse, the town would not be here. It lives and breathes through the harbor. The lively comings and goings of the vessels are the very core of the town's life.

In its waters have been reflected the evolution of the sailing vessels from the time the *Mayflower's* small, unwieldy bulk cast anchor here to the most beautiful of them all— the hundred-foot schooner of the fresh fishermen. The little pink stern two-master was its ancestor, and the schooner was born when, improving on the old model, a new two-master was set afloat.

"See how she schoons!" cried an enraptured witness.

"Schooner let her be," said her builder.

Over the years every sort of craft has come to anchor here, from battleship to Chinese junk. The *Bowdoin*, Commander MacMillan's vessel, came in before one of its trips to the North. Other explorers paid him visits.

In the old days the porgy fleet, fishing menhaden, put in here. In the great days of sail the harbor would be so full that a man could walk from boat to boat. Even today a storm brings all the vessels from everywhere scudding to shelter, until there's a forest of masts around Sklaroff's and Town Wharfs.

Until recently, three-masted lumber schooners came down from Maine; the white-lighthouse tender and the revenue cutters still make their visits. For many years a fleet of submarines showed their whale backs as they clustered around their clumsy repair boat, the *Hetty Green*.

In prohibition days lean, armored rumrunners came alongside the wharf. There are always yachts coming and going. Sometimes in a burst of triumphant beauty the New York Yacht Club makes our harbor on its cruise.

The Atlantic fleet has come in and made an iron wall in the day and a city of lights at night. Once on the *Molasses II* we sailed down to see what a battleship was doing down by Truro shore, and a voice with a megaphone called to us as we came near.

"Small boat on the port bow, keep off. We are at target practice." No small boat ever scuttled away so briskly.

II

A great place from which to see the harbor and its vessels is Tony Avellar's gas boat. Tony Avellar gasses the fleet for Socony. The boat is a great wallowing affair that the captain keeps as bright as a man-of-war. He pumps the gas with one hand, with as little effort as a baby needs in shaking a rattle, though many a landsman needs two hands plus a hard shove to work it. Tony has Mother Avellar's gift of storytelling and her friendly liking for people. He knows more about the harbor and the fishermen than anyone.

One day a boat with two dark-faced Portuguese came alongside. One of the fellows had a bandage on his nose.

"Gee, boy," said Tony, "how you going to tell your girl how you got your nose most bit off?"

The man clapped his hand over his nose.

"Tony, I don't know how."

"Some things you can't explain to a woman. How you going to explain you got your nose bit fighting over another woman? If you hadn't got to the dock quick, you mightn'ta had but half a nose, I hear."

"Warn't my fault," cried the victim. "I never liked that woman. She set someone on me 'cause I didn't want her nohow."

"It wasn't his fault all right," said Tony, as the dory pulled off. "But a most-bit-off nose fighting over another woman's awful hard to explain!"

Another boat came up. "Tony, what's the matter with my carburetor? It's as goddam sensitive as a compass."

"It's dirty, that's what's the matter with your carburetor. You fishermen keep your engines so dirty and you're so stingy with oil, it's a wonder your boats even go. How many times do I have to tell you to keep your engines clean? If a woman was to keep her sewing machine the way you do your engines, there wouldn't be a stitch sewed in all Provincetown."

Next a yawl came alongside, a beautiful creature on a cruise. Tony had his eye out for her as she came around the point.

One of the big seiners came up. "Fill her up, Tony. One-fifty."

"Any luck?"

"Didn't do so bad. They was schoolin' pretty good. Down to the Sound the sword fishermen ain't doin' bad either. But Delickity he ain't any luck. Engine went bad on him in the Race. Seen Wood End towin' him in."

So through an afternoon the stories of fishing, of fights, romances, of storms and rescues, pass over the deck of the gas boat.

III

If man had not been here, it might well be that there would today be no harbor. The sea breaking through at the Eastern Harbor on one end of the harbor and by Lobster Plain on the other end might have made an island of Provincetown and cut off the protecting curve from Wood End to Long Point. Or the swirling sand coming through the narrow entrance of the Eastern Harbor could well have choked the harbor by now.

Thousands of dollars were spent in vain to cut the Eastern Harbor from the bay. A dyked bridge was put across from Beach Point to Provincetown in 1854. Not until 1869 was the dyke finished which finally separated it from the bay, and what was a harbor within a harbor has become a fresh-water pond. The dunes come down to the edge of the pond and sand pours into it year by year. There was once a duck shelter built on the far side of the pond.

Within three years the shelter had been buried in the unhurried, advancing sand.

The harbor was menaced at Long Point end by an inlet which stretched up from the Bay nearly to the New Beach. Here, too, only a few rods of sand divided the creek from the Bay. At different times the sea had broken through. It was a lovely place to sail at high tide in a good wind, one of those remote spots where the complete isolation of wild country gives you the illusion of being its first explorer. But this inlet, too, imperiled the harbor, and in 1911 a breakwater was built across it. Albert Avellar was working on the breakwater and he told us when it was about to be closed, so Wilbur, Tony, and I solemnly sailed up it for the last time. The next day the final stones cut this waterway from us forever.

IV

Those who look out to sea have a different point of view from people who look out on stones or bricks or on mountain and meadow. There is perpetual beauty in the harbor and its shifts and change of boats. Never for an hour does it remain the same. Even on a calm day it changes, when at dawn it may be pale as milk, deepening later to a satin blue and ending in a crescendo of sunset.

The tide is sometimes so high that the Bay is seen bright and shining beyond the Point. The Point, a strip of sand, lies like the shadow of a cloud on the shining sea. On such days, the sea alters at every moment. Waves of color spill across like a changeable silk of blue and another color which is neither gray nor lavender.

Some days are so pale that the sea merges with dove-gray sky. The Bay becomes a mirror. The dories left at mooring are violent black dots. The masts of the fishing boats make long reflections. The lighthouse and its building are in dark-gray silhouette.

[151]

There are brilliant days with a fog bank dark and menacing beyond Highland Light which blares out mournfully. Of a sudden the fog comes inshore and the town is muffled and shrouded in it. The vessels cry to each other, while the bells and foghorns fill the air with their warning. An easterly lashes the bay to fury. The sea beats against the town. Vessels go adrift. Bulkheads break.

It is strange when one has lived within sight of so much beauty to be where there is no changing sea to watch. Life becomes uneventful and adventure ebbs from it.

More than anyone, the Bay affects the children who live by it and in it. In front of my house the children of the neighborhood come to swim. These children, both Portuguese and Yankee, are a different breed from the summer children who join them—so hard and so well muscled are they.

They are like the beautiful children of Capri, strong, adventurous, yet at the same time steady—knowing their world of water. It is a wonderful sight to see Milton at five, with Paul on the other side, between them launch a large dory and spring in and row off with the assurance of trained sailors. There is always a great raftmaking going on, not rafts that tip and leave you in the water, but weighted rafts, sometimes with a superstructure that indicates their builders are going to live aboard her or sail to foreign ports.

This summer, weighted planks formed a sort of surfboard, which the children skulled standing. The girls were not far behind the boys and there are some who swim so well by the time they are ten that one can imagine them later being Olympic swimmers. No wonder that Provincetown is the recruiting ground for coast guards when the children so early become familiar with the boats and the sea. From these dark-skinned, foreign-looking children comes a fine Cape speech saturated with sea terms. Bands of little boys have been drilling on the beach for the past two years. I heard one young commander, who didn't know what next to do about his troops, shout:

"Company *back water*!" The little girl sitting beside me on the beach, watching the clouds, exclaims:

"Oh, M's Vorse! See the clouds schooling." Even ring-around-a-rosy has been translated into sea terms. The children here sing:

> *Ring a ring a rounder,*
> *Daddy caught a flounder,*
> *Oysters, Oysters, Hooray!*

The harbor's importance from a military point of view has always been acknowledged, as has its vulnerability. In case of war, enemy ships swiftly have occupied it and planned its further occupation. At present in the State Department's archives is a German plan dated 1903 for the occupation of Provincetown Harbor as a base of attack for the mainland. Submarines and airplanes have altered its status, but there is no doubt that there are plans at present for its speedy occupation in event of war. This present summer again great naval vessels made a wall of gray between us and the horizon.

Yet the harbor becomes more and more empty, the fishing vessels fewer, and there are ever more vessels from the navy. It is as though the former actors had moved out to make way for another and more terrible scene.

CHAPTER SEVENTEEN

Postwar Years

I

No ONE could live in the midst of war and in the postwar days as they did in peacetime. Instead of the family coming first and personal affairs being of importance, the family became second, and personal affairs of no importance at all, in the dreadful unity of war.

During the summers of '18, '19, and '20 the time that I spent with the family in Provincetown seemed all the more precious. There was an unreality about it, however. It seemed impossible that our Provincetown world, and the world at war and as it was immediately after the war in Europe, could both exist on the same planet.

Through the war years and directly afterward, I no longer ran my house. I came and went as I could, while Miss Selway, the children's English governess, ran it despotically to an accompaniment of English tea and toast—being tyrannical to Ellen, indulgent to Joe, and following the English pattern of all for the boys and girls take what's left. The house ran evenly under her hand, but it was no longer mine. It was a house in which I now had the status of a favored visitor. The children were too young to have any deep realization of the war. So through them the household had recaptured the gaiety of the days of innocence. Pictures come back of that time: Miriam Hapgood and Ellen drawing one large picture after another with a box of pastels someone had given Ellen; coming home and finding a whole display behind the picket fence with a big sign—ART FOR SALE. Unself-conscious and fine pictures, too, of sea and dune and boats. All through those years there are pictures in my mind of Ellen and Miriam playing a series of games under the big willow tree. Ellen dark and Miriam blonde and both lovely, taking old point-d'esprit curtains and making veils of them or dressing up and acting some fairy tale for each other, encompassed about by a shining, imaginary world.

The *Molasses II* was dead. She spent her declining days in the garden between the barn and the house and was a play boat for the little children. Joe and Freddie **Dutra** and Mary Louise and the other small children made eternal voyages in it. The *Molasses III* was a homemade boat. There was a year when the older boys in Provincetown started building boats on a very simple model. Heaton owned the *Molasses III*, which fell off so much that it irritated me to look out of the window and see her sail, half forward and half sideways. I would wake up about light to hear the *"Preis Lied"* of the *Meistersinger* coming up from the Bay—then I would know that Heaton had gone fishing with Stuart McIntyre and had taken his phonograph along. Stuart was Mr. Stull's grandson.

"There they were out again fishing," I would say to Mr. Stull as I met him on the boardwalk.

"Leave 'em be," Mr. Stull would cry. "Leave 'em be. There's nothing you can do about it. Sent Stuart south to a military academy to get ideas of the sea out of his head. Comes back to the water like a duck, talking about the merchant marine. Born to the water, they stick to it. You can't get it out of them. Don't try."

II

That was the time of the dog trial. Our dog Timmy was a bulldog. He was buttercup-colored and had white stockings. His mother was a Boston bull. He had bat ears. His only parlor trick had been taught him by Heaton. He would wag his stump of a tail when asked: "Wag your tail for the navy! Wag your tail for the army! Wag your tail for Uncle Sam!" And he would wag with the enthusiasm of one waving a flag. Like most bulldogs, he had a temperament of extreme sensitiveness. He was loving and kind to all human beings, the playmate and guardian of the children, not only our own children, but all of the crowd who made our yard their playground.

Timmy had the habit of going uptown for the mail with us, when he would either walk with us or ride proudly in the pony cart or bound along beside it. Now the pony cart was gone and mail was delivered. Timmy missed those regular trips uptown where he could pick a few fights along the road, greet friends, and see the sights, and so daily he went uptown alone, going to the post office and returning.

The collector of the port was Mr. Atwood. He was already an aged man, but he rode a bicycle nevertheless, and one day a summons came to our house from his lawyer. Timmy was supposed to have attacked the wheel of Mr. Atwood's bicycle, which had thrown Mr. Atwood, and he had "suffered abrasions and contusions." "It's a wonder I didn't break my neck," he cried angrily. He wanted this dangerous dog done away with or confined for good.

Court was held to show if there was any good reason why this dangerous animal should not be rendered harmless to elderly bicyclists. Timmy was beloved in the neighborhood. There was not a child who hadn't gone out crabbing with Timmy or who hadn't had Timmy run ahead of him on a trip across the dunes.

He was one of those animals who had a human quality. He was an institution in our lives. There was never a stranger trial. Posy Hall and Joe led Timmy by a ribbon. The courtroom was crowded with all the children of the neighborhood, many neighbors had also come to praise Timmy's character. There was even Prince Freeman, who lived behind us, who had suffered so much from Kite's eating his lettuce. Joe, who was so little he couldn't realize

[156]

what it was all about, led the dog proudly up to the Judge and lisped: "Judge—thith ith our Timmy." Timmy fawned politely, pleased to be the center of attention. On one side sat the victim, Mr. Atwood, his hand still tied up in bandages, and with him sat his two witnesses.

Child after child testified to Timmy's good conduct. Neighbors, old and young, came to his defense. But the climax came when Bunny Hall took the stand.

"How long have you known this dog?" asked Judge Welch.

"Most all my life, your honor."

"What is your opinion of this dog?"

"I think that man there," said Bunny, pointing to poor Mr. Atwood, "would be more liable to bite your honor than the dog!"

The trial, which had begun with all of us fearing for Timmy, now took on the aspect of comedy. The courtroom roared. The Judge rapped mildly for order.

The two witnesses only said that they had seen Mr. Atwood spill, while a yellow dog with white legs ran away in the distance, but they had not seen the attack and could not identify the dog. So Timmy was triumphantly acquitted, with mild admonitions by the Judge to see that he did not take his daily walk to get the mail by himself.

Later, Timmy, who had never noticed any of the boys on bikes who swooped into the yard, or chased anything on wheels, was entirely vindicated.

My brother, riding his bicycle on one of the narrow streets down toward Steel's Farm, had a mongrel yellow dog run out and worry his bicycle wheels.

III

These postwar summers each saw the house crowded with visitors—friends of the children, of mine, and relatives. Seldom did we have a summer where we sat down less than eight or ten to table. We were feeling more and

[157]

more, in Provincetown, the results of the war. The days spent with the children were like living on borrowed time.

The country had been living under the tension of war, a united country fighting a war against war and looking forward to what Lloyd George called "a world fit for heroes to live in." Instead of that, we had the Versailles peace which thinking people realized would inevitably cause more wars. America had failed to join the League of Nations. The world fit for heroes to live in came neither to England nor elsewhere. The soldiers who were sent off with such enthusiasm found cold shoulders when they returned. Their jobs were gone. Disastrous consequences of the peace followed quickly.

America as well as the other countries made the change from a war basis to a peace basis with difficulty, with a resulting unemployment which spread like a blight all over Europe. People felt slack and disillusioned. The financial structure of the world was insecure. A great country like Germany could not go spiraling down with inflation without its having repercussions in other countries.

Within a year after the war ended, there occurred the incredible "red" scare and the Palmer raids. During the war the Department of Justice had become greatly enlarged. Naturally these people wished to retain their jobs and helped foment the widespread belief that there was a "red" menace in this country. In this they were aided by a number of unexplained bombs which were exploded in 1919 and 1920, one in front of District Attorney Palmer's house. It was never discovered who was responsible for the Wall Street bomb or who planted bombs at the houses of such public characters as the liberal Frederick H. Howe, then Commissioner of Immigration of the Port of New York.

In retrospect, the "red" raids seem an unbelievable nightmare, as though in 1919 and 1920 the Gestapo were rehearsing here. Throughout the country, people were arrested without cause. Meeting places, clubhouses of foreigners were entered and all the fittings smashed. In New York a Russian professor from N.Y.U. had classes for his countrymen to teach them the English language and American history, with a view to making citizens of them. His classrooms were raided, his blackboards smashed, and he himself brutally treated and, in a fall, suffering a concussion. There was a reign of terror through the Pittsburgh coal regions. Ridiculous things happened, like the arrest of a man who was then held incommunicado for three months because he was accused of reading "a Russian terrorist book" which told how to escape the police and make jail breaks, cause riots, and so on. When the case came to trial, it was found that the book he had been arrested for reading was *Huckleberry Finn*—in Russian! In Boston a large number of people were routed out of their homes and kept incommunicado. These arrests were so numerous that in many cases there was not jail space for them. Many people would be herded into a single room, without covers, without food. *Agents provocateurs* roamed around, getting up "Communist" meetings and informing on their unfortunate victims. It was during this period that Sacco and Vanzetti were arrested.

The Ku Klux Klan was revived. Strangely enough, it throve most vigorously in the Middle West and was powerful around Indianapolis, which had almost no foreign-born, no Negroes, and a very small percentage of Roman Catholics. This section of the country had been Debs' country, where the Appeal to Reason had flourished and where Young People's Socialist Leagues had grown up in the small towns before the war.

Intolerance, hatred of foreigners, fear and persecution of Negroes, spread like poison through the country and extended down Cape Cod to Land's End.

CHAPTER EIGHTEEN

The Portuguese of Provincetown

I

IN PROVINCETOWN a fiery cross was burned in front of the Catholic church. This act of intolerance was one of the greatest tragedies that had ever happened here. The Ku Klux Klan was powerful in Rhode Island and demonstrated against the influx of French Canadians from Canada after the immigration from Europe had been limited. The dormant prejudice against foreigners awoke in this atmosphere of persecution.

Until the World War, there had been a melding of two cultures, the like of which I do not know in this country. For the life of the Portuguese and the Americans was closely interwoven because the interests of both were identical in the difficult work of fishing.

The old religious bigotries seemed to be dying; the old racial antagonism stilled. There were numerous intermarriages between New Englanders or Nova Scotians and Portuguese.

The Fourth-of-July parade was an index that a racial synthesis was going on. The Sunshine Society, whose members spread sunshine to prisoners and shut-ins, writing letters and doing good deeds, had a float covered with bright-yellow streamers. The ladies dressed in yellow and white, amidst the yellow shower, would be followed by a Portuguese fishermen's float. A handful of veterans of the Civil War, in uniform, in a hack, were preceded by a

Portuguese band. Mothers dressed their children as little Priscilla Aldens or in Portuguese costumes. There were *Mayflower* floats and Indian floats and floats representing all the different epochs of the history of which we were so proud and which Portuguese, Bluenose Nova Scotian, and New Englander all felt were theirs. Shimilovitch, the old junk man, brought up the rear with his old junk wagon and his junk bell ringing. Everyone except the bedridden or paralyzed turned out to watch or march with the parade.

The Catholic societies, the Masons, the Portuguese, and other organizations of good will paraded one after another.

After the Ku Klux Klan burned the fiery cross, the Portuguese Catholics retaliated by organizing strongly in the Knights of Columbus and, to show their strength, staged a three-day Fourth-of-July celebration with a fair and fine fireworks. They took the celebration over. It was now Catholic against Protestant; old New Englander against foreigner.

The latent animosity of a dying dominant race, for the more fertile race which is supplanting it, flared up bitterly. The Portuguese had emigrated in numbers and now no longer needed to, to keep their balance of power. They had big families where the New Englanders had not and so they were bound to prevail.

These were the days when the old New Englanders would gather in the Board of Trade on Sunday and march two by two, with earnest, severe mien, to church. The Portuguese retaliated by attempting, and with success, to choose selectmen and tax assessors and to see that the schools, so far as possible, had Catholic teachers. Some of the larger Portuguese employers refused to hire anyone who did not belong to the Knights of Columbus. It has taken a generation to soften the bitterness of religious and racial intolerance of a quarter of a century ago.

In Provincetown's small bright mirror, the world's rising

inhumanity was vividly reflected. This is the sadder because the immigration of the Portuguese to Provincetown and other fishing ports was unlike any other immigration. They were invited here. What sort of people they are, I have shown in my mention of the Avellars. This family is unusual and outstanding, yet among the other people from the islands, the same dignity and courage and beauty abound. The gifts which they have brought to this country are incalculable. They, like other foreigners, have taken up the dangerous and difficult tasks which those of American blood have laid down to enter the professions or ornament the office chairs of the white-collar class.

II

When the big whaling fleet went out from Provincetown on voyages to the South Seas after whales and sea elephants, and our coasters plied from Boston to the West Indies, our skippers stopped at the Western Islands to recruit their crews, and the Portuguese sailors who were landed in Provincetown from our vessels liked this country and sent for their wives and children or for their sweethearts.

The Portuguese immigration which began in the great whaling days continued until legislation put an end to immigration. The greatest number came in the decade between 1911 and 1920. This immigration is divided almost evenly between the Atlantic seaboard and the Pacific coast. In the west more Portuguese work in the mills, while six thousand fishermen are divided between Provincetown and the other fishing towns.

Those who came to Provincetown were almost all from the Western Islands, the Azores, and in the early days there was a considerable immigration of Bravas from the Cape Verde Islands. These are people of pride and character, a mixture of Sudanese Negro, who were a proud and superior warrior race, of Arab and Portuguese.

Many Portuguese families have American names. A cabin boy would be brought over by some old sea captain and raised as a son of the family. First he would be known, perhaps, as "Snow's Manell," and then he would become known as "Manny Snow," his old name forgotten but his religion kept. Other names became Anglicized. Perriaras or Perez became Perrys, Diaz became Deers.

A little Provincetown boy once landed at Ponta Delgada in São Miguel. He looked around at the children and the sailors loafing at the water front, and the signs on the shops, and his comment was:

"Why, this is just like home!"

And no wonder. Fayal, Flores, Pico, São Miguel, began over seventy years ago sending their handsome, clean-blooded people to us and have been doing so ever since. "The Lisbons," people from Portugal, came much later.

III

By the first of the century, ninety per cent of the fishing was being done by the Portuguese. The great fresh fishermen were mainly captained by Portuguese and manned by Portuguese. The fleet of "gasoliners" was almost entirely in the hands of the Portuguese.

The Western Islanders bought their homes and their vessels, went into business, or became coast guards. The tax list of Provincetown shows more Portuguese names than it does those of Americans.

The Portuguese weren't tucked away in one little quarter of the town as were the early Irish settlements through the New England towns. On three-mile-long Commercial Street, that spreads along the water front, are perpetual little crowds of brilliantly colored Portuguese children; by Railroad Wharf are always knots of fishermen—handsome, strong-looking fellows—and as you go farther along toward the West End, " 'way up along," you seem to be in a foreign community altogether. The names on the shops are Coreas, Silvas, Cabrals, Mantas; the very language of the street is foreign.

At six-o'clock Mass, the priest still preaches first in Portuguese for the benefit of the old folk who had never learned English and then in English for the children who know English better than the tongue of their fathers. Saint Peter's Church was built by the Portuguese fishermen who each gave the money from a "fare" until the church was completed.

Formerly posters advertised the Thanksgiving Dance in the Town Hall: Dances—American, São Miguel, Flores, Pico, Fayal. Thus, this merrymaking, commemorating a day so essentially American, became half Portuguese. The American dances were danced upstairs; those of old Portugal, the Charmelita and others, were danced downstairs by young people and old.

IV

Almost everyone in Provincetown has a nickname. This custom is said to have come from São Miguel. The nickname often descends from father to son. So Louis Chocolate, whose tan was doubled by tarring nets, has a flock of little Chocolates. Captain Gaspy, one of the highliners of the great fresh fishermen, was known as "Vadee." Mr. Silva of the fish market was called "Begunna." And there is Mrs. Jazz Garters who lives to the westward. John Bull, Tony Fall River, Manny Bigfeet—there is no end to the nicknames. There is the Goddamn family, with Tony Goddamn and Manny Goddamn.

Formerly there were always men knotting new nets in their "stores," as they called the little sheds on the water front where the gear is kept. Making and mending nets

[164]

were as unceasing a work as that of housekeeping. Fish nets are fragile things, and the fury of the storms and the struggles of the fish are constantly rending their meshes. From the fishhouse would come the sound of a *guitarre*, the seven-string Portuguese instrument. Carts laden with nets to spread out to dry their accumulation of seaweed and sea creatures went down the street. When they were finally dried, the nets were tarred and piled, black and dripping, from the great tar kettles, to be laid again over the blueberry bushes to dry, like a mourning veil.

If you stopped inside the fishhouse you would hear stories of miraculous catches, of strange creatures seen—stories like that of Louis Tindrawers and his dory mate, Lopez, who were separated from their vessel by fog, and when the fog lifted the vessel was gone. They rowed for two days and two nights and finally came upon the back side, thinking themselves in hard luck, only to find they were the only ones left alive of their crew and that their vessel had been cut down by a steamer in the fog.

Or you might hear a legend like that of how the gray moss that covers the dunes and blooms with a yellow flower happens to be called "Mary's flower" by the Portuguese. A fisherman took his wife and baby to live in one of the deserted shacks up at Helltown. He was so poor he didn't have a power dory and still used sail. As he didn't return, food grew low and there was only enough flour left for one loaf of bread for his wife and baby.

One night there was a terrible storm and the woman heard a knocking on the door and hastened to open it. It was a woman with a baby wrapped in a shawl. The fisherman's wife warmed her visitors before the fire and gave them the last of the bread and used the last bit of coffee.

The next morning was beautiful. The woman said good-by and started off across the gray moss of the dunes, the baby in her arms. Then a wonderful thing happened. The gray moss bloomed under her feet in golden flowers, and as she went away in the mist, the fisherman's wife could see a shining halo around her head, so she knew she had been visited by the Blessed Virgin, who had come to comfort her in her husband's absence, and that her husband would soon return. So Portuguese story and song and legend and nickname have been woven into our lives.

While the antagonism of twenty-five years, between old New Englander and Portuguese, has been softened, the Portuguese, who became politically conscious at that time, have kept their political dominance. Building and business generally are more and more in the hands of people of Portuguese blood, and it will continue to be so. When my children went to school, half of the school children were of New England blood and half were Portuguese. Today ninety per cent of Provincetown school children are Portuguese.

CHAPTER NINETEEN

The Fresh Fishermen

I

ANOTHER effect of the war was the disintegration of the fleet of fresh fishermen. Some vessels were bought as cargo vessels, some went south, others moved to South Boston and Gloucester to be nearer the market; and the great beam trawlers changed the whole complexion of fishing when they scooped 100,000 pounds from the bottom in a single haul.

A quarter of a century ago, if you looked out of the window at sunrise or just before, you would see a sight of glory. The one-hundred-twenty-five-foot schooners would be getting under way. No more beautiful boats have ever been built than the great fresh fishermen. One after another would make sail until as many as twenty-five of these beauties rounded the point. They restored one's faith in man that he could conceive of anything so beautiful and so adapted to its purpose. Some authorities claim that for speed and safety they outclassed the famous clipper ships of the early days when American vessels were the wonder of the seas. Down the ages man had been striving for a vessel like this of perfect beauty and seaworthiness.

These boats were made by the greatest shipbuilders in the country; the same men who designed the cup defenders designed these fishing schooners along the same lines, though these vessels were heavier and schooner-rigged instead of sloop. Gloucester was their home and the Essex shipyards built them. There is a long-standing argument whether the elder Burgess, who never designed a slow vessel, or Mc-Manus was the greater designer of these handsome boats. McManus designed the fishing vessel with the long overhang; yachts adapted them after the fishermen had been sailing them a year.

When the knockabout rig appeared in Provincetown, which brought the jib inboard and took away the peril of the bowsprit, nothing could equal the pride of her crew— "Boy, she's keen!" The beautiful black vessel shone; her sails were pale gold. She was a triumph, another step in man's long struggle with the sea. These vessels were evolved from the two-masted schooners, the bankers which fished off the Great Banks, of the *Captains Courageous* type.

Their tale of adventure and daring has never been told completely and probably never will be told, for while their exploits were taking place there was no one to record them. Certainly the fishermen would not. The stories of the fishermen's races in Gloucester are great stories of magnificent sailing; the race that brought the Lipton Cup to Provincetown is a great story. But the real stories and those that will never be recorded are those of the races to market.

The legend here in Provincetown is that the great highliners, like Captain Gaspy of the *Valerie* and Santos and Marion Perry and Joe King (Antoine Joaquin Sousa) of the *Jessie Costa* or Manuel Enos of the *Annie Perry*, never hove to in their race from the George's Banks. They left their fishing grounds with a "keep 'er full and drive 'er." Drive her they did. A coastwise steamer came to anchor in Provincetown Harbor reporting, "Had a fishing boat pass me sailing underwater."

They sailed their vessels with water swirling around the waist of the helmsman. They kept on canvas until the water came around the helmsman's neck. They tied their halyards aloft so they couldn't shorten sail. Fishermen claimed a good Provincetown boat sailed better when her cabin house was "most draggin'." They said that a vessel like the

Annie Perry couldn't sail at all if her rail came up for air. There are stories of Gloucester boats winning races with "their sail just level with the water and their crew sitting on the keel."

The race of these rival skippers for market has probably outfooted any of the formal fishermen's races, though we have no record of them. In those days when fish were scarce and the man who made market first got the high prices, if he came in after stormy weather with halibut he might make a fortune for himself and his crew. The racing of two of these great boats was one of the romances of the sea, the winner coming in with a broom tied to his mast, indicating he had swept all before him.

The great captains strode the streets of Provincetown with the security of great rulers. Here was the moral equivalent of war. Here were danger and adventure. Here was a gamble so great that it included risking one's living and one's life. The men who sailed under these great captains were as proud of their vessel as if they owned her themselves.

What made a captain was a combination of a nose for fish and an ability to know how much canvas he could keep on—a daring that came close to instinct. Keep on too much canvas and you broke your spars and blew your sails to ribbons. Such men knew how to take advantage of the slightest shift of the wind and would pile sail on sail, not only because who made market first made money. They raced for sport, for pride, and for the devil of it.

A nose for fish is still a fisherman's greatest gift. A captain will sense that there are fish nor'ard and he will up anchor and follow this hunch. A nose for fish is like second sight, or it's perhaps a syntheses of a knowledge of weather, of the habits of fish, of some evanescent clue, come and gone too quickly for a man's brain to record it. Yet it's as real as two times two. Year after year a captain with a nose for fish will come in, his gunwhales awash, when his less gifted competitors come in empty.

[169]

Of these captains James B. Connolly says in his *Gloucester Fisherman*, "By all the laws of chance such men should be lost at sea, but they are not so lost. They were daring but not foolish men. Knowledge and intelligence were theirs; and theirs also an extra sense—call it intuition or genius— that subconscious sense or faculty in seaborn men which makes it safe for them to do things which other men say cannot be done."

These great sailing captains are passing, though there are still skillful and daring men on the fishing vessels.

II

For two centuries the American fisherman fished over the side of their vessels anchored. Then at last they adopted the method long used by the Frenchmen, that of fishing with trawl, two men to a dory, with two nests of eight to ten dories piled one inside the other on the deck of the schooner, and then put overboard to fish. Trawl is a long heavy cord. At every eighteen inches a smaller line is attached on which is the hook. The heavy cord which may be a mile long is paid out and lies on the bottom, anchored at one end with a buoy marking its other end. There are fifteen hundred hooks in the trawl, eighteen inches apart. The baiting of this trawl and the coiling of it into the trawl tub so it will run look little short of a miracle to a watching landsman.

The long, thin knives flash so quickly you can hardly see them cutting off pieces of bait; baiting and coiling the trawl into its tub is another sleight of hand. Sometimes the men baited by the light of flares, the whole vessel alight and the men's faces crimson, their knives flashing silver, their hands moving machine fast. A good fisherman can bait thirty hooks a minute. The coiling and uncoiling of the trawl are an art.

After some hours they pulled their trawl in and if they had luck there would be fine cod and halibut on their hooks.

[170]

They might row back "gunnal awash." If they had no luck, it was one dogfish after another.

It's the work of a stout man to haul in the line with a great fish on every hook and kill them with a gobstick as they come overboard in a dory that may be tipping at an angle and that has to be kept head in to the incoming waves. Into this tipping, lurching boat comes the flood of fish.

Halibut fishing is the heaviest fishing of all. Here come fish that weigh a hundred pounds, still fighting and unmanageable while the dory may be rearing like a horse on the incoming waves. Nothing but heavy, strong men were chosen for halibut fishing.

Steam has changed all this, though one of the best of our Provincetown fishermen, Manny Zora, went hand-lining after halibut not long ago, and with profit, when the other fishermen were getting nothing.

The crews of the fresh fishermen were from twenty to twenty-four and they fished share and share alike after the vessel's portion and the great overall were deducted. The captain got two shares and the cook got a share. They might go out for two weeks and come back with one hundred dollars apiece. Chances were they came back with only a few dollars. Anyone who got over thirty dollars a week felt he was doing well.

The men work eighteen or nineteen hours out of the twenty-four. They bait, fish, clean the fish over gutting tables, ice the fish, sleep briefly, and are off again. Sometimes they work two days on end.

The Provincetown fishermen usually went on trips of about two weeks, from Provincetown to George's Banks and back to port. They fished generally off the dangerous ledges of George's Banks.

George's Banks have been a gold mine to the Cape towns. The discovery that you could fish there was like the discovery of gold and forever it became the great fishing ground for the fresh fishermen. How many vessels have perished there and how many men drowned no one knows. In 1861 an article appeared in the *Cape Ann Advertiser* urging that winter fishing on George's Banks be discontinued, forty men having already been lost there that year, by March 15. Records have it that nine hundred Gloucestermen were drowned there during the years of the Civil War alone. How many were drowned out of Provincetown there is not recorded.

George's Banks is a terrifying piece of water. These famous fishing banks are eighty miles east of Nantucket. They go seaward one hundred twenty-five miles, and seventy-five miles north and south would span them. So treacherous is this water, so full of rips and shoals and crosscurrents, that for many years no one fished there. The devil was supposed to reside under George's Banks and set the water a-boiling.

Shoals would appear on which gulls settled. It was a terrible anchorage, a place of storms and, worst of all, a place of fog. The early fishermen didn't believe it was possible to anchor there.

For years fishermen had known that there were fish on the George's Banks. But it was long before three Gloucestermen first dared to fish on the George's, though Gloucestermen had been fishing for two hundred years before these venturesome men made this attempt.

George's Banks is a small piece of water. Here the big fishing fleets, three hundred vessels out of Gloucester, Provincetown, Salem, and New Bedford, anchored. When gales came up on the Banks, anchorage was always precarious. Vessels went adrift and ran each other down. It was terrible to see the bobbing, irresponsible lights of a vessel whose anchor no longer held her, running amuck and bearing death with her.

No more dangerous fishing has ever been done than that of the fresh fishermen of the latterday off George's Banks. Let a blow come up and a vessel drag its anchor and come into collision with another and there is no record of the crew of either one surviving. The short waves come in an incessant roll and when they fall square on a vessel's deck they founder it and everyone in it. Yet year by year men have gone out for fish and still go to George's Banks.

Fog is the fisherman's greatest danger. The large ship drifts between the dories, at several miles' distance. When fog shuts in, the skipper makes an anxious search for his dories. He whistles, listens for the answering shrill screech of the conch, and, as if led by instinct, manages to pick up one dory after another. Often there is a dory lost, a dory that cannot be found. Frequently the dorymen save themselves by rowing ashore. A body of legend has grown up around the fresh fishermen.

There is the story of the vessel that sounded her foghorn for twenty-four hours and heard no answering sound of conch. When the fog lifted not a dory was to be seen, yet these dories, attached to one another, triumphantly made Provincetown Harbor. They had been picked up by a Gloucesterman, put overboard at Race Point, and they rowed into harbor after having been given up for lost.

There is the tale of the young fisherman who was courting the same girl that his Old Man courted. He got the consent of the girl but the Old Man got the consent of her father. The lovers parted in tears. The girl did not dare go against her father's wishes. But the young suitor, overboard in a fog, made harbor first and when the vessel made port, after her trip, the Old Man weeping crocodile tears over the loss of his rival, the girl had vanished with the young suitor.

Some of the stories have a sourer ending, like that of the widow who had already spent the life-insurance money and was outraged at her husband's reappearance, going back to her folks to stay.

And the story of the man and his wife who got on none too well. They got on so badly indeed that each had consoled himself surreptitiously with another love. Finally the husband was lost at sea, the widow married again and put up a fine tablet, LOST AT SEA, in the cemetery. But there was quiet gossip that he had not been lost at all but had shared with her the life insurance and had settled down elsewhere and married his sweetheart, under another name, and that once a year he and his old wife met in Boston and went "on a time" to commemorate his death.

There are not only legends of improbable rescues but legends of second sight, of the foreseeing of inevitable tragedy, of ghost ships, and authentic stories of incalculable disaster.

The adventurous days of the fresh fishermen are over. The most beautiful and most romantic of vessels now carry sail only to steady them. The radio beam gives them a bearing that is truer than the compass.

One by one, the fresh fishermen left us. In 1939 the *Mary P. Goulart* was the last of this great race and she too was sold. In the summer of 1940 she was here again, transformed into a dragger under another name. Pure beauty vanished from the sea with the great fresh fishermen.

CHAPTER TWENTY

Great Fishing Captains

THESE fine vessels bred great captains. When you think of the great captains of the fresh fishermen, Captain Marion Perry, who won the Lipton Cup, springs to one's mind. Wilbur Steele went fishing in his vessel. Men were baiting trawls by flares and a young fisherman and an old fisherman began to quarrel about whether the world was round or not. The old man finally shouted,

"You're uneducated and you're a son of a bitch," and they drew knives on each other.

Marion Perry was a big-barreled man with a short neck. He walked with a springy catlike tread and stood over the two men and shot his head at them. He didn't speak a word. The quarrel died like a lamp turned out.

"God," he said to Wilbur, as he walked away, "what'll a captain do when he can't hire nothing no more but sons of bitches and bastards! Fish to the nor'ard," he growled, "and them quarreling about whether the world is round or not!" He said the last in a high falsetto.

"When they draw knives like that, aren't they dangerous?" asked Wilbur, who came from Colorado. "I should think you would need a gun."

Marion Perry looked at him with amazement. "Gun?" he said. "Hell, ain't I got hands?" and he raised his two hamlike hands slowly above his head. "At that," he mused, "I've a mind to chuck one of them bastards overboard anyhow."

He was the kind of captain who didn't need to maintain order and discipline on his vessel. There just *was* order. He was a great captain and a great killer. He had the *Rose Dorothea* built and named after his wife and when he saw how elegant it was, "Gor," he growled, "fishing vessels don't need all this bright wood. I've a mind to tear it all out. It ain't fittin' in a fishing vessel."

I have seen him sitting out on the porch of the eight-thousand-dollar house he had built his wife, the bowler hat he always wore clapped down tight on his head, and a baby on his knee. For this silent, hard-bitten captain who needed only his bare hands to drive his crew adored his blonde wife and her blond children.

Captain Marion Perry, folks say, won the Lipton Cup because he was in a rage. He thought that racing anyway was an effete business and fit only for a yachtsman. "Hell," he said, "don't I race for market most every trip? Don't I get in first? What would I want to race for a cup? I know I got the best boat. Why should I waste time yacht racing? Let them yachting fellows do the racing."

When he was trying out the *Rose Dorothea* the topmast broke. Captain Marion Perry was not chary of words when he told the boat builder what he thought of his rotten spar. Then, during the race which he finally entered to please his wife, the spar broke again and his fury had no end.

He drove his vessel hotfoot for Boston pier with one single end in view—not the gaining of the Lipton Cup, but to tell the boatbuilder what he thought of men who gave not one, but two rotten spars. But as luck would have it, his rival, the *Jessie Costa*, crowded too much canvas, and as luck further had it, the broken spar made it possible for Marion Perry to point up closer in the wind. So his crew tied a broom to the masthead and he sailed in first, with every vessel in Boston Harbor giving tongue to his triumph.

He stormed back to his boatbuilder to tell him what he thought of him.

When he got the Lipton Cup there was some talk of keeping the trophy in the State House in Boston. "What good," inquired Marion Perry, "would that damn cup do me up to the State House? I want it in my own Town Hall where my own folks can get some good of it."

Probably no man ever suffered more than he at the presentation, and that was nothing to what he was to suffer at the hands of his proud townsmen when they gave him a welcome such as no one had ever seen.

The *Boston Herald* of that date said:

Now, this Captain Perry is a combination of daring and timorousness—that is, he is all to the good when real dangers threaten and courage and brawn and brain are needed, but a veritable greyhound for the backwoods when men seek to haul him into the limelight of publicity. Then he shies like a terrified horse.

What he suffered during his ride through the streets decorated in his honor and packed with shouting admirers, the town officials seated beside him, a full brass band preceding, and a rousing big band of new broom carriers constituting the rear guard, may never be learned; but he certainly endured an ordeal more to be dreaded by a man of his bashful make-up than the perils of a lee shore in a winter's smother.

During all that triumphal march, Captain Perry sat mute.

It was because of his natural shyness that he didn't come to meet President Theodore Roosevelt when he was in Provincetown laying the cornerstone of the Pilgrim Monument. Delegations went to get Marion Perry who was busy about his vessel. One hundred and fifty fishermen had sailed over from Gloucester beside the Provincetown fishermen. All met the President—all but Marion Perry.

"If the President wants to see me he knows where to find me," he muttered.

To make amends he wrote a letter to President Roosevelt, inviting him on a fishing trip with the *Rose Dorothea*:

Provincetown, Mass., August 23, 1907

To Theodore Roosevelt
President of the United States
Washington, D. C.

Honored Sir:

A report is current that you said to the fishermen assembled in Odd Fellows' Hall, at Provincetown, Tuesday, Aug. 20: "Mr. Connolly has said that it was a sacrifice to meet you. It is no sacrifice. On the other hand, I am glad of the opportunity of seeing you. I would like to go out on the Banks to have a chance to talk to you."

As master and part owner of the trawling schooner *Rose Dorothea* of Provincetown—the craft which won the Lipton cup in the fishermen's race, off Boston, Aug. 1—I cordially invite you to be my guest on that schooner during a trip to the fishing banks, the date of departure from port to be of your own selecting.

Speaking for myself and crew, we shall be glad to have you with us; and we shall do our level best to make your stay on board ship both pleasant and profitable.

Yours, with respect,
MARION AUGUSTINE PERRY

Captain Antoine Joaquin Sousa, who became captain of the *Jessie Costa* in 1911, one of the great Provincetown vessels of that day, was among the famous captains. He was generally known as "Joe King," because when he first came to America in the whaling vessel he was asked by the mate what his name was.

"Joaquin," he answered.

"Oh yes, Joe King," said the mate, and he was Joe King all his days.

It was only lately that I heard about him from Mr. Lavender, whose father Joe King saved. Robert L. Lavender captained vessels that were in the foreign trade. He was a great captain. On the day of the Portland gale he was standing on the beach. There had been one futile attempt after another to launch a lifeboat to save the men of the *Lester A. Lewis* from Bangor. Her men had climbed into the rigging and there they had frozen to death, and the coast guard had been able to do nothing about it.

[178]

Another schooner, the *F. H. Smith*, came in, and Mr. Lavender told me she went aground in shallow water.

"My father was watching her and there in her rigging was a man and he waved his arm. 'Twas more than my father could stand after seeing those men frozen to death on the *Lester*.

"There was a whaleboat on the shore. My father righted it, got him a volunteer crew of ten in no time, and sprung into the boat. The kickback of the steering oar was so big that it knocked him clean into the water.

"Wet as he was, my father got right in again and somehow or other they made that vessel and took off the man. My father was most frozen to death himself when he made shore. He was unconscious and had to be carried home." If Joe King hadn't saved him he would have been drowned between boat and wharf.

Captain Robert Lavender got the Congressional Medal for that cold day's work and so did the improvised crew of the old whaleboat, including Joe King, later highline captain of the *Jessie Costa*.

Most of the stories of the fishing captains are unrecorded. Gloucester had the good fortune to have a lover of boats and a great teller of tales, James B. Connolly, to record the epic of the exploits of Gloucester captains like "Bat" Whalen. Of all the authentic stories that of Captain Tommy Bohlen of the *Nanny Bohlen* out of Gloucester tops them all. He had put in at Hammerfest, Norway, when he heard that the *Valkyrie III*, the cup challenger, was leaving next day for America. At the hour that the *Valkyrie III* sailed so did the *Nanny Bohlen*. He raced the cup challenger across the Atlantic and got here six days ahead, though he had a thousand miles further to go. He explained modestly that the *Valkyrie III* was sailing on as safe rig as she ought, while the *Nanny* was carrying everything she had.

One of the greatest fresh fishermen who ever sailed from

[179]

Provincetown is Alfred Mayo. Though he doesn't need to, he still goes fishing. Only a little while ago a dory was seen almost foundering around the Point and everybody said, "Who the devil is that out in a sea like this when there is nothing else afloat?"

The coast guard put out to give a hand to the reckless sailor. Who was it but Alfred Mayo with a fine catch of mackerel.

"How in hell did you think you'd get back in weather like this?" they asked him.

"Oh, I knew someone would see me," he replied.

Another time, not long ago either, he was jigging mackerel around the Point and he jigged so many and the fishing was so good he didn't notice his boat was sinking under him so full it was of fish. He put two of his casks open side down under his armpits and waited for the coast guard to fetch him in.

Alfred Mayo is a tall New Englander who still gives one the feeling of youth. He owned one of the most beautiful vessels in the harbor, a great sloop called the *Iris*. The exploits of the *Iris*, the risks she took and the fish she caught, are part of the fishermen's legends in Provincetown. Mayo has a nose for fish that has never been surpassed.

Jot Small was fishing with him one time over toward Billingsgate. The tide was out and the water was shallow and Alfred Mayo said, "We're going to row in," so they rowed in with their nets to the dry sand and they dragged their nets over it. The tide was so low that you could hear the water running through the guzzles at the shallow harbor entrance, and here they were dragging their nets over sand in the dark night. Jot Small didn't say a word because he trusted Alfred Mayo, though it seemed insane going fishing in the sand.

And then Alfred Mayo said, "Now we'll set her," and

they set the nets across the guzzles—the little streams of water which flow out of the harbor at low tide.

Then came the noise of the rustle of great fish caught in a net, and that night they pulled in 1800 ten-pound bluefish and made $250.

Jot Small asked, "How did you know they would be there?"

And Alfred Mayo said, "I've been waiting for just such a night as this and figuring when they would be here, for some weeks."

The bones of the *Iris* to this day lie somewhere over toward the Truro shore.

CHAPTER TWENTY-ONE

Days of the Locust

I

WHEN I returned to Provincetown in the spring of '23, after a long absence, the *Annie Spindler*, a rumrunner, lay wrecked on the outside shore, just where the road to Race Point ends, and the town was full of Haig and Haig pinch bottles.

This vessel was beached here in the winter of 1923. She was supposed to be proceeding from Nova Scotia to Jamaica, with a fine cargo of Haig and Haig and other good liquors, when she sprang a leak. She could claim the hospitality of international law. When a vessel is wrecked it is the duty of our government to provide guard for her goods for trans-shipment. Another vessel came into Provincetown to receive the precious cargo. Under guard it was transferred across to the waiting vessel. But in the meantime many a Provincetowner had seen the fine liquor and a large portion of it was said to have come back quietly by night, or perhaps never to have left the harbor.

The story of the *Annie Spindler* should have warned me

that a new era had begun in Provincetown. The old life whose pace was slow and easy, like the tide coming in, lasted until 1920. Now it was gone.

People say Provincetown has changed much in the last few years. The real change, the deep spiritual change, happened long ago. The end of the war left a vacuum. The fine phrases with which the war ended bore bitter fruit. People had hoped for a new world; instead there had been intolerance and oppression. Fascism had triumphed in Italy. Unemployment was spreading through Central Europe. The young people who had grown up hungry now found no work. There were cynicism and disillusion everywhere. The revolt of the young people of Europe against the authority which had made the world so frustrated a place in which to live caused different youth movements, such as Germany's *Wandervogel*. These movements found their repercussion in America.

During 1921 and '22, prohibition and cars changed the whole life of the country. Directly after the war everybody took to wheels. But we in Provincetown were still cut off, more accessible by sea. Long, sandy, winding roads kept motorists away. Now the state road had come through. Cars had come to Provincetown, and there was a never-ending line of them. Horns honked, loud-speakers blared on the front street. The town looked as if there were a costume ball. Clothes were up to the knees over pink stockings. Little girls wore knickers flapping around their legs, their bosoms strapped flat in tight bras. They had as much as possible the look of young boys. Old ladies in cardigan jackets, visored caps, and pants waddled through the crowd. We were no longer an isolated place.

The summer crowd had come to stay.

II

Prohibition drinking came slowly to Provincetown. We had always had prohibition here and the people who wanted to drink had their liquor sent. Drinking was not a part of life, it was an occasional matter—a gesture of festivity.

After prohibition, people drank as if this were going to be the last drink in the world. It became an obsession not to leave a drink within the bottle. In Provincetown, people who had not drunk at all or had sent to Pierce's for a little beer or wine to celebrate a birthday were now always on frantic voyages to bootleggers. While you waited for the bootlegger to go out and dig up some stuff, you would sit around his kitchen hobnobbing with the miscellaneous customers. The bootlegger's kitchen, with its surreptitious air, was a cross between a smuggler's cave and an old tavern. There would be an old-time soak, one or two drinking companions, some slick pretty girls with their boy friends, an elegant young couple, and some elderly ladies in search of a snifter. Conversation led by the bootlegger would run like this:

"Well," the bootlegger would say, "then Joe went thundering down the Cape. How it happened I can't tell you. The police was all fixed. How long his truck stayed there empty with him and O'Donnell dead inside nobody knows. A truckload of booze gone and not a soul on that highway seen a truck go past. They must 'ave done it in cars. There must 'ave been a file of them. And we thought we'd cleared out every hijacker between here and Boston.

"You can get rid of hijackers easier'n you can sea pirates. A couple months ago my son was fishin' off Hyannis and he saw a vessel driftin' an' no hand on the wheel. When he boarded her, sure enough, the crew was all dead. Lyin' around dead as herrings with their throats cut. Queer too. Why wasn't they shot? Sea pirates I always say are worse than hijackers—harder to get after, tougher, too."

This rushing to the bootlegger's was quite uncivilized but like many other uncivilized things it was picturesque. Adventure had come back to daily life. The old pirates and smugglers had risen from the dead. With the rumrunning and rum chasing and hijackers and rumrunners shooting each other back and forth, the young people were bursting with excitement. A hot breath had blown over the whole country.

III

This was the time of flaming youth. Youth was conscious of itself. Young people dramatized themselves as "the lost generation"—"the Beautiful and Damned." I remember girls of sixteen, who had been charming, unself-conscious little girls, saying in an affected voice:

"All I need is my cigarettes, my little flask of gin, my lipstick, and I'm set." The kids walked around to the perpetual accompaniment of ukuleles. Boys toted flasks to dances in Town Hall, where shortly before a boy with "liquor on his breath" was not tolerated.

Young people handed each other what was called a "line." The line was a sort of jargon, an extravagant kind of compliment that no one was supposed to take seriously, a studied insincerity, to which an older person could listen and not understand a word.

In 1923 the postwar madness was in full swing. The tremendous upheaval of war and revolution had swept out a great deal of traditional debris, long due for the ash heap. Sexual freedom, which had long been practiced under cover, came out in the open. Young people and old talked sex.

This was the time when young people did what they called "face the truth." They believed in honesty. The cartoon of the little girl waving, saying, "Yoo-hoo, Mother, I've lost my virginity," was, like all good caricatures, based on truth. No one stood still a moment. The excitement of cars was new. Life was passed rushing from this place to that place, off on the cocktail chase, off to another dance. Necking was about as public as the amours of a horseshoe crab. Jazz was God. Life bumped along to a boop-a-doop.

Parties became not an incidental adornment to life, but the reason for being.

Social life in Provincetown was completely changed from the days when we danced in Town Hall and walked to the outside shore for a picnic. New people came into town and gave big parties where drinks were served kids who didn't know how to drink. I remember one charming, fluffy-haired blonde child lamenting on the stairs, "What'll I do? I've never been like this before. I'm tight—I'm tight. I can't go home like this!" Youngsters unaccustomed to drinking "passed out."

The young people liked to go to the roadhouse dances which began at midnight Sunday night, to which cars came from all over the Cape. I have a note made about such a dance.

"Music blared out, people's bodies wiggled. Their bare-looking legs flew out sidewise and they toed in en masse before the evening went into a kaleidoscope—drinking, necking, legs of girls going sidewise, shuffle, shuffle.

"Girls and boys in strange contortions, chuckles and slitherings of saxophones, laughter of saxophones, syncopation of trap drummers, an excited welter of young people, toes turned in, heels kicked up, laughter, wails and chuckles of instruments. More drinks, more necking. Shifting of cars whose lights cut the darkness. Everyone was potential fireworks. Another drink, another bit of music, another shuffle of feet, and they would be off, whish, like rockets."

IV

People drank whether they wanted to or not. After a time drink became somewhat regularized. Instead of making trips to the bootlegger everybody kept a gallon of "alky" in the house or a still in the cellar.

If the young people had broken away from former standards, so had the older people. Women whose like hadn't drunk since the great temperance movement swept the country took to drinking. Everybody joined the nation-wide strike against prohibition by drinking as they never had before. The war of the generations was on. Children no longer took their parents' authority for granted. This was part of the revolt war had left in its wake, an unconscious saying, "Why should we respect you or obey you when you have made such a mess of the world?" On the other hand, youth had lengthened for men and women. The teen-age children found they had young parents who were drinking more and dancing as much as the young people.

It would be hard to know if the older people were more appalled by the young people or if the young people were more appalled by the older people. In many households the boys would come home with friends, hoping and praying they'd find their parents sober.

Long before, the old folks had taken up dancing again. Now they went at it with renewed vigor. This was the time of "the life of the party," when a squiffy old boy with a false nose and a small paper cap on one ear was at every party, in every ship's company. He was fat and along in years but he danced and drank and capered and pretended he was as young as ever he was.

V

I had lived the summer before in a little town on the Jersey coast where the entire fishing community had taken to bootlegging. We had plenty of bootlegging in Province-town now. The rum ship would anchor fifteen miles out to sea. Beautiful, swift, armored rumrunners would tie up to the wharf. They would be clean as whistles when they came in to victual up and get gas. They were manned by hard-faced young men who would make the average gangster look like a parson.

It was quite the rage for the young folk to get to know the rumrunners and get taken out to the rum ship for a midnight drink. Lonely roads like Long Nook made good landing places for liquor. Harriet McGinnis came back from a picnic there with stories of seeing a lantern wink on the high bluff and an answering wink at sea. They saw them come in landing the stuff and presently a truck went whizzing down the Cape, perhaps to be hijacked.

The temper of the coast guard was changed by prohibition. Rumrunners enlisted in the coast guard for the purpose of helping get the stuff ashore. Bribery was everywhere. Captains became suspicious of their men. No one knew whom to trust. It was easy money. The coast guard had only not to be there. He had merely to turn his back and be paid for it. Fast little rum chasers were added to the equipment of the coast-guard station.

"I enlisted in this service," one captain told me, "to save lives. Now I have to order my men out in a speedboat to chase smugglers and maybe to shoot them. I'm nothing but a sea policeman instead of a captain." A frightful corrupting thing happened to the cleanest of services.

These social changes happened everywhere. Here they came suddenly. From one year to another the social atmosphere had changed. Too much had come to Provincetown too quickly. The invasion by car, the altered morals, and prohibition were too much for the town to assimilate all at once. The changes were too much for me too. In these years the children had grown up and they were whirled away in the town's new excitement. They took the house over. I was out of tune with the new world of jazz where the young people were avid for amusement every hour of the day. I couldn't adjust myself easily to this new Provincetown.

CHAPTER TWENTY-TWO

The Back Country

I

DURING this time there were two escapes from the young confusion of the house. One was out on the water and the other was the back country. I don't know any other place where the wild country is so close to a town. You can walk out of your door on the back street into it.

I would leave the town behind me, plunge into the woods, cross the railway track, and go up the Atkins Mayo Road, up a steep sand hill, and then turn right into a trail, scarcely visible between blueberry bushes, which we called the Little Trail. This was the shortest road to the dunes. The trail cut through the blueberry moors, dipped into pine woods, and arrived in a little valley where the light filtered through the green leaves of young trees. Wild lilies of the valley were underfoot. The green from above and that underfoot made one feel as if one were in some magical atmosphere between air and water. The dunes came down sharply and there was a swift ascent through the tops of wild cherries and gnarled beach plum bushes.

Suddenly the dunes spread their majestic immensity before one—beyond them, the blue line of ocean. The only sign that man had ever been here was far off the top of Peaked Hill Bars station appearing behind a high dune. I would sit there and the quiet of dune and sea and sky would pour over me and heal me from the new, bewildering world.

Often I went over to the station, or swam on the outside shore. Sometimes I would only stop on the dune's edge, and one of the coast guard would say to me reproachfully, "Saw you on the edge of the dunes yesterday from the watchtower. Was expecting you over. Why didn't you come?"

Although it has been a long time since I was at Peaked Hill, I still feel as if there were an invisible path between that far station on the outside dunes and our house, so often have I crossed to it.

Sometimes when I couldn't sleep, I would go out through the back country at night. I knew the trails so well that I was night-footed and would let my feet take me, trusting them to find the way up the dunes and sit and watch dawn break.

The back country is like a wild little animal that crouches under the hand of man but is never tamed. It has been left to grow wild generation by generation since the time when people were forbidden to pasture sheep and cattle for fear of the encroaching sand.

The woods of scrub pines are all trees of second growth. The moors that are covered with blueberry and wild cranberry have little trails made by Indians or by animals going to forgotten water holes. There are few people who know the dunes well enough to leave these trails, for on one hand there are entanglements of bull brier that only a machete could cut, and on the other hand unpassable marsh in your way. People have become hopelessly lost in the back country and have had their clothes torn from them by briers or been bogged to the waist trying to cross a treacherous marsh.

II

Once on a snowy day we went out to the dunes and came back by the Atkins Mayo Road. In the snow were fresh tracks of a wheelbarrow and feet which suddenly began in the middle of the dune. Someone must have pushed this wheelbarrow from the back side and then the tracks were blown away by the wind and snow. We followed the tracks, wondering why anyone in winter should push a wheelbarrow through this wild country and what he had found in the back shore that would make this work valuable. The wheelbarrow track followed the Atkins Mayo Road for a time, then branched to the left and came to the railway cut. The railway cut is sixty feet high. Right to the edge of this high precipice went the foot tracks and the track of the wheelbarrow, and then they vanished. There were no signs of feet going down the perpendicular side and there were no signs on the sand that had blown across the track.

There was never any answer as to how that wheelbarrow flew through the air or what it was doing on the back country. It was one of the many mysteries of the back country and the dunes to which there is no answer.

The mystery of the wheelbarrow had for a companion piece the mystery of the kitchen stove. We walked over to Peaked Hill Bars at least two or three times a week. One day as we were walking across, we saw a black spot. It was quite a way to the left of the Snail Road. We went up to see what it was. It was a kitchen stove in good repair. There it sat for no reason at all, near no road, near no wagon track, a fine kitchen stove. There also it remained year by year and rusted away and the sands covered it. You can be puzzled by the hour as to why or what brought the kitchen stove. Sinclair Lewis made a legend about it. He said that one of the wives of the lifeguards got mad and left for home and, naturally, took her stove along and didn't notice till too late that it was gone. He pointed out that that was the only way that a kitchen stove could have got there unless an airplane had dropped it, which seemed unlikely.

III

I do not know of any country which is so wild and so diverse within so small a compass. This little piece of land, small when you measure it in square miles, is unlike any other place; nor have I found anyone who has seen anything like it.

In the fall the sweep of its color is incredible. Then the moors are washed with purple of the wild cranberries. The blueberries and blackberries are scarlet. In some places the wild country leads down to the orange-colored salt marshes, and the maples around the edges of ponds turn scarlet and the bull brier are plates of gold. The whole back country is spicy with bay and sweet fern.

In the spring there is a bloom of wild fruit which spreads like a bridal veil of shad and juicy pear and wild cherries and beach plum, growing in great quantities where the dunes and the woods meet. The high dunes over by Mayflower Heights are dappled with white in the spring.

All through the season there are blueberries and huckleberries. Later the high bush blueberries ripen near the swamps. Every season of the year there are berries to pick, from the wild strawberries through blueberry and huckleberry time, till fall when one goes wild grapin' and beach plummin'. The last fruit of all, is the cranberry; all through the back country are little wild bogs of cranberries that have planted themselves or that someone once planted and let go wild.

The Cape is dotted with secret ponds, one after another. Shank Painter Pond which is shrinking to a marsh has water lilies and floating islands. Around these ponds on the shore one will often find the sharp, delicate tracks of deer.

They are all stocked with fish. Carp, bass, and perch are plentiful and no one troubles to fish them. Some of the fishermen used to take a busman's holiday and put on hip boots and come back with strings of fine fish. At Herring River up Wellfleet way, there are trout.

The back country is so wild that it abounds with little creatures. Many of them, like the rabbits and puff adders and toads, have turned dune color. Foxes slide through the underbrush. There is a man in Provincetown who traps him a score of foxes every winter. Formerly when I used to go up the little trail I often raised a covey of quail. They would erupt almost under my feet and go whirring past me.

The beach grass makes beautiful circles on the dunes. The patterns are so lovely that wonderful photographs have been made of them. The little dune mice feed on the grass and at the edge of the dunes there is a complicated pattern of the feet of the wild things, and finer traceries yet of the insects which also are dune-colored.

There were foot tracks that we could recognize, of squirrel, coon, rabbit, and of turtle, who drag their tails when they walk, and there were other foot tracks we couldn't recognize at all. The legend is that there are ghost animals left by the Indians. We would divide the tracks into those of regular animals and those of irregular animals, the ghost tracks of non-existent creatures of a distant day. Some times inland on the dunes there would be enormous bird tracks we could not recognize.

Once down the steep side of a dune we found a track as though of a large ball. It ended suddenly. There were no foot prints leading to it or going away from it and there was no ball. It was the track of some large thing that had rolled.

IV

The dunes have many legends. One of the first that I heard was of the white stallion. Many years ago there was a vessel bound for Nova Scotia, with a cargo of fine horses and cattle, wrecked off Peaked Hill Bars. All were drowned but a beautiful white stallion who swam ashore. For a year he ran wild up and down the dunes, the most beautiful creature that one could imagine. Many people tried to catch him and bait him with oats or trap him in various ways but always he went free again and galloped the dunes to his own liking. Then they made an enclosure and brought a mare and he went to the mare. When he found he was trapped the fury of the free filled him. He threw himself against the palings again and again. The dunes resounded to his neigh and the pounding of his angry hoofs.

At last, as though he had wings he sailed over the high enclosure. But two lines of men were stretched out over the dunes. He ran from them and stood on the top of a dune, his great figure with its white mane silhouetted against the evening sky. As the men again approached him on both sides, only escape by sea was possible. He saw his pursuers to right and to left, as he stood pawing the sand. Then as a man with a rope approached him, he reared his head and plunged furiously into the sea. They could see his white mane tossing above the water as he swam on out and out, defying them to capture him and preferring death to captivity. When I first came here the old coast guard still spoke of the waves as white horses.

V

Once the dunes were covered with forests. The early settlers cut them down and made their houses and vessels of them. The old houses in Provincetown are made from timber cut here.

Today the only sign of this ancient woods is a line of old cedar trees peering through the sand, weathered and polished, a ghostly reminder that this was once a wooded country. Today there are no cedar trees in Provincetown

[194]

or in Truro. Cedar begins farther down the Cape. But in the order of advancing sand dunes you may find small woods, like cranberry bogs, sand all around them, about to creep up on them and whelm them.

There are many places in the dunes where fresh water is near the surface and shows itself by a grassy patch. We used to pass one such place on the road to Peaked Hill Bars. As soon as we got near there, the dog would race and begin to dig, and presently there was a little pool of fresh water from which he lapped. If we came past the next day there would be the tracks of small creatures who had been there to drink.

The dunes walk. A great wind will lift them bodily. A vast crater appears where last year there was none. The wind piles up a mountain of sand and things may even begin to grow upon its top. Then the mountain will be again leveled off. There is space here. There is an expanse that gives the illusion that the other side of the dunes is a long way off, as one feels in the West, looking over a great mesa.

The austere beauty of the dunes is almost impossible to paint. No one has rendered their magnificence or their violence. Most attempts to paint the dunes make them look like insipid sand piles.

Where woods and dunes meet there goes on a tremendous and unending struggle. The dunes have been moored down in the Provinceland the last years, but toward the point where the dunes are all prevailing on the other side of Snail Road near the Eastern Harbor, a never-ceasing struggle between trees and sand goes on.

Over by the Little Trail the dunes have been cutting in. There is a trail that's called "The Side of the House" because it ends in a perpendicular dune, almost as straight as the side of a house, with a narrow trail zigzagging up its side. Here are tops of buried maple trees that have arrested the flight of the dunes for years.

To the west of the State Road there's a place called the

Buried Forest, where the dunes began coming in like a waterfall with a motion as slow and inevitable as a glacier's. Gradually the sand is silting up the ponds and in another hundred years there may be no Eastern Harbor. The mighty force of the dunes walking wins each year another victory.

CHAPTER TWENTY-THREE

The Two Theaters

I

FROM the time that the Provincetown Players gave their last production here in 1916, people talked of getting up another theater. There was a tradition to be carried on.

In 1923, a new theater group was organized entirely through the initiative of Mary Bicknell. Many people have confused the Wharf Theater with the Provincetown Players and have thought of one as the continuation of the other. They had nothing in common except the fact that they both gave plays in the same town.

The Provincetown Players had come together almost by chance. Their foundation was the plays that many different people had written. They had also gaiety and spontaneity and earnestness.

The new group at once thought of building a theater and having a publicity director. The Provincetown Players had nothing but plays and the new group had everything but plays. It had an ambition, which was to be a prominent summer theater. It was a strange thing to hear publicity discussed when there was nothing as yet about which to make publicity.

With enormous difficulty, two plays were produced that summer in an empty moving-picture house. That they were produced at all was through Mary Bicknell's energy.

The next year Frank Shay's barn was transformed into

a theater. We were playing a bill which included Eugene O'Neill's play *Before Breakfast*, a play by Raymond Moore who founded the Cape Players, and one by William Gaston, which I directed.

I have notes written at that time of one of the rehearsals.

"When Ellen and I get to the theater all the cast except Myron Viera is there. We shall never rehearse with a full cast. The Shays and Agnes and Gene O'Neill are just sitting down to supper. The rehearsal is smooth as far as lines go but without heart or vivacity. The barn is littered with benches and chairs. There are dark-green backdrops from some set of the O'Neill cycle. The ground is covered with shavings.

"Fern looks very pretty and young and says her lines better than the rest. She is a witty actress. Dogs bark outside. Cars stop. Little Jean Shay shrieks, 'Mammie, Mammie!' at the closed barn doors. John Souza cannot get his cues for music right. He cannot remember to cry, 'Last call for dinner.' He is short and shiny-looking with nice brown eyes and teeth splayed far apart. Bill Gaston gets cranky and tells him to 'lay off the music cues.' We are bored and disorganized, lifeless too. We hurry through early, though we might have had a good rehearsal, as Frank's cast fails to show up.

"A cloud bank rises from the northwest and makes a rapid, menacing way across the sky. To the east the horizon is a green turquoise like the sky in Morocco. To the west as the cloud bank leaves the horizon the sky is red. There is a sense of disaster that turns everyone's head toward the high fog bank which creeps past the monument, eating up the blue of the heavens. Down the village street everyone is looking at the cloud. The barometer is low. There is a gray spiderweb of masts and rigging in the harbor. All the fishing boats are in or coming in from around the Point.

[198]

"We all stand aimlessly around a large table placed out of doors. Gene O'Neill tells Frank Shay he should cut down the locust trees which interfere with the view of roofs of the town and Betty Collins complains to me about the woman who was making her costume.

" 'She seemed so embarrassed because I was in my bloomers and brassière, perfectly covered, yet she was always worrying for fear someone would come in.'

" 'She probably didn't want her husband to see you,' someone suggests.

"While we talk, the wind blows cold and we watch the storm sweeping up. The strange cloud bank is hurrying over the sky. The Portuguese women watch us curiously.

"The Parks and Frances Hyde come. They are excited at meeting Gene O'Neill. Park is a Princeton man. Gene was there for a year. 'Then I had a difference of opinion with the Dean,' he boasts.

"Frances Hyde is to play in *Before Breakfast* instead of in Wilbur Steele's play which we had to take off. Gene wanted me to play this part when it was first given by the Provincetown Players. I couldn't, so Mary Pyne had it. I remember Mary Pyne's subtleties as Frances gives the lines.

"The benches have filled up with the cast of the *Moon of the Caribbees*, who have come at last. The door is crowded with dark Portuguese faces. Some of the children are extraordinary, with smoke-black eyes and sharp, birdlike faces. Frank says there are several families who are Bravas but do not admit it. They have 'passed.' This northern town takes them at their own valuation.

"The children make too much noise. This, together with Gene and Agnes being there, disturbs Frances. Agnes whispers:

" 'You almost have sympathy for the woman the way she plays it.'

[199]

"Frank drives the swarming children away. Frances goes bravely on to the end. Gene coaches her quietly, away from the crowd. He is well, but has lost the look of security and sweetness which made him so lovable last summer. His face shows the pain he went through at his brother's death. He is remote and absorbed within. Jim's unexpected death still with him."

II

It was after that bill the split occurred that became a Provincetown legend. Before the first program had been given, two factions had arisen. One was headed by such people as Frank Shay, William Gaston, Harry Kemp, and other members of the first Provincetown Players; the angel, Mrs. Aldis, and Mary Bicknell and Raymond Moore were adherents of the other and more conservative side. Each group wanted to dominate the theater. Each side was maneuvering to get the other side out.

Mrs. Aldis took the initiative. She arose early in the morning, during a temporary absence of Frank Shay, and got a truck which she had backed up to the theater. From it she removed all the benches, all the props, even the light bulbs, and carried them off to her studio. It showed energy and a ruthless determination to win. The theater was split in two. The goats and the sheep were separated.

The rest of the season Mrs. Aldis had plays in her studio by the water with the furniture from the Barn Theater. The Barnstormers pulled themselves together again and Frank went on with the plays of Eugene O'Neill that he was giving. The Glencairn cycle was given as a unit for the first time by Frank.

Rita Byrd and a friend went to the costume ball as sandwich men, advertising the two theaters. One advertised the LEWD AND STEWED and the other the RUDE AND PRUDE.

III

Frank carried on in the Barn. Next year the theater was enlarged and the tower was built. There was always a vital feeling about this theater, something robustious and rollicking and alive. Though it made no special mark on the history of the theater and though it was disorganized, it still had the breath of life.

During this summer, Raymond Moore, who looked like a young robin peering over the edge of his nest, was making his plans. He had a large Adam's apple which jerked up and down, and his ideal in plays was something like Tarkington's *Seventeen*. His own plays were water with a touch of Tarkington. Yet this young man had the most profound sense of how to make a theater succeed.

Next year he hired Frank's Barn, brought down a company of serious young actors and actresses, many of whom later made a name for themselves, such as Zita Johann.

There could be no greater contrast with the atmosphere of the year before, with its rollicking gusto and its disorganization and its handsome performance of the Glencairn cycle, than Ray Moore's summer in Provincetown, which was really a dress rehearsal for Dennis, though probably he himself didn't know it.

He spent the winter in Provincetown very broke but busy with his plans for the next year. He had seen that Dennis, which was passing its declining years doing some lobstering and having a few summer visitors, was ideally situated for a summer theater. It was only forty miles from everywhere on the Cape. With Plymouth on one side and Provincetown on the other, it bordered on the Cape's Gold Coast—Hyannis, Osterville, Wianno. There was an old church which could be bought cheap.

It was a brilliant idea, from which came the successful Cape Playhouse.

IV

Meantime Mary Bicknell had got money together and had built the Wharf Theater. How she had accomplished this was little short of a miracle. Frail-looking and gracious, Mary Bicknell had under this charming exterior a driving force. In her mind's eye she had seen a real theater in Provincetown and intended that it should exist. The financing in itself was a tremendous feat. The Wharf Theater was built on the remnants of a wharf in the west end of the town. It was not on the end of a long wharf, but inshore, and it was a charming theater.

Mary Bicknell ran it the first two years and while some good plays were given, it lacked what the Provincetown Players had had—playwrights. In the ten years between the two theaters, the theater itself had changed. There were now many places where young playwrights could try out their work. The old hegemony of the Shuberts and the Frohmans had been broken. The war had shattered the demand for bright society plays alone. The Guild Theater had been formed, largely by people who had served their apprenticeship in the Washington Square Players, and the Guild was hungry for original plays. New playwrights could get a hearing.

The Wharf Theater was good fun the first two years. It had the element of something fresh and new and untried, but the financial burden was too great for Mary Bicknell to carry. There has never been a theater audience accessible to Provincetown to make a little theater pay. In its day, the most one could say of it was that it produced a number of plays very charmingly. Young actors tried out there and a summer school of acting was added to the theater.

After 1925 it changed hands many times, and each group failed to make a success. The last few years the Neil McFee Skinners ran the theater. Under their direction it had some of its most interesting years, since the days of Mary Bicknell. But still it always remained a liability.

For fifteen years, the little theater that Mary Bicknell had built with so much courage and so much hope was a feature of Provincetown. We had a great many gales in the winters of '39 and '40 and the fishermen warned that the piles which held it up were becoming shaky. They offered to repair it from their own stock and many offered to donate their labor. Their warnings were not heeded in time and in a great gale in the winter of '41, the theater fell into the sea.

CHAPTER TWENTY-FOUR

The Painters of Provincetown

I

How is anybody going to write about the painters of Provincetown? Who can deal with this complicated and complex subject? To me it is as enormous and as difficult to handle as would be the love life of whales. When I approach it I feel as if I knew as little about it as about love and leviathan; yet I have lived all my life among painters. When I was young I even hoped to be a painter myself.

If there were two rival theaters in Provincetown there were and are two rival schools of art, but the rivalry between the theaters compared to the artists' differences was as brief as the life of a mayfly.

The profound gulf between the two schools in Provincetown is so deep that the respective members fight freely together, pound tables, and even heads. Enormous vocabularies of so great a magnitude were developed during this warfare that a philologist should find here a rich store for observation. One of the first plays given by the Provincetown Players, *Change Your Style,* written by Jig Cook and Susan Glaspell, was about the two schools of art. The play was built on the stark bones of reality, though it had the playful tone of a farce.

Perhaps the most effective voice of the old movement was that of Richard Miller. For those who liked colorful and expressive language, it was a treat to hear him. His words flowed like a river in spate, hurling to destruction the whole modern school. It was probably at that time that he earned the title of Tiger. Cubism and the abstractionists generally "goaded him like a goblin bee that will not sate its sting." Their indecencies haunted him even to his subconsciousness.

Richard Miller was among the élite of the old school. A museum without a Richard Miller is hardly a museum. Burly, vigorous, impatient, with a brilliant gift of invective and a manner of speech that has the restraint of a sledge hammer, he paints delicate and beautiful pictures; lovely girls sewing, mirrored in a looking glass. While he paints loveliness he bellows like a bull walrus on the subject of the surrealists and the abstractionists.

The school of the extreme left had no such eloquent voice, though a subtler note came from the vocal and clever Hans Hofmann. For him could be heard those superior and pitying overtones in which the new order speaks of the futile vociferousness of the dying order. There was a serenity among those of the new school, those accents of certainty with which the Communists refer to dying capitalism. As someone said, "The old school shouts the loudest, but the new school flies its nose highest."

Before coming to America, Hans Hofmann had earned a reputation in Germany as a progressive teacher in art. Many of his students came to him from America. When Hitler came into power, Hofmann moved to the United States. In the summer he holds his classes in Provincetown; in the winter, in New York. As a teacher he is very successful. He is in a class by himself, a complete abstractionist.

The many art classes and schools in Provincetown run the gamut from ultraconservatism to the most extreme of modern painting. At one end of the scale is the well-known academician, George Elmer Browne, who holds forth to the westward. While on the opposite end is Hofmann's School of Modern Art.

[205]

From the earliest days Provincetown has drawn artists to it. Marcus Waterman came first to paint the dunes as a model for a picture of the Sahara Desert. Other painters followed. Ambrose Webster started the first school of modern painting in Provincetown. He was mainly a colorist, who believed in light and bright pictures; later he adopted and became a follower of the French impressionist school. Such men as Cézanne and Matisse held his interest.

Then came Charles Hawthorne, and the morning and the evening were the first day. No painter has ever had such a following. Year after year students came from all over the country, and as many as eighty-five to ninety would crowd into his class. His pupils set the tone of the student art colony. It was a sight to see one of his classes on the beach, painting together, like a flock of bright-colored birds, trying to follow Hawthorne's words and block out not the detail but the essential quality of the scene before them.

He was generous in praise to students who deserved it, and his laconic criticism could flick the hide off a student as cleverly as that of any of the great masters in the Paris academies. But even his criticism was the sort that was inspiring and not crushing—the sign of a great teacher.

Probably Hawthorne's classes worked no harder than other people's, for the art students of the early days were a hard-working lot, but there was an *esprit de corps* that discouraged the frivolous as in the old French ateliers where the last word of scorn that could be spoken of a student was *"Il n'est pas serieux."*

On Saturday morning, Hawthorne would exhibit his dexterity in painting and demonstrate how it was being done. A model was posed on one of the wharves in bright sunlight. Hawthorne would arrive like a prima donna after the stage was set. He would look over the situation carefully and, after everything was right and his palette had been carefully set by one of his favorite students, would splash in his rich colors while his students would sit spell-bound.

It was truly inspiring to watch Hawthorne paint. With dexterity his brief brush notes accomplished what none of his students would ever be able to equal. Perhaps some of his best work was these quick and brilliant sketches. He was a tall man, as New England as his name, and immensely popular. His was an ample personality which Provincetown will never forget.

Curiously enough, although Hawthorne was a conservative—in fact, an academician—a great admirer of the Italian primitives whose trend of painting he followed closely, many of his successful students reacted from his teachings.

Among Hawthorne students who have become well known are: Edwin Dickinson, Ross Moffett, Agnes Weinrich, John Whorf, Charles Kaeselau, Henka and Jerry Farnsworth, Lucy and William L'Engle, Charles Heinze, and many others.

III

There were important artists in Provincetown who derived nothing from Hawthorne. Three enthusiastic young artists from New York came to Provincetown because O'Neill liked it here. These were Charles Demuth, Arthur Fiske, and Zorach the sculptor. They quickly associated themselves with writers of the Provincetown Players such as O'Neill, Susan Glaspell, George Cram Cook, and Wilbur Daniel Steele and others, all of whom had one idea in common—that Art was the great universal refreshment.

Niles Spencer was another independent who has made a notable contribution to American art and who has painted the modern industrial scene as well as anyone.

Fiske, Demuth, and Zorach worked independently for a while. They produced work conceived according to their own conviction, undoubtedly stimulated by the European postimpressionism or cubistic painting.

Up to this time Provincetown had been dominated by artists of the conservative clique, while the younger set who experimented with modern ideas were still in the minority.

These three newcomers gave the younger set in Provincetown a fresh inspiration. For them it was a new dawn. Webster, Oliver Chaffee, and Karl Knaths fought desperately in the Art Association for a modern independent group, which they finally won, but not without strong opposition from those they termed the "Old Hats." Later on, the modern group was augmented with such painters as Coulton Waugh, Floyd Clymer, Tod Lindenmuth, Reynolds and Gifford Beal and Agnes Weinrich and many others. Many of them are very successful and are considered leaders in the American art world today.

Karl Knaths, perhaps the best known in this group, has made some very interesting and highly successful experiments in geometric abstractions. He has won an enviable position among the best-known modern American painters of today.

In the early struggles against the conservatives Max Bohm was a mighty figure. Having been acclaimed in Europe as one of the foremost American painters, he could well afford to be generous in his attitude to younger painters who were still struggling and experimenting with new ideas. And while it is true that some of these young men had already achieved a slight recognition, they had not yet gained any great success. They followed mostly the French painters and the sound doctrines of such men as Picasso, Matisse, Dérain, Braque, or such American painters as Sterne, Weber, and Kuhn.

IV

One of the most fascinating personalities who ever came to Provincetown was John Nobel. He was a big man who always wore a ten-gallon hat and a flaring Windsor tie. Nobel, a native of Wichita, Kansas, came to Provincetown via Paris, where he had lived and painted and earned a good reputation as an artist.

With an unusual flair for publicity and a spectacular picturesqueness, embellished with a vocabulary of such colorfulness that he shocked people into something between coma and admiration, he was promptly elected Director of the Art Association. When he conducted a meeting his language made Richard Miller's expressions sound like a high-school girl's recital. He can be credited with advancing Provincetown's reputation as the most important art colony in America.

One of the most beloved painters in Provincetown was the late Frederick Waugh. He was the outstanding marine painter in America—with perhaps the exception of Winslow Homer, whom he admired. He earned the highest award throughout the country with both popular and academic prizes, and his works are hung in all the great museums in America.

V

One of the most frequent questions of the tourists is, "Where is the art colony?"

They figure the artists as living together in a species of art ghetto, perhaps with bars in front of them through which one may watch them painting, with maybe a keeper and a sign saying, "Do not annoy or feed the artists!"

Only this week a neat but firm-looking old lady approached me on my own beach and said accusingly, "Where will I find the celebrities?"

Poor woman, she probably thought that the celebrities walked around like the members of an Elks' convention, a disk suspended from their necks telling their names.

This is not the case. The artists are sprawled from one end of the town to the other. They dress like everyone else and there is no way in which you can tell them from other citizens. If you see a fine new car, however, it is apt to belong to the captain of a vessel or the foreman of the electric-light company, whereas artists usually only have jalopies.

The townspeople should have got used to artists long ago. They have indeed taken individual artists into their bosom, but by and large their attitude is that of a puppy to a June bug or to a firecracker. He thinks that it may bite or go off.

Many an old Provincetowner has the same point of view toward the art colony as that held by the young fellow who drove me over the Nantucket moors to 'Sconset.

"There are a good many colonies around here," I said, to make talk. "There's a spiritualist colony over at Oak Bluffs and there is a theatrical colony at 'Sconset."

"Yes," he answered cordially, "and there's a leper colony down to Pasque, and down to Provincetown there's an art colony."

VI

Provincetown breeds painters on its own soil. In Silva's fish market in the old days there was a beautiful painting of a mackerel. Hawthorne, looking at it one day, said with generosity, "No better painting has ever come out of Provincetown."

No one knew its origin. There it stood with the veracity of a great painting, anonymous.

When Marion and Tom Blakeman bought the house of Mr. Atwood, who had been the collector of the port, they found in the attic great rolls of paintings of fish by Mr. Atwood's brother, a famous ichthyologist. They were in *gouache* or water color, painted on a soft paper, and they had the flow and abbreviation of the great Japanese. Whale and shark and halibut and cod and all the fishes of the sea had been painted and rolled up and put away and forgotten.

Some spontaneous painters have arisen here who late in life suddenly began to paint pictures which surpassed the work of long-established artists. One of these was Pa Hunt. Pa Hunt, Peter Hunt's father, began painting pictures during an illness. His pictures were primitives in the best sense, naïve and humorous and delightful.

Just how Pa went at it, nobody knows. He asked no questions about material or technique. All of a sudden, Pa came out with a dozen canvases that staggered the entire art colony. This old man got intuitively, in less than a year, with apparently no trouble, something that "the boys" had slaved for years and tried to get, in vain. The art critics lavished great praise on his work and he was promptly invited to exhibit his paintings in various places in America.

Not in the same class with Pa Hunt, but a most interesting phenomenon, nevertheless, was John Enos, known to everybody as Kitty Enos, a former fisherman who took to painting clamshells and selling them to tourists after he had had a fall from a roof.

"Go'dammit," said Mrs. Enos, " 's lucky he fell down the right side of the roof. If he'da fell down the left side he mighta been a writer instead," so voicing in one pregnant sentence a section of public opinion in Provincetown concerning writers and painters.

A small, merry-eyed man, Kitty Enos liked "going ducking" better than anything else. No longer able to do this, he took to painting. The thing he was proud of was the accuracy with which he could paint a vessel or a lighthouse. Some of his pictures, the little restrained snow scenes, for instance, were beautiful. Like a child, he felt no subject was too great for him to tackle; his pictures of storms had the sudden violence and movement that artists strive for so often and seldom get. When he sold a picture for $100, his surprise was beautiful to see.

Since he valued his paintings for their accuracy he charged more for a schooner than for a sloop and more for a ship than for any other vessel. When John Whorf, the famous painter of water colors, whose work is known throughout the country, sold a picture called *Derelicts* for many hundred dollars, Kitty Enos was scandalized. "Why, he's a fraud!" he cried. "Wasn't no riggin' in the hull durn picture!"

The works of Provincetown artists are found throughout the world. All American museums know them. All schools have been represented here. It is impossible, without writing a long book, to appraise them or even list them. Even at present there is no art colony which has the importance of Provincetown.

CHAPTER TWENTY-FIVE

Unsettled Days

I

DURING the "days of the locust," when everything was so chaotic and old standards were being broken and there was a hot feeling to the life that flowed through the town, the upset state of things reflected itself in people's lives by strange romances.

Some were tragic stories, like that of Johnny Blackfish and Sarah Underwood. She was an artist and a beautiful woman. Any place she lived in became a home, warm and like herself. She had one of those modern husbands who said everybody ought to "go their own way." He certainly did and she tried not to mind it. But he began telling her she ought to have an affair herself.

"I lead my life, you ought to lead yours," he told her.

So she began feeling old-fashioned and behind the times. There were lots of men at that time who made their wives feel they ought to have an affair. From Bertrand Russell down, people talked that way. Wives would obediently have affairs that they didn't really want. But it never worked. It didn't work with Sarah.

She began having an affair with Johnny, who had lived for two or three years with a much older summer woman and had broken off with her because she was too bossy.

There was something young and tragic about Johnny and something tragic about Sarah because she wanted children. Her husband didn't want children. Johnny's mother had died young and he kept on looking for a mother in those older women he liked.

So these two people, so unlike, so far away from each other in their upbringing and their knowledge of the world, really fell in love with each other and Sarah's husband used to come down and visit them just to show he was big-minded and meant what he said.

Their house had something warm and good about it. Sarah would cook wonderful dinners and Johnny would sit around telling stories about the coast guard and about himself. It didn't make any difference if they were true or not, they were fine stories. But there was always something tragic about him too. Johnny loved Sarah so much that he would meet every train and boat when she had gone away, days before she came back. And they stayed together until this union came to a tragic end, for Johnny was killed in an accident.

II

Not all the strange romances were among summer people. Take the case of the Williamses. There never was such a good housekeeper as Mrs. Williams. Her house was a model. She baked her own bread. She had two children of high-school age and she and her husband were devoted to each other. Then Williams went into the trucking business and had to spend a lot of time away from home.

There was a no-account summer fellow named Andy Brown who was a girl chaser. He had come to town several summers and it was a wonder that any girl would look at him. He had curly, greasy hair and a fat red mouth, and he looked soft, as though when you poked him with your finger it would stay in.

When first he began hanging around the house people thought he was hanging around Kitty, Alice Williams' daughter, who was nearly sixteen.

Neighbors used to say to Mrs. Williams, "I should think you wouldn't let that Andy Brown hang around your Kitty."

She would answer, with her head up, "You don't need to worry. I can take care of my Kitty."

She was a proud woman with a dark flush in her face and she was nearly old enough to be Andy Brown's mother. After a while people began thinking that Andy was hanging around Mrs. Williams. The children began suspecting it. Kitty had stood nearly at the head of her class. Now she brought in bad report cards from school. She couldn't eat, for she worried all the time. What she was worrying about was that her father would find out. She was crazy about her mother. Both the children were crazy about her. They thought she was about the best mother in the world, and they were proud of their home and they were proud of her. They were fond of their father too, but they had heard her beg and beg him to get some business near home so he wouldn't have to be away all the time.

You just couldn't imagine a woman like Alice Williams taking up with Andy Brown. She couldn't imagine it any more than anybody else could. She'd kick Andy out and tell him never to come back again, but he enjoyed getting around her. He enjoyed making a fool of this proud, handsome older woman. It was a bad, unnatural affair all through. She knew just how no-account the boy was and she really didn't want anything but her own husband. She couldn't get rid of Andy. She had a passion for him which was beyond her. She despised him but couldn't keep away from him.

Of course, Williams began hearing rumors. It got so that the men at the filling stations a hundred and two hundred miles away would make a wisecrack at him. At first he didn't believe it. Then when his mother began croaking like everybody else he turned around one day and came back and found Andy and his wife together. He saw red and almost killed Andy and told Alice to take her things and get out.

So she did. She went down the Cape where her folks lived and she stayed there two or three weeks. All this time she got madder and madder. She kept thinking how she'd been a good wife all these years and what good children she'd raised and what a fine house she'd made, and she thought of things she'd had to forgive Tom Williams for. He hadn't been any more perfect than any other man and what did he do when he was off on those long trips! She knew well enough what he did.

So one day she packed her things and came back. She was a mad woman when she got in. She said, "You've got a nerve turning me out of my own house that I made. You've got a nerve to try and separate me from my children. Who brought them up, you or me? How've you acted all these years? Perfect? I don't think. This house is mine and my children need me and you won't be a mite o' good without me either, so I've just come home to stay!"

Then both the children came forward and took her side and bawled their father out good and told him if he tried to pitch their mother out they would go with her as she was fitter to bring them up than he was and why hadn't he stayed home when their mother asked him to.

So all the Williamses were united again and it took a great load off Tom Williams' mind to have his wife act with so much sense.

III

Love affairs happened in these times with every attribute of farce, like that of the two fishermen to the westward who each fell in love with the wife of the other. All the neighbors knew that each one was having an affair with the other's wife, but the two men didn't know it and they raced like mad to get in so each could have a glimpse of his sweetie without the husband being there. One time Manell was ahead when something happened to his engine and so Fernand got ahead of him. When Manell finally got his engine going and got home he found that Fernand had run off with his wife and his three children.

"Gosh," he said, "this makes everything simple."

And he went right over to Fernand's wife and told her the good news and what a big fool he had been not to know his wife had been carrying on too. So all that happened was that the women and the children changed houses.

IV

It had always been the fishermen's code that if a man wanted to go on a time he had better do it away from home, when his ship touched Boston, for instance. But now, once staid fathers of families suddenly had romances with members of the summer colony. The authentic flame struck in strange places.

There was a fisherman to the westward who was a very personable man and who had a very plain wife. He was a kind man and a good provider. He had everything that a husband ought to have.

Near him lived a beautiful woman, young though she had a family of children. Her husband was a worthless fellow. He was a plain, mean-looking little man with a long, drooping nose and sloping shoulders which seemed to be following the nose. He had little to recommend him. He got tight and beat his family. When he had money he kept his family poor by gambling it all away at the fishermen's game.

There is a story that there is a fishermen's game of poker up to the westward, which has not stopped night or day for thirty years. Great sums have been won and lost at this game and people like Nick the Greek are said to have left as much as a thousand dollars behind them in a night. I do not know if this is merely a legend, but there is surely a fishermen's game where the fishermen lose money that their families ought to have. And this little man, with his long nose and bad disposition, probably gambled in one of these.

Now the strange thing happened. The two homely people had a grand passion. It was one of those grand passions that one reads about and that become classics down the ages. It had all the qualities of great romance, except that the man and the woman were swart and ugly and small.

The lover would wait to pursue the course of his passion until the husband had gone fishing. The wife, God knows why, wept. Maybe it was the hurt pride of a beautiful woman who sees herself put aside for a plain one.

Nothing could keep the lovers apart. It was one of those passions so great that it flames out and can be seen like a fire, that even reached the trusting, wronged husband, who probably could not imagine that Eros had flown to the cot of his homely and middle-aged wife.

One night he didn't go out fishing. He waited awhile and came home and there indeed he found his wife with her lover. When, like a traditional outraged husband, he was about to fall upon his rival, the rival, who was prepared for such an emergency, drew his revolver and told the outraged husband to get out of there damn quick.

When suit was brought, nothing of a scandalous nature was mentioned at the trial. He was merely found guilty of carrying concealed weapons and was "bulkheaded off the Cape"—in other words, he was exiled. But exiled only to be joined triumphantly by his beautiful wife, who soon presented him with another beautiful baby.

What went on here was going on all over the country. Men and women experimenting with love. Women demanding freedom. Someone asked, "Freedom for what?" Young people having brief, meaningless affairs. Society was making such books as O'Hara's *Butterfield 8* possible.

CHAPTER TWENTY-SIX

Tired to Death

I

THIS upset time was too much for me. It seized the children and whirled them off. It was a time when all life was topsy-turvy. Instead of the people with initiative having the right of way, the unproductive ones took the lead by the very impetus in their flight to nowhere.

It was then I broke the most important of the Ten Commandments of the house, which is: *You must not get too tired.*

These commandments of a house are more relentless than the moralities which we are taught. One may evade the consequences of lawbreaking if one is adroit enough, but the laws of the house have the inevitability of material laws—fire burns, for instance.

When a woman gets tired she only seems disagreeable and unreasonable. She makes no new friends. Her old friends find her changed. Inside of this unpleasant shell is a creature crying for help—needing help as much as if she were lying on the ground with a broken leg. Her children, used to seeing her adequate and potent, only escape from her or see in her a spoilsport.

Fatigue is the great enemy of all women, of all their houses, and of all the affairs of their houses. It is the enemy of all those in the house. It is a disease, a calamity, a misfortune. Lately we have located fatigue as an actual poison, and it is a poison; it poisons hope and life itself. It is the enemy of peace and of joy. It kills people.

This was the time when no young people went to bed if they could help it. The house seemed always awake. I would come down and find hordes of young folk eating egg sandwiches at strange hours. It seemed to me better that they stay up late at home than somewhere else.

There was no way I could shout across the gulf to them. There was nothing I could ever tell them. I could not say I cannot carry this house alone. I need help. I need care. Why is it one needs to have pneumonia before anyone notices that you are so ill you can't go on?

The insufficient, apprehensive nights were like the respite between the smothering comb and the successive wave. Each day left me gasping and drowned, trying to struggle to my feet. I was so tired that my thoughts went clattering around like the bits of glass in a broken kaleidoscope, making a jangling sound, but no pattern; so tired that I was beyond the help of change. My house was now against me and fought against my uncertain hands. I was a sick soul poisoned by bewilderment and fatigue. Sick and well souls should not live together.

I was so tired that when I woke up in the morning it seemed to me I was coming up painfully, from some smothering depth below the surface of the water. I have always thought that being rescued unwillingly from drowning must be very much like being waked up in the morning when one is tired to death.

I had once had a poor neurotic housekeeper of whom I was contemptuous. She had never been in a household like ours with all its youthful fun. I was in New York when the costume ball came off, and she wrote me she had "lived through the confusion." I had in my innocence always liked the costume balls. Now they were a time of darkness and terror to me.

I knew I couldn't go on, and still I had to go on—there

was no stopping. All the normal things of life were more than I could bear, even to a joke or the small, ever-recurring demands of the children.

I have a picture of myself in those days, sitting in a chair, trying to make myself get up from it, knowing that there was a great deal to be done. Usually knowing this was like the steam in an engine—it drove me. But now something had slipped. I must wake up to action, and yet I couldn't get up from the chair to walk across the room. It was as if nature revolting now kept me quiet in some waking trance, though I felt as if I were whirling around and around in space like an insect.

I had never felt like a whirling insect before, and I said it in those words; then I said: "This is crazy!" Tears came to my eyes, but they did not fall; I was too tired even to raise my hand to wipe them away.

II

It was at that time I wrote a piece called "The Hole in the Wall." It was about a mother who, exasperated by a story in a woman's magazine of how beautiful in these days of the locust were the relations between children and parents, threw the magazine at the wall, where it made a hole. She looked through the hole and there she saw her children as they really were, without the veil of illusion, without which being a mother is almost impossible.

She saw herself going down the stairs and all of them assailed her at once, shrieking, "Why can't I have a car?"

"Stockings, stockings, stockings."

While the maid echoed, "The plumbing is bust. The man hasn't come for the lawn."

The older children shrieked for dances, objects, lipsticks, and the younger continued to chant, "Ten cents, ten cents, ten cents."

This was the period in life when boys have no face at

all and when girls fly through a house, leaving chaos behind them, and look upon home only as a place in which to dress or have a party. The change from the co-operation one gets when children are smaller comes very quickly and it overwhelms you. A touch of madness is in their avidity for pleasure and a stony and violent dislike of anything that may stand in their way—one's need for sleep, for instance, if one is working.

The real name of the story was "The Stinkin' Chillun." It came from an old Negro in Amherst, who used to carry my baggage to my mother's house. We always had a stereotyped conversation. I would say,

"How are you, Pettibone?" and he would answer,

"I'd be all right, Mis' Ma'y, if 't wasn't for my stinkin' chillun."

I meant the story to be a funny allegory of a woman trying to cope with the modern young. Miss Viola Roseboro read the story. She said, "My child, the story of a nervous breakdown and its causes are never funny."

III

Then at the end of summer came the collapse. I had pneumonia it seemed. In reality I was tired to death. My own much-loved Mary got sick about the same time, and I, who had always had good help, found myself with strange girls passing through my house, one after another, as though mirroring my own disarray.

There was a woman who had been an old trouper. She had run away when she was fifteen and had played vaudeville all over the country. She still played the part of four-a-day and still dramatized life. I think she gave up after the time she went home, leaving only Ellen, Joe, and me, and came back to find Agnes, Gene, and Shane O'Neill and Fifi, Shane's nurse.

Shane had been bitten on the lip by the Irish terrier, who

[222]

was jumping for food and didn't mean to bite Shane. Besides these, there were Fern and Jean Shay and their maid, and the children and the extra maids were a little too much for the former vaudevillian.

Queer little bodies, incapable of work, would stay for a few days and wander on, uncomfortable in a house where the mistress was sick and where they had to take more responsibility than was natural for them.

There was Rosabella, perhaps the plainest girl who ever worked in Kibbe Cook's house, with peaked face, thin large nose, and the kind of pale freckles that look like a skin disease. Rosabella, moreover, was perfectly bald and wore a wig. She hated work and, ill favored though she was, had a taste for romance. Indeed, perhaps because she was bald and plain a need for romance nagged her, which was incompatible with housework.

There followed her complete opposite, a neat girl who had been sent to normal school by a rich woman. She loved it there. She liked the fact that plates were changed and that there was silver and good table linen. Later on, when I saw her home, I knew why.

One day when she was bringing a tray downstairs she stumbled because she was out of balance. This girl, so full of ambition, with such a desire to change her mode of life, had unfortunately, as the saying goes, got into trouble at normal school.

Her story was one of sheer tragedy, for when I saw her at the door she kept crying, "It isn't so. It couldn't have happened, Mrs. Vorse. It isn't so!"

I went with her to her house. It was a dark and dirty house slopped with the washing her mother was doing. Her father sat by the table, drunk. Her own room was a little cubicle of order and brightness in the midst of the general disorder. The girl had a pretty, ruffled counterpane and ruffled curtains at her window and pictures. She was going to get away from all the disorder.

Now that she had got into trouble, the dream embodied in the neat room was over. She couldn't go back to normal school. This girl, who was going to be a teacher, and spoke such careful English, when her time came cursed as she had heard her father curse; dark, filthy oaths poured from her as they took her to the hospital.

Finally there was no one to take care of me except a dour girl who was a stenographer and highly educated and who had an insane hatred for men. By now the older children were at school and at a job and Joe was then very small, doing his best to look after me.

IV

As if to add to the picture of disarray, I had strange bedside visitors. One time Tommy Atwood and Harrison Tree came to call on me just at dusk. They apologized deeply for coming at such a strange hour but they had noticed my light and wanted to see how I was. Then it turned out that they had been drinking so long they thought that it was half-past five in the morning instead of half-past five in the afternoon. But I will always remember them both with something essentially good and sweet and kind showing through their drunkenness. You could feel that they had been drunk for quite a while and had almost got to the outward edge of sanity, but just the same there was nothing bad or dark in either of them.

Old Mr. Steele, the milkman, came to collect a bill. His wife had died recently and he told me her whole story, and if anyone could have written down Mr. Steele's words just as they flowed from him they would have written a great lyric. I never met Mrs. Steele, but there is no one more vivid in my mind.

This time kind neighbors looked after me, too. The Dutras would go out hunting and bring birds back to me because their mother had said there never was anything like wild birds to put strength into a body who had been pretty sick. When finally I was well enough to go walking, I met Jim and Tony, in back.

"What you doing here?" I asked, because nobody walks in back unless they are going shooting.

Tony said, "We didn't like your looks when you started out. You looked feeble. We didn't think you ought to be alone in back. Might've fallen down."

My good neighbors had followed me to give me a helping hand if necessary. In spite of illness and strange maids and accidents, I felt surrounded by my friends' kindness.

CHAPTER TWENTY-SEVEN

The S-4

I

ON A December afternoon in 1927, a neighbor put his head in the door long enough to shout,

"The *S-4* has been sunk off Wood End."

Later Edith Foley came in to say that Coulton Waugh, Edwin Dickinson and Floyd Clymer were going over with a crowd of men to stand by at Wood End all night. All we had had was the core of the tragedy—the *S-4* and her crew and officers were sunk.

The news ran like fire through the town. The sinking of the *S-4* blotted out all other interests. There was no one who could think of anything else. It was as if we ourselves were imprisoned below decks with those men. There was no consciousness of anything else in the town except those men under the water. We had never seen them. We did not know them, but they were there with us, in the room with us. Our own living and dying stopped. We lived, all of us, with the imprisoned men. The town had formed itself into a formidable mass that was like a prayer for help.

That first night was a strange night. People all over town kept vigil with the men on the *S-4*. Their own men had all gone out to see if there was any help that could possibly be given. Lights burned all night in houses along the street. Late that night some of the men who had been out on guard passed by with a little more news.

"I've been over to Wood End, talking to Frank Simonds. He saw it all. He was on watch over to Wood End. The *S-4* was making its trial trip and cruising between those two can buoys. By and by he saw the *Paulding* rounding Race Point light. Pretty soon Captain Gracie came into the observation tower and asked Frank if he'd seen the submarine lately.

"He swung the telescope around and seen a stream of spray from the periscope. He dropped the telescope and was half down the tower yelling back, 'There's goin' to be a collision!' "

It was getting near the holidays and the rumrunners were busy, so the Destroyer *Paulding* had come out of Boston, looking for rumrunners. Frank Simonds at the telescope saw what happened. He saw the *Paulding* swing to starboard, trying to reverse engines. He saw the submarine break surface under the port bow of the *Paulding*. He saw the *Paulding*'s bow rise with a terrific crash when the destroyer struck and he saw the stern of the submarine heave above the surface. You can read his testimony yourself. The *Paulding* stopped. A boat was lowered, but the *S-4* had gone down.

Captain Gracie launched the surfboat a few minutes after the collision. He dropped a grapnel and commenced sweeping the bottom. For four hours Captain Gracie worked back and forth over the spot where the *S-4* had gone down. At last he struck with his grappling hook. At three in the morning the grapnel gave way and his boat went adrift.

The only salvage ship the navy had in the Atlantic, the *Falcon*, was in New London, a part of her crew ashore on liberty. But the *Bushnell*, the mother ship of the submarine, hurried from Portsmouth. Boston sent several destroyers and tugs and these had already been arriving. When his grapnel gave way, Captain Gracie got a better grappling equipment from the *Bushnell* and went back to work through the rising storm.

There wasn't a small boat in all the vessels that the navy sent that could live in that sea. Gracie lowered his new grapnel in the freezing spray and the darkness and began his dragging under the searchlights of the navy mine sweepers.

II

At Burch's next morning and on the street knots of people were talking. It was as if one had gone into a town in mourning.

Everywhere groups of people were saying to each other, in low tones, "Why ain't they done nothing? We'd save these men with our own hands."

As I went down the street toward the Avellars' an old woman came up to me. Her face was brown as leather and her head was done up in a handkerchief. She gestured at me and at the sea and tears were running down her face.

At the Avellars', Ma was crying. She said, "It's like my Raphael was down there!"

People were crying in every house you went. They had all had their own boys in danger. They identified their own men with the men on the submarine.

I have been in a mining town when men have been trapped in a mine. Provincetown was like this—everyone waiting for word from below, only there wasn't even a pit mouth to wait around.

All through the freezing night Captain Gracie dragged his grapnel back and forth. The divers from Newport had come down the Cape overland and at seven o'clock the salvage vessel, *Falcon*, got to Provincetown and stood by with the divers. There was no use in them going down until the S-4 had been located and the lines were hooked over the vessel's side to guide the divers.

Not until quarter to eleven did Captain Gracie's grapnel catch again. There has always been a question as to what might have happened if he'd had any boat to help him when he first located the S-4 at eight o'clock the night of the disaster. At half-past one, twenty-two hours after the S-4 sank, the first diver went over the side. There was a head sea but in the sea's depth there was no sound but the diver's weights against the steel hull. Through the silence a faint signal was heard. He went across the torn deck toward the sound, which came from the torpedo room.

He banged on the cover of the hatch. From inside six raps came clear and distinct. Six men were alive in that torpedo room. The diver signaled the news. He went aft to the conning tower and he signaled. Only silence there. He went to the steel hatch over the engine room and signaled again. Again silence.

III

Admiral Brumby, flag officer of the Control Force to which the S-4 belonged, had arrived on the *Falcon*. He consulted with the other officers as to what steps to take. They knew that six men were alive forward. The rest of the crew might be alive in the rear battery room. There were two emergency air lines, one leading to the ballast tanks and one to the crew compartments. Edward Ellsberg, the famous diver writes as follows in *Harper's Magazine*:

To which of these two emergency connections should the next diver hook the air line? . . . Carefully the situation was discussed. That no sounds came from aft probably indicated, Brumby thought, not that the stern was flooded, but that so many men crowded in a small space aft were either unconscious, or so weak from bad air, they could not answer. If so, prompt lifting of the stern was all that would ever save those aft. . . . The decision to blow ballasts first and try and float up the undamaged stern was concurred with by all present (but which turned out to be wrong because two compartments were flooded; in addition a ballast tank was ruptured) and was promptly put into execution.

This decision was a death warrant for the six men still alive. With a rising storm, a desperate attempt was made to connect a hose to the compartment air line to feed air to the torpedo room. The attempts of the divers to accomplish this from the *Falcon* is an epic story which has been overshadowed by the tragedy of the men entombed in the *S-4*. Mired to their waists in muck, entangled in broken wreckage, frozen in icy waters, one gallant attempt after another was made.

Chief Torpedoman Fred Michels, Chief Boatswain's Mates Carr and Thomas Eadie were later joined in their heroic efforts by Edward Ellsberg. To save Michels' life, who had been brought up unconscious and frozen stiff, the *Falcon* left for Boston. This reason for the *Falcon*'s leaving Provincetown was not understood and made a further bad impression. The townspeople were openly cursing the navy.

By now much time had been lost. The greatest wrecking concern in Boston, which had raised one great vessel after another, offered its services to the navy the day of the accident and sent its wrecking machinery over at once. The navy's nearest wrecking equipment was in New York. It would have gone against all precedent for the navy to allow a private wrecking concern to raise the *S-4*. The navy equipment had started its long voyage through the Sound, where it encountered bad weather, and some of the equipment went adrift from the tug. It took three days for it to arrive in Provincetown.

The question has always remained as to what might have happened had the wrecking concern immediately raised the

S-4 to the surface before the storm broke which made diving impossible for a time.

Now that it was known that men were alive down there, a fury against the navy seized the town. The fishermen said they could raise the vessel themselves. As if by wireless the messages sent by the *Falcon* and answered by the men on the submarine flew through the town.

The *Falcon* signaled, "Is there any gas?"

They answered, "No, but the air is bad. How long will you be now?"

"How many are there?"

"There are six. Please hurry."

The *Falcon* replied, "Compartment salvage air line is being hooked up now."

The air connection was never made. The divers could not go down. The weather was sunny and seemed calm enough for some salvage work. The fury of the town rose higher and higher. Had there been some leader, the feeling ran so high, the town and the fishermen especially would have demonstrated against the navy.

IV

Meantime the weakening messages imploring help came from the men on the submarine. The town had become the center of the whole world. Vessels of every kind had arrived. Town Hall had been made into headquarters for the press. Relatives of the men, too, had come to Provincetown. Admiral Brumby had forbidden people, and even the press, from hiring small boats to go to the scene of the disaster. When he peremptorily sent back the father of one of the entombed boys, anger again swept through the town. The days dragged on and nothing seemed done. The feeling ran so high that to lessen the tension one of the townsmen invited the officers of the *Bushnell* and *Falcon* and other vessels to meet some of the principal captains of local fishing vessels to explain the technical difficulties which caused the seeming inaction. The officers and fishermen got on very well; the officers explained that the bad weather had prevented any diving. A better understanding had been reached when about two o'clock the fishermen got up to go.

"Don't go so soon," their host implored.

"We got to go fishing," they answered simply. The weather, they implied, might be too bad for the navy, but it wasn't too bad for the fishermen.

They did not realize that the short, choppy sea would have banged the divers to death. Certainly it was a hard situation for the town to understand. The weather was good enough for small boats to go over the surface under which lay the S-4. Until they were forbidden, boys in rowboats offered to take out passengers. Little motorboats cruised freely above the surface. The wrecker belonging to the private company was anchored in Provincetown Harbor and the navy wrecker didn't arrive. Meanwhile the town was being aroused to frenzy by the continual messages that were being tapped out.

"How is the weather?" they asked.

"Choppy."

Later on, "Is there any hope?"

The answer came, "There is hope. Everything possible is being done."

It seemed to Provincetown that nothing was being done. The Navy Department ordered a message to be sent to Lieutenant Fitch, "Your wife and mother are constantly praying for you."

All through the night they kept on tapping the message through the water, through the silent ship.

"Lieutenant Fitch, your wife and mother constantly praying for you."

At last, early Tuesday morning, the last word came from the men on the S-4, "We understand."

The town did not understand. They did not understand

why the line to the *S-4* was lost again or why the divers didn't connect any air hose to the torpedo room.

V

Later, on March 3, three months after she sank, the *S-4*, a tomb of thirty-four men, was brought to the surface. The tragedy could then be reconstructed.

First of all, it was established that the only way to have saved the *S-4* would have been lifting the stern immediately. The *S-4* went down bow first at a steep angle and struck the bottom hard. She leveled off at an even keel and there she lay waiting for the rescue which didn't come.

When finally she was raised, it was discovered that a strange, unforeseeable accident had caused the death of most of the men. When they leveled off, Lieutenant Fitch and his five torpedo men were forward. Lieutenant Commander Jones was in the control room. The majority of the crew were safe. They had possession of the control room and its machinery. Banks numbers three and four were undamaged. When water suddenly came in and they tried to close the forward ventilation valves, the bulkhead valve would not close. What must have happened is this.

The sudden pressure of the sea had caused the collapse of the ventilation duct in the battery room. Water rose on the floor. The captain's stateroom was just forward of the control bulkhead and the door was draped with a green baize curtain. Water flowing in floated up the curtain, which got tangled with the valve body, and the valve disks could not close.

Men must have fought to close it as the sea streamed in, the water rose. They were beaten by a valve in which a harmless green curtain had lodged. They then were forced to leave the control room which had compressed air and controls, where they would have remained alive, for the flood of water from the entangled valve drove them into

[233]

the engine room. And there in this small black hole they poisoned each other. They were dead long before any help could come to them. One awful thing is clear—that when the *Paulding* struck the *S-4* there was a chance for every one of the men to be saved, and a green baize curtain and human error killed them all.

Provincetown never forgets the *S-4*. There is a special terror in the memory of those men waiting, tapping their patient messages, and dying. Everyone in Provincetown had a feeling that it was their individual task to save these men and no one could do anything. But every year a service is held for them at St. Mary of the Harbor. The town gathers. The colors are presented in the little church close, and taps are sounded for these never-forgotten dead.

CHAPTER TWENTY-EIGHT

Eating the Arequipa

I

ALL that winter of '27 and '28 was a time of storm and of disaster. A great gale tore Provincetown to pieces. I drove to Race Point and back to town. Bulkheads were cracked like eggshells. Sand and seaweed in patterns of disaster strewed the road. There was seaweed on the Givens' roof and on the roofs of many houses where the sea came close.

The bulkhead of the Arequipa, which had only been finished, was smashed in and the sand had sucked out. Since the wharf went, the earth had been eating away alarmingly in every easterly. Neighbors stood around saying:

"Never was built right. Saw when he was making it 'twouldn't hold."

"Always knew 'twould go in the fust storm. That feller made it never did know nothin' 'bout buildin' bulkheads."

My expensive and futile attempt to save part of the wharf was nothing but wreckage. Great bulkheads were cracked. Up-Along a cement bulkhead was in pieces.

One of the strangest accidents had happened that night. A revenue cutter was anchored in the harbor. The captain had repeatedly sent in requisitions for another anchor. When the storm came up, people who knew what an easterly can do to this harbor had felt that the vessel might drag its insufficient anchor in this gale. It did.

In the night it ran amuck among the shipping, crashed some fishermen's dories, and rammed and wrecked the

[235]

Casino which was out on a wharf. The Casino was one of the first eating places and night clubs in Provincetown. It was a pleasant place with a lovely view of the harbor, and now it had drifted ashore, lolling drunkenly on the beach. A wrecked house is an unnatural-looking thing.

A gangway had been thrown to the Casino and one could walk up its steep, inclined floors. The wharf on which it stood had been wrecked and the heavy piles had gone hurtling down the water front, pounding the bulkheads to pieces like battering rams.

One could hear their steady smash-bang through the night. It was a noise that seemed to have a conscious fury, as if the storm was intent upon tearing the town to pieces and was using wrecked piles to make a breach for the sea. The wind had shifted and mountainous waves were piling up at Race Point and along Peaked Hill.

Of all the losses, the fishing boats were the worst because they were uninsured, though later the government reimbursed some of the damage done by the revenue cutter.

II

There were other storm signals than those that flew from our signal tower. The gambling mania which had seized the country, the belief that you could get something for nothing and that securities would only go higher and higher, was at its zenith. It was the time when everybody speculated, scrubwomen, office boys, professors, workmen; everyone who could get a few dollars together gambled the stock market.

There were plenty of people who warned that this couldn't go on forever. The financial structure was already uncertain. We couldn't be prosperous when unemployment stalked through Europe and England. In our own country the farmers weren't prosperous. The disparity between the cost of farm products and the cost of manufactured goods was widening every month. Depression had come upon New England already. Capital was going South. The spindles in the large textile towns were slowing down, but no one except a few economists paid any attention to the signals of coming disaster.

III

Joe had been in school in France and Ellen and I joined him there. When I got back from Europe in the fall and came back to Provincetown with Joe, our house at first seemed strange and cold and unlived in. Other people had lived in it that summer and there were yet traces of them in the house. The house hadn't liked them. Moreover, the house hadn't been mine for four years. It had belonged to the children and their friends and had always been full of noisy young people. I had worked hard to support it, and had become a mixture of unwelcome watchdog and a provider whose need for quiet seemed unreasonable.

Now my house was again my own. Gradually I took it over, and the furniture fell into place once more. It seemed lived in again. Joe and I no longer felt as though we were very small peas rattling around in a large pod.

That was the winter I learned I could write a book without any money. I started *Second Cabin* on the assumption that I had some royalties coming in from my play, *The First Stone,* Eva Le Gallienne was putting on. Some mistake had been made, or I had misunderstood, so in the end there weren't any royalties.

Family finances are predestined things. They have to do with your whole make-up, your attitude of mind toward life. Years before, when I was first beginning to write, Miss Viola Roseboro had said,

"My dear, you'll make a great deal of money but you'll always be poor. Having a lot of money will never make you any richer."

Families are like that. I remember a friend of mine who suddenly realized that her own family would always be slack, that tradesmen would always be clamoring to be paid, that the house would be tumbling down and the children would need new shoes and she would be living in a depressing slack poverty unless she got out.

Miss Roseboro was right. Times when I have had a sizable income and times when it has been much smaller made very little difference. No matter how much money I make I never have money saved for taxes; on the other hand, no matter how much I pay for rent I am always forehanded. It is as obscene to be always in a mess and clutter about money as it is to be in a mess about sex. These are both things with which decent people should make an adjustment. This year the certainty I was going to get royalties gave me a serene and quiet attitude toward my finances.

It was a calm household with Joe and myself and his gang who came in perpetually—Freddy Dutra, Irving and Junior Rogers, Jimmie Cordeiro. Louis Ding, whose real name is Silva, Qualey, Isaiah Turner, and Khaki Captiva, who is now one of the best fishermen out of Provincetown, were in and out of the house by couples or the whole lot at once. They were kids, and I could cope with them and the house liked them. If they didn't go home early their parents knew the answer. The house hummed along like a bee.

Evenings when the girl had gone home and Joe was in bed it was like living in a pool of quiet. Days, Harriet McInness came to work for me and I drove through my book. I would look out at a gray-green sea. The wind from the northwest crested the waves with white. All the fishing boats would be out in spite of bad weather and now and then a small boat would come out through clouds of foam.

When you live quietly in a house and your window looks out to sea, you know every change of the weather. It becomes part of your consciousness. At night sometimes the house has a creamy quiet; and when the wind roars over it one is snug and secure within. Sometimes there are strange noises through the house, sounds of footsteps, creaking of floors, and doors opening and shutting. These are the times when the dog bristles and shivers and stares at things that you can't see. For the house has moods, and when you live intimately with it, it changes all the time.

With the bay before me, the house gay with kids, I worked happily. Then, just as I had learned I had no royalties, I sold a story. It had all been as smooth and precarious as a flight on an iceboat.

IV

In the early spring, the *Robert E. Lee* was wrecked near Boston Harbor. Great quantities of her cargo came ashore on our beaches and all Provincetown went beachcombing. She was carrying a cargo for the coming carnival season down to Revere Beach. The cargo consisted of great vats of uneatable material called pie fillings, cosmetics, and O-Boy chewing gum, a loathsome sort of bubble gum. It was an undermining sight indeed to see little boys running along with wheelbarrows laden with chewing gum. They chewed all day and went to sleep chewing, gobbets of gum stuck on doorknobs, walls, and under tables; your feet squooshed chewed gum on the pavement as you walked.

My neighbor said dryly, "It's a wonder we haven't gum in the meat grinder, Mrs. Vorse. There's gum on every doorknob in Provincetown."

Another fearsome sight was the little children going to school with rouge and lipstick and mascara on their faces. Little girls had only to stroll on the beach to pick up cosmetics. Wellfleet got more than Provincetown—"enough cosmetics to last a generation," someone said. Little painted girls shrieked past the house, chewing violently a mass of gum, while every house in town feasted from the horrible ersatz fillings of carnival pies.

There were also such inedibles as made-up codfish cakes. One thrifty man to the westward kept his family eating them until his wife finally left him. But more terrible than anything was the pie filling.

Joe and his friend Freddy Dutra took the wind, located the wreck, and made a neat calculation that the wreckage would be coming ashore down toward Beach Point. They both hopped on a bicycle and came back triumphant with a pineapple pie filling. For weeks, this pie filling came on daily for dessert. Harriet and I used every device to get rid of it without hurting Joe's feelings.

V

In late March my secure existence blew up. It was one of those complete disintegrations that is like an actual explosion. First there was a disaster which at that time seemed so great that I, who had been writing fruitfully and well, did not write another thing I could sell for nearly a year. At the same time, the maid who had been with me for a long time suddenly went insane and Harriet also got sick and had to leave.

That was the time that the Smooleys rallied around. "The Smooleys" was a composite word for a family of friends who lived together—Stella Roof, Kate and Bill Smith, and Edith Foley. I was ill for a time and there wasn't a day when they didn't come to see how I was, bring me magazines and things to eat and, more than all, companionship. No one had better friends than I.

One day Kate and Bill came to me, wanting to buy the Arequipa. I had many offers for it but never wanted to sell it. I had wanted to live on the wharf, and now that the wharf was gone I wanted to live on the Arequipa when the children were grown up.

I hadn't enough tenacity and courage to keep it. Fire and ice and the sea had destroyed the Lewis wharf. The Arequipa was now defenseless. Days when there would be an easterly I would think, "Well, if the tide changes in time, all right; if it doesn't, good-by Arequipa."

Every storm took away a little bit of the Arequipa's land and left it more exposed to the sea. Besides that, we had no money and I didn't see any way I could make money. So I sold the Arequipa to Katie and Bill.

By joining the two buildings and lifting it, they made a magnificent dwelling of it, which they called Smooley Hall. Katie, who married John Dos Passos later, lives in it to this day. But I, during that spring and summer, ate the Arequipa.

CHAPTER TWENTY-NINE

Dragging the Weirs

I

THAT was the time when we went trapping a great deal. Joe used to tie a string to his toe and throw a stone tied in a handkerchief out of the window. This was a sign he wanted to go trapping. When Tony Dutra, who was working in Crosby's weir boat, came past before daylight, he would always look up at the house to see if the white handkerchief was flying. Then he would give a pull at the string, and Joe would be out of bed and into his overalls and shirt and sweater and down to the wharf where the men were putting off. Sometimes I went along.

Never a weir boat was conducted with such decorum as that of Captain Crosby. He was a slender, gray-haired man with refined features; an ardent Christian he permitted no cursing whatsoever on his boat. It was reported that when a tuna had torn his nets to pieces, he referred to that "ding-dong fish." Casting off with Captain Crosby was almost like a church service. As though he were on a large vessel he spoke to all his men as "Mister," with the exception of the younger boys.

"You may cast off now, Mr. Sousa," he would remark quietly, and they would chug across the harbor which was only now filling with light.

Often the bay had that satin smoothness that comes with dawn. Then the dawn wind would ruffle the water and just as we rounded the Point the sun would come up. Seeing sunrise at sea in a little boat is not like seeing a sunrise anywhere else. You are closer to this daily miracle than you are on land or in a larger vessel. The silence is scarcely broken by the throbbing of the motors of the weir boats going to their traps.

A fish trap is built in a circle around weir poles. Two converging lines of net lead the fish into the trap. As the school of fish swim along they run into the net barrier which they follow until they get within the trap itself. Once in they are unable to get out and mill around with flashing fins. On a good day the whole surface of the water is a-glitter and a-whir with fish.

Captain Crosby would say, "Mr. Silva, you may now stop the motor. Mr. Henderson, would you care to man the dory at the gate?" In calm silence the men went through their work. A dory entered the bowl of the net. The door of the trap was raised. The bowl of the net was pulled up while the fish were brought nearer and nearer to the surface until they were a-flop and a-glitter in the shallow purse of the net, making a rustle like no other noise in the world. The men in their high boots ladled the fish into the weir boat. Some of the older men with their gnarled hands looked like Father Neptune.

Of all the catches of fish there is nothing like the herring. The fish are of such a clear, royal blue that the catch is like an enormous agitated bowl of precious blue stones. In all nature this piercing blue is the rarest of colors whether in gem or flower, and here it is multiplied and magnified, flashing sapphire without end.

Next in magnificence and much more profitable is the mackerel catch. Fortunes have been made on a single catch. In the days when weirs were owned by individuals, Thomas Knowles had no luck at all. When there was a good price for fish he got nothing but dogfish. When he got a good catch the bottom fell out of the price of fish. He didn't make enough to pay for his crew or his twine. Then one day, after weeks of despair, there was a glitter and a flash and a rustle of thousands of mackerel in the trap. There had been no mackerel at all; they hadn't run yet, and he made $5000 in that one haul.

There are terrible, discouraging times when one dogfish after another has its head beaten in against the side of the boat, or when the catch is so mixed that it's hardly worth bringing in.

In the old days before the filleting of whiting, there would be a stream of whiting pitchforked out of a weir boat either to float ashore or be retrieved by screaming gulls.

Every year there is a time of great excitement when the horse mackerel are trapped in the weirs. These great tuna-fish weigh sometimes as much as three and four hundred pounds. They are a great game fish and full of fury at their imprisonment. Before they can be gaffed a terrific battle takes place. It's one of the sights of the sea to behold these furious fighters rush around the nets. The fight can last for a long time and before the end serious damage can be caused, for the great fish rip the nets to shreds in their attempts to make a getaway.

This summer the tuna have been running, and a weir full of one-hundred-pound tuna lashing the water white is a spectacle never to be forgotten.

II

Strange things have been found swimming in the weirs. Manuel James' trap was near Truro and one morning as he went out to draw it, he saw an animal swimming around and around that he recognized as no fish.

He said to his helper, "I never seen a fish with horns yet. We got some sea monster, I guess."

His helper said, "Your eyes is funny this morning. Fish ain't no horns."

The creature with horns milling round and round the

bowl, the fish threshing about it, was a young deer. It had swum across the bay from Provincetown to Truro, had run into one of the lead nets, and, like a school of fish, had been led into the weir trap. He had no more sense than a fish and could not find his way out again. So frightened was he that they had "a time" getting him out and he swam so fast for shore that he left a white wake behind him as big as a destroyer, so Manuel James said.

Once they saw a funny creature with a little black head swimming around Captain Crosby's trap.

"Danged if it don't look like we caught a nigger in our trap this morning," said he.

But it was not a Negro boy swimming round the net. It was a little seal, for seals are not at all uncommon along this coast.

A single bluefish will appear when no bluefish have been seen at all in these waters. Small sharks are frequent. Not a year passes that some strange fish is not caught, fish from the sea's innermost depths, fish that have strayed from their latitude.

III

By the early part of the century the majority of the weirs were already owned by the cold storages. In Provincetown, the cold storages paid wages to the weir fishermen and in some cases a small percentage. The cold storages bought every kind of fish. It was an interesting thing to sit in the cold storage office and see the different catches come in. Sometimes a couple of little boys with a bucket of fish, sometimes old men with a doryload of squid. It was surprising in those days how many older men made just enough money fishing in the harbor to carry them along.

The fish were weighed and the men paid over the counter immediately. But the greater part of the catch was brought in by the weir boats and dories. They were carried in by great buckets running on a runway into the building and frozen quickly. A sign displayed outside read, FOOD FISH AND BAIT.

Fresh fishermen coming in to be baited and iced flew a flag at half-mast, signifying bait. Great blocks of frozen squid and herring and other fish were stacked aboard for the trawl baiting. Today Provincetown has only three of its cold storages left in operation.

In 1906 new cold storages were being built with local capital. People bought shares with their savings. The cold storages in Provincetown were owned and financed locally. Gradually weir fishing went over from individual ownership to corporate ownership. By 1932 the Atlantic Coast Fisheries owned the cold storages and most of the weirs, which they acquired by buying up the majority of the stock. Today they own all but one.

Weirs are as old as fishing. No one knows when the first weir was planted any more than he knows when men first made boats. When they were digging the foundation of the Boston Public Library they found weir poles, where hundreds of years ago Indians had made primitive weirs. The coast of South America is outlined by weirs made by the Indians.

Originally weirs were owned by individuals who sold their fish to whatever buyer they chose. Weirs came before the cold storages which they serve today.

IV

Why the cold storages bought the weirs is best explained by the failure of the cold storage in Truro a few years ago. In the teens the cold storage in Truro was run by a man named Atkins Hughes. He was a great driver and a person who had command. He ran the fishermen. He didn't need to own the weir boats. The weir fishermen and the cold storage rocked along together. But after he died the cold storage burned and a bigger one was built.

In the earlier days, too, the Truro weirs sold fish to Jess Paine, who had a fish-canning factory, but it too failed and remained on the Truro shore an empty specter, until it fell into the sea a few years ago. The cold storage offered a steady market to the fishermen, but instead of selling their fish to the cold storage they sold them to a Guinea boat. Guinea boats are fair-sized boats belonging to an Italian firm. When they would draw the traps in the morning, the *Mayo II*, owned by Peter Bussalacci in Boston, would slide alongside with plenty of whisky aboard. The fishermen had fun with the captain of the Guinea boat. They would get drunk out there in the morning, and the Guinea boat would offer them five cents more a barrel than the cold-storage price and would puff back to Boston with all the Truro fish.

The cold storage would meet the price and perhaps for a little while they would bring in some fish, but as it was fun to go out in the morning and drink whisky with the Guinea-boat crew, the cold storage presently failed. Then came the beam trawlers who scraped the fish off the bottom in a great net and so needed no bait, and the Guinea boat didn't come any more. Fishing got in a bad way in Truro. Traps were being abandoned and fishermen found that they had cut off their own noses.

John Worthington reorganized a company to open the cold storage again, which is now doing well and has re-employed the weir fishermen.

There are between fifty and sixty weirs from Billingsgate, just out of Wellfleet, to Race Point. Thirteen trap boats serve the weirs. The Atlantic Coast Fisheries own nine of the trap boats and forty of the weirs. Fewer men do more work in the weir boats today. Thirty-five years ago seven men to a crew tended two traps, now five men tend four or five traps. Instead of the fish being shoveled out by hand, a great power shovel is used that can lift two or three hundred pounds of fish.

The Provincetown Cold Storage is still owned by local people. It is capitalized for only about $15,000, so it pays large dividends. The Atlantic Coast Fisheries is after it, too, but has not yet a majority of the shares.

Formerly the cold storage froze fish for bait. In the winter bait would bring prices that today seem fantastic, five dollars a barrel for frozen herring. With the beam trawlers and the draggers replacing the catching of fish with hooks, the cold storages now freeze fish for food. But with all the changes weir fishing is still a great industry in Provincetown. The weirs bring into town a catch of twenty million pounds of fish annually.

CHAPTER THIRTY

The Firebug

I

DURING these upset days, the core of unrest was symbolized by the firebug. There was a time when every Saturday night we listened for the fire whistles. Generally some small building or cottage owned by a summer tenant was set afire.

There were other fires that were terrible, like that on Steele's farm. That night a wind was blowing and the cattle were trapped. As one fire followed another, speculation grew as to who was the firebug. Different men would fall under suspicion. People would point out that when so-and-so was out of town the fires stopped for several weeks.

For years so regularly did these unexplained fires happen that Saturday night was a nervous night, everyone alert, everyone waiting. A legend grew up about the firebug. Boys would see someone scurrying away from an empty barn that then went up in flames.

The greatest fire of all was the fire where the town nearly burned. There is no doubt now that a fire or fires were set in the woods. The fire lasted a week. There was no hope of putting it out. The town was so menaced that Judge Welsh packed his valuable legal library and sent it out of town.

Some of the time the schools were closed. A pall of smoke hung forever over the town. It did queer tricks.

I walked toward the railway track with Sue. The horizon was veiled with smoke. Suddenly I saw the engine apparently flying like the Valkyrie through the skies. So heavily was the track cloaked with smoke, and the bushes burning on the sides, that the illusion of the train's flying in the air was complete.

Everyone fought fire. Everyone went to the woods and thrashed out some new blaze. Fires would appear in the most distant places from the main blaze, as though they had been set. The fire worked underground. You could see the conflagration jump from one tree to another far off. It burned for yards under the mossy coverage to flame up again. Heaton wrote a good account of it:

II

"The first day the wind blew toward the town. After that the wind blew from the east. There was nothing to do but let the fire burn into the sea. On the last day it was impossible to go through the new road. One fellow did and he had a tire burned clean off.

"Unless you were right in it the smoke was rather pleasant except for what it meant. It had a rich pine smell. Night and day smoke hung over the back country. Our quiet woods were strange. One was just as alone in them as always. The smoke pushed you into solitude at twenty feet. But now the woods were full of voices and shouts.

"At night you never knew exactly where you were. You found parked automobiles where you expected to find the middle of a lake. How the cars got there was a mystery. The woods were filled with parked cars. I sat down on a running board for a rest and smoke. Sounds came from inside the car. I stood up and looked in. A girl giggled. I moved on.

"Jimmy and I found an old model-T Ford that had been

parked too long. It sagged to one side, its cushions still smoldered.

"Tony drove us up on Town Hill early one evening. Out there was a shifting kaleidoscopic city of smoke. Everything always changing except for the firm red rim of flame on the hilltops. It was beautiful and horrible. Near us stood a young woman, thin, tired beyond her years with worry and children. The youngest was in her arms. Another clutched her skirts and looked out at the fire, wondering if he should cry. The woman turned to Tony and said something in Portuguese.

" 'She's not going to bed tonight,' Tony translated.

" 'I was standing by a field near Shank Painter's this morning,' said Tony. 'Boy, how that fire can go! A spark lit in the field an' she went.'

" 'It must have been something to watch.'

" 'I didn't watch it,' he remarked, 'I was runnin' too fast. She nearly caught me. My shoes were scorched. I was poundin', I'll tell the world."

"What Tony meant was—'If the wind changes to the westward . . .' "

III

"You'd hear men calling, 'This is bigger than the school-house fire.'

" 'Sure it's bigger. I guess it's worse in some ways.'

" 'If this ever catches a house and the sparks start flyin', Oh baby!'

" 'Pray the wind don't change.'

"Patrick and I were fighting an isolated blaze on the side of a hill. We had it except for a small rim of flame. A half minute's work. Came a soft puff of wind.

" 'There she goes,' said Patrick. The whole side of the hill became a furnace. Out of the smoke came a rabbit, one leg burnt off. It jumped into a patch of bushes. The fire followed it. Seven men came up to help us. It took half an hour to get the fire on the hillside under control."

" 'It's them artists what set the fire,' said Mrs. Enos. 'Them artists is all reds anyhow.'

" 'But why would they light a fire in the woods they like to paint?'

" 'You never know what them artists'll do for a thrill.' "

IV

"I looked up at the town clock and waited for a wisp of smoke to drift by, to see the time. A man next to me was doing the same thing. We smiled.

" 'Nice weather.'

" 'Yeah. Think the wind'll shift?'

" 'Well, it might.'

"Our eyes said if—if—if. Our eyes said damn this dry weather, let it rain. The whole town wondered *if* ——

"Darrow Adams called up Phyllis Duganne.

" 'Better not send Jane to school. There's only one road out of town. It might be needed.'

"People prayed or cursed. You grunted at your friends and spoke to strangers.

"The kids had a grand time. They were all let out of school to fight the fire. And for the same reason they never went home at night. Night-time was particularly enjoyable. A group would assemble on the top of a hill.

"One yelled in an excited tone, 'Hey, Joe Brown!'

"Joe Brown, thinking that the boy had found a new blaze, would answer hoarsely, 'What is it?'

" 'Joe Brown, you're a so-and-so!'

"You could hear them guying each other a quarter mile away. They let their tongues, lungs, and imaginations fully out. Joe Brown came crashing through the underbrush. Each boy darted away, anonymous in the night.

[252]

"Some people thought the kids set new fires for the devil of it.

"Clean, precise Mr. Parmenter, a smudge streak down his face, his white shirt the color of smoke, his forehead red and sweaty, his mouth firm and thin and tired. Withal he was having a grand time.

"Saturday and Sunday is the time for parties. The fire didn't stop them. A road in the woods going from noplace to nowhere. Down rambled a Ford fire truck plowing slowly through the sand. Bell ringing. Horn, too. Half a dozen men. Three sang. One drove. One cocked a bottle. Fat Alves was blowing tunes on the hose nozzle. He waved it cheerily as he passed.

" 'Does your mother know you're out?' he yelled at me. I imitated the hose nozzle.

" 'Well, pray the wind don't change.' And he returned my salute. I ducked an empty bottle. Over the horn and the bell,

For she was a Lulu,
Every inch a Lulu . . .

"What was the use. Everything was so dry. I shoveled sand on a blaze. Bull brier scratched my legs every time I moved. My shovel struck a tree root. I drove the fire ten feet back. Fifteen feet. I wiped the smoke from my smarting eyes. My back ached as I straightened up. Twenty feet back. The tree root in the hole started to glow dull red. The fire was burning underground. I wanted a drink of water.

" 'Hey, you guys, she's workin' in to Roger's barn. Better come 'long. Put this one out later.'

"To hell with Roger's barn. I was hungry. I put my shovel on my shoulder and trudged along with the others.

"Someone said, 'Go' uh cig'r't?' I gave him one. He nearly burnt his nose lighting it.

" 'Better not try to blow it out.' He winked at me gravely and dug his shovel in the sand.

" 'Pray the wind don't change.' "

[253]

V

"One A.M. I was getting ready for bed. A car drove up and stopped next door. It was a fire truck.

" 'Hey, Clarence, Clarence Nelson!' Someone stumbled on the steps and pounded on the door. 'Get dressed and come on.'

"I grabbed a shovel and ran out. We drove off.

"Clarence asked, 'Where is it now?'

" 'Right next to the pumpin' station.'

" 'But we put one fire out there ten o'clock tonight.'

" 'I know. But whoever it is has it in for the pumpin' station.'

" 'I'd like to catch the son of a bitch.'

"We got out. There's a hydrant at the pumping station. John Allen came out of the darkness.

" 'Lucky you fellows come. If she catches those poles there'll be no lights in town.' His cheeks were sooty and his eyes red with smoke.

" 'How much hose is out?'

" 'Only a thousand seven hundred. There's three thousand out by the new road. They're pumpin' it out of the creek.'

"Way off in the darkness I saw a small flicker. It took me a minute to walk there. I found an old dead tree right in the middle of an unburned patch. The fire was funny that way. A spark had drifted into a low crotch and caught. Soon it would send off sparks of its own. I put it out. I walked back toward the rapidly diminishing blaze that was being drowned.

" 'Hey there!' A man came up in the dark. 'I just found another small fire and put it out,' he said.

" 'So did I.'

" 'I wonder if there's any more.'

" 'I don't know. I don't see any. Everything's so dry.'

" 'Well, pray the wind don't change.'

" 'Hey, give us a hand with the hose!'

"Five or seven silhouettes against flame. Bent with the weight of a clumsy hose, tumbling through half-burned wet brier. Everything burns but thorns. One step filled shoes with hot ashes. The next plunged into a puddle ankle-deep and cooled the ashes.

"The shovel was a blessing. No one else had thought to bring one. My job was to run along the hose line and keep it from getting burnt. The chief put his hand on my shoulder.

" 'We got some sandwiches and hot coffee up't th' fire-house. Come along after we've got this out.'

"When the fire was out no one thought of coffee. We thought of beds."

VI

"Next day it rained. It was all over. The fear was gone. No one had to say, 'Pray the wind don't change.' "

The great fire did not stop the firebug. Lonely houses still continued to be set. A fire started in my barn not long after. The menace of someone wandering in the night and finding an empty house and gloating over the beauty of its flames still remained. Probably through the years different thwarted people got their excitement that way. Last year they caught a firebug just as he was setting my brother's cottage afire. There have been no set fires since then.

The burning of the barn was not an unmixed disaster, because we caught it in time. Mrs. MacIntyre for once had been out late and as she went to put some things away, she glanced out of her kitchen window. She saw a bright reflection. She telephoned the fire department and came over to warn us. We had not gone to bed yet. Neith and Hutch had come for dinner which Heaton had cooked.

The big children, Sue and Heaton, were staying in Kibbe Cook's house. By now the fire department came and put out the fire.

The box stall which still had Kite's name on it had been charred. The whole place had been fumed by the smoke as if on purpose. I had long wanted to turn the barn into a cottage. The garage was joined to the main room, a staircase was built into the loft. Now no more boys would break in here through the loft skylight as they had had the habit of doing. There they played poker until the fishermen coming through the yard to go to work would catch a glimmer of light where there should be no light and hear the words, "I raise you twenty." This would happen no more with the barn made over into a cottage. A wide, screened sleeping porch with a view of the sea was put along one side and a deck over it as a porch for the top floor. The house was again on an upward swing.

VII

We had touched the all-time low when we ate the Arequipa, but from then on there has been a steady, if snail-like, progress. That winter, for once, the budget was in hand. We lived for less than we ever had before because we were all anxious to keep Joe at school. We made a game of living within our budget and had a great sense of triumph when we had a few dollars left over. Sue, Heaton, and I would divide the small surplus to buy the things we wanted most. Small regular savings even were made.

Heaton had a fine dog given him, a German police dog which we called Halyard. Halyard grew to young manhood in an extraordinary state of innocence. He had not learned that dogs bite or men kick. There was no old Cape Cod bulldog up the street to teach him fighting. All the dogs in the neighborhood were young and they raced and frolicked together like lambs in the spring. Halyard was not even orthodox in regard to cats, for he felt like a father to Marmola's kittens and they curled up between his paws and slept warmly in his long coat.

Toward spring some people appeared who wanted to

make a miniature golf course in the back yard, for miniature golf was the game of the years of depression. It seemed an awful thing to have a golf course in the back yard and yet I was not intending to live in Provincetown next summer but was planning to go off some place with young Joe. The summer before, I had found the atmosphere somewhat too stimulating for a young boy, and I wanted Joe to have a job. The advantages of the golf course were that they would plant shrubs and bushes and put on fifty cartloads of loam, for the soil in the yard was sandy. But alas, they got nothing out of it and neither did I. The golf craze collapsed as suddenly as it began, and though they must have put a large sum of money into it, few people came. The caretaker sat there every day letting his radio blare out an incredible noise. Neighbors complained and still he blared. It was only later I realized that this was so they would be refused a license the next year. There was a clause in my lease which said that if a license was refused at any time he could break the lease.

Not even the coverage of the soil remained to me because when I was abroad in '33, the turf I had come by, through letting the neighbors' ears be assaulted with such a high count of decibels, was sold in cartloads by the children, who thought to turn an honest penny for me. When I came back, the back yard was as bare as a newel post and the feet of ball-playing children had stamped through to the sand.

VIII

During the winter of '32, the depression deepened. It became harder and harder to sell stories. It was at a time of very low ebb in finances that several bricks fell from the underpinnings into the cellar leaving a large yawning hole. The sand began to sift down as if to undermine the very house. Hastily I got a mason. He in turn called a carpenter. The two consulted. They were both aged New England workmen. I could hear one pecking away at one of the beams with his pocketknife.

"Nawthin' but punk," I heard him say, "cut through it just like cheese. All rotted out."

They appeared triumphant before me, with the knowledge that a large beam would have to be replaced before we could put the bricks in.

Meantime I had noticed a small leak at the top of the boiler and called the plumber. He investigated and turned on me a beaming countenance.

"That boiler," he said, "is a miracle."

"A miracle?" I quavered.

"A miracle it holds together. It's nothin' but a mere shell. Just been held together by capillary attraction, just waitin' to collapse on you when the boiler was good an' hot, I s'pect. Just yest'd'y, got jes such a collapsed boiler put in about the same time yours was, likely."

It was at that moment that there came a letter in the mail telling me if I didn't immediately pay the insurance on my car, my license plates would be taken from me.

Even Sue and Heaton's sanguine natures were stumped as to how to get the side of the house fixed, a new boiler, and the new license plates.

It was that night the smell came into the house. It seemed as though a skunk were coming rapidly to my bedroom door. It was only Halyard, who had had an encounter with a skunk and, innocent as he was, was coming to me to rid him of the horrid smell. But even with Halyard out of the house the smell didn't go. It seemed that the skunk had moved in through the hole in the underpinnings and was now in the smuggler's cellar or lurking under the house.

It turned out that almost everybody has, at one time or another, had a skunk. From far and near, friends came with advice as to how to get rid of the skunk. One had given a party and danced on the skunk. The skunk had

[258]

left, but so had the guests. Others had lain in wait and shot the skunk which has to go out to hunt at times. One of the mail-order houses advertises scooter-skunk. Others suggested the loud ringing of bells and the beating on dishpans because skunks are sensitive and insecurity makes them leave. At last I got a message from an old lady from the West End who said there was only one way to get rid of skunks and that was to write them a letter. So I printed a letter in red crayon. I wrote:

DEAR SKUNK:
I would not willingly hurt the feelings of one of God's creatures, but circumstances beyond my control make it necessary for me to ask you to go.

Regretfully,
MARY VORSE

Heaton connected a long extension that reached under the house and turned a light on to illuminate the letter. Sure enough, the skunk left. The hole in the wall was bricked up, the beam of pure punk replaced, the new boiler put in, and the family began to get ready for Christmas.

IX

That Christmas there was a great party which was at once sad and beautiful. Lawrence Grant was dying and he knew he was dying, so he wanted to see all his friends around him once more in a gay Christmas party. Lawrence and Alice Grant had always loved entertaining and there were no parties that had more warmth in their hospitality than had the Grant's parties. There was a feeling of gaiety and inexhaustible kindliness in the way they lived. Now this would be their last big party, the next time we all came together in that house it would be because Lawrence, whom all of us loved so much, would be dead. It sounds a little dramatic for a dying man to give a big party and superintend all the decorations himself, but it wasn't dramatic,

[259]

because Lawrence was a simple person, and he loved having his friends around and he wanted to go as he had lived.

Lawrence had too great a sensitivity to endure the shocks of life; but he was one of the unforgettable people who live on. Alice Grant was a woman of strength and power, much older than Lawrence, and there was between them even in their best days, an unescapable element of tragedy. So these two people, whose hospitality had been such a part of the town, gave their last party with all the bountiful spirit with which they had lived. Lawrence Grant was a peculiarly lovely human being; a man gifted in friendship and kindness. His going and the breaking up of that household which had seen so much hospitality, was among the things which crumbled the fabric of our social life.

The depression winters of '31 and '32 merged themselves into each other as something good arrived at in adversity. The whole family was now together. Ellen was home for good, Joe was going to school in Provincetown. During the depression years many people stayed in Provincetown all winter.

The Colony had been enriched; Alice Kelly, Alice Grant's daughter lived near us; the old Arequipa had been transformed into Smooley Hall, which now became one of the centers of our social life. John Dos Passos had married Katie Smith and between journeys to distant places they spent a great deal of time here. Possessed of enormous physical vitality, Dos, as soon as he stops writing, goes swimming, sailing, or works in his garden, or paints. It is as if he were obsessed with the shortness of life and cannot bear to lose one precious second.

From one moment to another he is off to the other side of the world, to Russia or South America. He is as accessible as Eugene O'Neill was solitary. Yet I have never known anyone well over a long time who so seldom talked of himself. Always his talk was about the world, or politics, or what he has seen or what he thinks; never himself. There

[260]

is no one who ever combined so bitter a criticism of the world in which he lived with greater intellectual courtesy. A stream of interesting people pour through the Dos Passos house; unexpected guests are always arriving. There is always a feeling of a heightening in life when Katie and Dos are around. Sometimes there is so much life that Katie is almost swamped by it.

About this time Edith Foley, another of the beloved Smooleys, and Frank Shay were married and Frank and Edith's house to the Westward was another center for us all. Betty and Niles Spencer bought a house on the hill near the Gifford house, where Betty made an exquisite garden. Ida Rauh Eastman, who had been so much a part of the Provincetown Players, bought a place near the Hapgoods' summer house and lived here summers with young Dan Eastman.

Another house where life always seemed intensified, was the Hapgoods'. There was always a crowd there at tea time; Hutch talking abundantly and Neith throwing in one single word which crystallized the talk swirling about her. Trixie Hapgood was at our house a great deal during the depression winters, and with her instinct for life and living, was a great addition to our household.

Phyllis Duganne sometimes would take a house in Provincetown for the winter and with pretty Jane and her mother, Maude Emma, whom we all adored, made another center of gaiety, while at the other end of the town were the Frederick Waughs and the Coulton Waughs, and the Floyd Clymers. Tom Blakeman, one of Provincetown's well known artists, and Marion Blakeman, bought a house to the west, and Chauncey and Mary Hackett came to Provincetown to live.

At that time there was in Provincetown as pleasant a society as I have ever known. It had begun in the early days before the Provincetown Players, and it continued uninterrupted until a short time ago—a society composed of summer people who had bought houses here and often stayed all winter. Few of these families left before Christmas, but when one family, such as the Wilbur Daniel Steeles, moved away, there was some other family to take its place. The center or meeting place would change—now people gathered at our house—then it might be at the Kaeslaus' or the Hapgoods' or Susan Glaspell's or at Phyllis Duganne's.

There was no afternoon when this group did not meet in one house or another. All of us went away so often and had traveled so much that it had none of the ingrown quality of people who see too much of each other. There was a peculiar quality to these informal meetings. There was almost no gossip, because everyone was interested in things outside—in writing, painting, or in the affairs of the world. The occasional parties had a real gaiety. It would often seem to me as I looked around a room that I had never seen more good-looking men and handsome women together. Each winter had its own quality and color.

It is hard to put into words the charm of these meetings composed so pleasantly of hospitality and friendship and intelligence. In all my travels and in all the interesting groups of people I have met all over the world, I have never known anything more satisfying than that small society which existed in Provincetown for over twenty-five years. The group shifted, changed, but it was like a brook running along where the water is never quite the same but the brook remains. It is hard to put a finger on what caused its disintegration, for many of us are still here. The death of beautiful and talented Marguerite Kaeslau was one of the things which took the heart out of us.

At this writing, in '41, there still remain more interesting people in Provincetown than in any town of its size, yet we live isolated from one another to a certain extent, no longer forming the society which continued so long and so fruitfully through so many years.

CHAPTER THIRTY-ONE

Likker Ashore

I

ONE day I looked out of my window and saw a puff of smoke behind a vessel, but the vessel was at anchor. Unless the vessel was afire, how could she have a puff of smoke? It was a day in March. The sea was deep blue and cold-looking, with small, choppy waves. The sky was cold and bright and filled with white, round trundling clouds. Black and white gulls screeched in front of the house.

There was a puff of smoke away from any boat, out in the middle of the bay. Still I didn't know what it was.

The harbor looked queer anyway. All the boats were fishing in the harbor. I couldn't remember boats fishing inshore in all the years I had looked out of my window.

There was another puff of smoke down near the gas boat. Then leisurely, quietly, a gray side, smooth and slippery and big as a submarine, heaved itself out, glistened, and dipped.

There were whales in the harbor.

The puffs of smoke were whales blowing. Not in the wineglass shape of a waterfall like the old prints, but in enormous sprayey smokelike puffs.

I went out to go to the Red Front. I met Captain Whorf on what we call the boardwalk, though it has been made of concrete these ten years.

"Good morning, Cap'n," said I. "What are they fishing for out in the harbor?"

"Fishin'?" he said. "They ain't a-fishin'. They're *rummin'*. Whar you been? Ain't you heard thar's likker ashore? The hull danged town's beachcombin'. Ain't any fishin' boat fishin' this mornin'. S'prised your boy ain't ben out. Your beach an' every beach had a patrol all night. . . . Seems they was goin' to land likker to Beach Point last night. Come 'long the coast guard, an' they dumped their cargo. Seen the whales in the habbor?"

"Yes," I said. "I've seen them."

"Ain't ben whales in fer years. Come in a hull school of 'em, come in after herrin'. Th' herrin's runnin'. Runnin' kinda small, too. Traps all full o' herrin' this mornin'."

II

Down at the Red Front a crowd had gathered. Cap'n Ellis was narrating.

"Coast guard come 'longside me and sez, 'Whut you doin'?'"

"I sez, 'Ef you ain't dumb you can see I'm fishin'.'"

"Sez he, 'You're putting down trawl in a mighty queer place fer fish!'"

"Sez I, 'Thar ain't no law yet against me fishin' wharever I see fittin', without permission from the coast guard! An' I ain't got what you think I got, nuther. So you can take you an' yer nosey ways off back whar you come from!'"

"Sez, 'Ef you got what I think you got, you won't keep it, nor it won't do you no good. I know what kind o' fish you fellers ketch in the habbor!'"

"Sez I, 'You think a awful lot. You're gonna split yer brains a-thinkin'!'"

"Coast guard got Mr. Souza," a woman said. "He was just comin' in, towin' a case, an' up comes the coast guard an' took an' broke the likker in front of his face an' eyes! Mis' Souza sez he went in the house an' most cussed himself into apoplexy. He's cussin' yet."

[264]

"I guesso! I guesso!" people sympathized.

A bunch of boys ran past the Red Front. Their eyes were bright and they were giggling together. Everybody turned around. "Looka there. I bet them boys' pockets is full!"

III

Downtown, everywhere people were standing in knots. The town had poured out into the street. There were groups standing in front of the stores, in front of the post office, and in front of the Board of Trade. Everywhere, up and down the street and through the whole length of town, there had flown tales of treasure trove—something for nothing.

The ordinary toilsome ways of the town, the hard work of fishing, had been interrupted. If you fished out in the harbor you might fish a case of liquor. The treasure trove came in twenty-four pints to the case, twenty-four pints of good whisky. You could sell that twenty-four pints at two dollars the pint—forty-eight dollars. Or twenty-four pints at three dollars—which you could get from the summer folk—seventy-two dollars!

Rumors flew around. The Jasons had eight cases. The Deavilas had found three. Little Minnie Crummins had been out that morning in her canoe and bumped right into a case. She was just towing it ashore when along came the coast guard. . . .

Something for nothing. Illicit gains. Liquor ashore. The old red gods were riding through the town. The old days of smuggling and buccaneering were back again. Everyone's blood ran quicker. There was a full stop to the workaday routine. Everyone was dreaming of a good time, of free liquor. Our town in the old days was a great pirate town. The smugglers and wreckers of the old days have worthy descendants.

[265]

IV

In front of the bank I saw Jerry Tate and a bunch of young men about his own age. Jerry has a brain, from which comes insecurity. He reads books. He likes talk. He loves ideas. He loves to get tight. He has never worked hard at anything. He feels himself superior to the townspeople and inferior to the summer people. So he is neither flesh nor fowl.

Now the breath of adventure had blown over Jerry, and he bloomed. His eyes were bright, he looked taller. He was talking with staccato, gangster gestures that held an abbreviated command. He was planning something. The other boys who do nothing but drink too much and hang out with Jerry were all alert, ears cocked up like terriers in front of a rat hole.

Captain Crowley came along. His vessel was in the harbor. He is the captain of a deep-sea, one-hundred-twenty-five-foot schooner, one of the few of our beauties still left us. He wore a gold watch chain and store clothes. He has fine shoulders and a chest three feet through. His hands hang down like hams beside him. His eyebrows are as heavy as his mustache. He jerked his head sideways at the group and said laconically:

"Plannin' a hijackin'."

He was right.

The rumrunners stored the salvaged liquor that night in a vacant barn in back and set guards. Jerry Tate got to know that the liquor was stored in that barn. Jerry had found two or three cases, and he planned how he would get a lot more education and buy books. He'd keep it all winter and sell it high to the summer folk, and be all set. He had a bright idea. If you got a big enough mob you could go and take the liquor away from the guards. For there couldn't be more than two or three guards, who wouldn't dare shoot into a crowd of twenty fellows.

So a mob of young men and older men, too, "snuck up on the barn," and when the guards saw that they were twenty to three, they gave up; for, just as Jerry thought, they didn't dare shoot. They couldn't shoot to kill. The mob lit in and divided up the liquor and carried it off. That gave Jerry a good lot to keep for summer. He thought he might just as well have a little party with some of it, with some friends. When Jerry woke up next day he felt he needed a pick-me-up. What with one thing and another, Jerry drank all his liquor himself before the summer people got there. Then he thought it was just as well, because anyway his mother would have hated to have him bootleg. There are plenty of people in our town who feel that it's one thing to find liquor on the shore and keep it yourself, and another to sell it. They feel it is socially inferior to go selling liquor.

Other boys tried to find out where Jerry Tate kept his liquor, and Jerry Tate tried to find out where the other boys kept their liquor.

It was contraband, it was illegal, and there was now no more law. People who wouldn't think of stealing a piece of salt fish would not mind stealing the liquid gold of their friends' treasure trove. It was surprising how quickly moral values ceased to be. Surprising how close, all of a sudden, a quiet, hard-working town was to the city gang. Little cliques of young men banding together to hijack each other's find.

V

In the meantime, the bootleggers had salvaged another load of the liquor. They started one night to take it out of town. They might have got by, except that Will Staunton tried to pull a hijacking stunt on them. He and two other fellows tried to hold up the rumrunners with a gun, but they jumped Staunton, blacked his eye, and beat him up good, and chucked his gun into the water. With the best of intentions our town tried to act like a city gang or like a gang in the movies. The good will was there, but they were amateurs always—not killers.

The activity of the town was now twofold. One was finding treasure trove, the casks that might bump ashore any time, money, a good time free. The other was trying to take away the money, the free good time, from someone else.

Nights the whole town was aprowl. Those who had liquor tried to take away liquor from other people who had it; and those who hadn't any skulked around like lean and hungry dogs watching if they could find out where their neighbor's cache was.

Our girl reported that men were every night skulking around the fisherman's house next hers. People took to guarding their houses. In the nights there would be a scuffle of feet on the streets—voices—shots. The night was never still any more. It was hard to go to sleep with the sense that the men were prowling around to steal from each other. That people shot at each other even if they didn't shoot to kill—yet.

VI

Some people's lives were changed for good. Old Man Kettle, for instance. Old Man Kettle lived on the back street. He was so old people had forgotten his name wasn't Kettle. Only old-timers remembered that his name was Ben Morgan. Only old-timers remembered how it was that he got his name of Kettle. They had forgotten about his brother, Johnny Pots, who had died years ago. The two old men had lived alone in the small Cape Cod house. As long as anyone could remember they had gone "sweetmeating and cocker-rinkling," which is to say sea-snailing and periwinkling. They had a trap box that they kept for their sweetmeats and cocker-rinkles out below low-water mark. When Johnny Pots died, Old Man Kettle kept right on sweetmeating and cocker-rinkling.

He would go out in his dory with his long boots on, and his old coat hanging around him, and times when he came laboring up the steep ladder down at the fish wharf he looked like some sea monster, something that had come up from the depths of the sea, with his rheumy eyes and his leathery cheeks and his hands that were like claws. The way he got his name of Kettle was this.

Some thirty-five years ago, Cap'n Long's lobster pots out by the Point kept getting robbed. Cap'n Long lay in wait over on the Point and said he was going to shoot anyone who went a-robbin' of his lobster pots. He lay low, and he saw someone rowing out toward the point. So Cap'n Long followed, and there he found Ben Morgan.

"What you doin' round my lobster pots? You been after my lobsters!"

"No, I ain't!"

"I seen you round here by my lobster pots!"

"Waal, 'tain't me, it's my brother. I'm a-fishin'." Ben jerked his thumb out to another dory. So Cap'n Long went to the other dory.

"What you mean, I ain't been robbin' no lobster pots. It's my brother. I'm only a-fishin'."

"Waal," screamed Cap'n Long, "it's a case o' the pot callin' the kettle black!" So from that time forth it was Johnny Pots and Ben Kettle.

Old Man Kettle beachcombed every morning. He brought home funny things that the sea threw up. He found three hooked rugs with holes in them. He found old towels. He found life preservers and mooring buoys and corks from the fishing nets. He found an old ship's lantern. No week but that the sea threw up something which he could pick up in the early-morning hours.

Old Man Kettle went out to look at his sweetmeat and

cocker-rinkle box. He saw the square corner that looked like his box floating off a ways. He said, "Cain't be that box o' mine is adrift—couldn't drift off from my nigger." The cocker-rinkle box was moored by a "nigger," which is a big stone with a hook in it and a chain attached to it, in a sunken barrel filled with sand and rocks.

He rowed after what looked like his sweetmeat box, and there was a case of liquor. He heaved it aboard his dory, looking all around fearfully to see if the coast guard were coming or if any of the other fishermen had seen him. He hadn't heard about the liquor ashore, for he was kind of hard of hearing and didn't talk much nowadays with other people. He saw Bug Lummis' dory roll past.

Bug rested his oars to cry out, "Find anythin', Cap'n Kettle?"

He roared back, "How? . . . No, I ain't found nothin'." He had thrown his slicker over the case. He rowed inshore and looked around fearfully all the time to see if anyone was watching him. Everybody was intent on his own business. He got the case up to his house without meeting a soul, and he hid it under his bed. He took out one pint.

"This likker," he thought, "ain't safe to my house. Best I bury it up some'res else. Someone might come in and look under my bed. No tellin' who might come in when I'm gone—for lately no one's liquor is safe. Young men lie in wait near houses where they think is a can of alky, and go in and pinch it. No tellin' who saw me come up here with it. Might nobody've seen me, or might anybody've seen me come from their windows." So he waited till dark, and he hid the liquor in a deserted henhouse in the back of his yard.

But he got to worrying about the liquor, so he covered it up with a lot of wood. That worried him too, so he spent a whole day spading up his garden, though it was pretty early. After dark he buried the liquor in the middle of his garden. Then he was sure that someone had seen him bury it in the garden. He thought he heard someone outside. He was sure that the Lummis boy and his gang were after his liquor. So he spaded his liquor up again. Then he thought he'd like a drink, so he drank one bottle; and then he drank another bottle. This was only the third bottle he had drunk. When he came to, the liquor was nowhere to be found.

But he knew he had hidden it somewhere. He remembered taking precautions, before he had passed out, to hide the liquor. He spaded his whole garden up again. He couldn't find the liquor. Now if he could have been convinced either that the liquor had been stolen or that he had hid it, it would not have gone so hard with him. But ——

"Dang it," he said, "I dunno if I hid it or if 'twas stolen!" So now he goes around looking and looking. He has almost given up cocker-rinkling and sweetmeating because of figuring where he hid the liquor and looking for it.

CHAPTER THIRTY-TWO

More Likker Ashore

LITTLE boys like Bug Lummis had more fun than anyone. Bug was a stocky, lusty boy, and comical. He was the head of the gang, partly because he was a little older and partly because of his vitality.

Mrs. Lummis was a big, heavy woman, who was often on the street swearing at her children. She could swear wonderfully. When Bug first ran away, she swore for two days.

Other mothers hated to see Bug come rolling in, with his wide, impudent grin and his stub nose. The younger fellows in his gang followed Bug like the Pied Piper. Bug found a couple of cases, and he hid them so his old man and old woman wouldn't drink them up or sell them on him. He said to the other fellows:

"Let's all of us go rummin', and let's pool what we find. Then we can sell it and share the money." But they were too smart for him.

"No, let's each one keep what he finds," said Jeremiah Wilson. "S'posing you don't find any, Bug? S'posing you didn't find any, what's the great idea o' *you* gettin' any money?"

Bug hadn't told the gang that he had already found the two cases. He pulled a flask out of his pocket and took a swig, then he passed the bottle to Jeremiah. Corkscrew, who had curly hair, took another swig. Squealey took a swig, and everybody took a swig but little Tony, who was the youngest of the gang and only fourteen. Squealey began acting tight. The liquor burned their throats as it went down, so Bug bought some ginger ale. It was better in the ginger ale. Little Tony began drinking too. It went to his head very quickly.

Bug and Squealey and Corkscrew all went staggering off, saying "Whoopee!" But Jeremiah went and bought some Lifesavers flavored with wintergreen, so his mother wouldn't smell it on him.

Little Tony went to sleep under a wharf. He felt awful when he woke up. He was sick at his stomach under the wharf. The tide had come in. He saw a box bumping on the piers, and, sure enough, it was a case of whisky. He pulled the case up and went right down the road to where he knew some summer folk lived. They called them summer folk, just the same, though they had lived here all winter.

Little Tony was still pretty pale and felt queer, but he wouldn't have touched any more whisky, not if you paid him. He offered the case for thirty-five dollars to these summer folk, and they bought it from him. He took his money right to his old man. There had been sickness in the family and his father hadn't done much fishing that winter, and the thirty-five dollars was a godsend.

"That's how good a boy little Tony is," my boy told me, "he gives every cent to his father when *he* goes bootlegging! I always told you Tony was a good boy!"

Bug's old lady swore at him good. You could hear her hollering most any time what she thought about Bug for not bringing home any of the money or the whisky. But he had saved a flask for her and gave her the first five dollars he made trucking. He had to. She took it out of his pocket when he was in bed. But he was always good-natured when his old lady swore at him and never said anything back to her, except "Shut your trap!" Sometimes when she called him a bastard, he said, "So's yer old man."

II

Likker coming ashore brought with it other instances of filial piety. Mr. Silva fished with his three sons. He was a good fisherman and had a very nice home with every convenience in it. He was noted for having good luck, and keeping up his boat as well as he did his house, and for his high temper. There was hardly any other fisherman with a higher temper than his. Being the captain even of a small vessel gives a man authority and dignity; and Cap'n Gaspy with his watch chain, his blue store suit, and vessel that carried a crew of twenty-seven men had no more dignity than did Mr. Silva in his forty-foot boat.

Mr. Silva's sons made a big liquor haul. They went out beachcombing in their dory and found eight cases, one right after the other. They said, "Whatdya know! Pa, we found a lot o' cases!" They told him because they knew someone else would, and then they would get the dickens.

"That so? Well, you bring 'em right here to me. I'll take care of them cases. 'Tain't good fer young fellers to have too much to drink. When you want a drink I'll give you a drink, ef I think it's good fer you. . . . And don't none o' ye try to sell any of it, neither!" He didn't believe in bootlegging. He'd have died to have a boy of his make a few dollars by anything so common as peddling liquor. So the boys did what they were told. They brought in six cases and only held out two cases on their old man, which they stored in a place they knew about. They would get a bottle from time to time and take it to a friend's house, in friendly fashion, to drink. But you couldn't have bought a pint from them.

III

People took to hiding their liquor in queer places. Rumors sped around the town. Wherever you went—to the post office, to the bank, the Red Front—there were men and women talking about where things had been hidden. If you went out to the dunes, men would pop up. You knew they were following tracks and looking. In the woods, where usually you could go day after day and meet no human being, there were now always voices. People were hunting in the woods for a cache.

There was talk that fifty cases had been sunk in Shank Painter Pond. The whole town was out on a treasure hunt. Few people cruise in back nowadays, except hunters and berrypickers. Now, all of a sudden, the back country was populous with stealthy characters looking for what didn't belong to them.

Some old men remembered that in the old country, Manuel Ferrera was a great one to find wells, and that when he came to America he brought with him his divining rod.

One of the fishermen said, "Let's go get Man'el Ferrera an' pay him to go around with us through the woods with his divining rod. Maybe it'll dip over buried whisky."

Manuel Ferrera was an old fisherman from the island of Flores, who lived on the back street. He was a little man who had never learned very much English, and his wife scarcely spoke it at all. She grew flowers indoors and had a fig tree growing in a pot. Great fleshy begonias climbed up from her windows, every window.

They are one of the few old-fashioned couples who still at Christmas observe the *Menin Jesu*—"the little Jesus" —in the old way.

Manuel Ferrera's friends went to see him. They offered to share with him if his divining rod would find the whisky.

"It won't work like that," Manuel Ferrera said. "It only dips for water. How will it dip for alcohol?"

"But you don't know, you never tried to have it dip for alcohol. So how can you tell?"

"It won't do you any ha'm, Man'el, an' you may get a lot of whisky." It wouldn't do any harm to try, his wife urged. So for days Manuel Ferrera walked through the woods in the-back country with his divining rod balanced. He walked up and down and up and down through the thick woods, among the little pine groves, but the divining rod never dipped.

IV

Word came that liquor had been tossed overboard down the Cape a ways. Brewster and Dennis were finding liquor, too. They were telling how at the girls' camp only champagne and brandy were washed up, while other places the inferior stuff came ashore.

The bootleggers kept busy disposing of their wares and playing hide-and-seek with the coast guard. Everything was watched so, that the rumrunners down Brewster way decided one night they would have to plant their liquor in the bay. They got a fellow who knew the shore to pilot them to a place where no one would be able to discover it, near one of the fish weirs, which would be a place they could mark.

The rumrunner said, "I don't think we need pay this fellow a second time to pilot us in. I've been taking notes where he went. I'm sure I can lay my course to this fish trap myself and save us the money we'd pay him for piloting us a second time." So that night they ran along to plant their liquor, as word had come there was no use trying to land anything with the coast patrol so active. Fog came in, but they sped along through it and happily found their fish trap. Here they sank the load.

There was a fish trap rather far inshore; and as there are long flats off that shore, at low water the trap stands high. This fish trap belonged to a man who had been doing very poorly. It seemed as if this hard winter even the fishes of the sea had deserted him. Without much hope he went down to his trap one morning, and there piled high were untold riches! A whole boatload of liquor was piled around his trap, case on case, moored securely, and some half out of the water.

The bootleggers had mistaken the trap and had come to the inshore one! Trying to save twenty-five dollars for the pilot, they had lost thousands.

The poor fisherman could hardly believe his eyes. It was like a romance to find that by night riches had been piled around his trap, which had given him so poor a living this hard winter. With hands trembling with excitement he filled his boat full of the precious stuff, as fast as he could. He came back, filled it again, before people began to suspect. Soon his trips roused suspicion. Presently there was a group of townspeople down by his trap getting the liquor too.

Soon the rumrunners came down, reconnoitering. The bootleggers stood on one side, the townspeople on the other. Each was afraid to start something. There sat the liquor, in plain view, yet each was afraid the other might fire. But there was no shot. They made some arrangement to divide the liquor quickly, before the coast guard should get there.

Around Brewster way, government agents seized more than two thousand cases of uncut "salt-water whisky." One hundred and fifty thousand dollars' worth of liquor was owned publicly or privately. The beach became a place of mad picturesqueness. When the coast guard and the police stopped work at four—for apparently "Old Caspar's work was done" at that hour—it was the citizens' turn—prominent men vied with poor clam diggers in hunting liquor.

Western Special was auctioned on the beach. It brought

three to six dollars a quart. The poorer people auctioned off their hauls to the more fortunate who could afford to hold on to their whisky until the summer people would come, or to those opulent enough to keep it for their own use.

It was on this beach, Charles Point, that the chariot race occurred the next morning. Horses were still used over these beaches to haul out the nets in long, flat carts. They can go on soft sand where cars cannot. So men driving "teams" raced each other through the heavy sands to the rum fields. All the "citizenry of Brewster," as the newspapers said, "turned out with wheelbarrows, with sacks, beach wagons, carts, trucks, carry-alls, even baby buggies and boys' handcarts." Anything that had a wheel to turn, anything in which liquor could be transported. Men, women, and children; high-ups and lowly clam diggers; Portugee and New Englanders and Bluenoses were at Charles Point, going out over the low flats as the tide receded. "Just as the chariot race was clattering over the sands, the government agents descended out of the fog which had drawn a soft curtain around the lively operations, and the race was stopped at the pistol point."

V

In these times there was no quiet of night. The night was full of queer sounds. I know in Provincetown there was never a time when I didn't hear voices, the sound of oarlocks, or the thump of oars on thole pins; the chug of dories, the glint of flashlights on the beach. It went on all night.

It did in Brewster, too. Some clever folk thought to fool their neighbors by putting sack and bags around their horses' feet. The muffled hoofs were all right, but they forgot to grease the axle hubs. Treacherous squeakings betrayed virtuous men hauling contraband in the night's darkness.

"Peculiar noises" coming from one of the houses led the government agents to the doors of a "prominent citizen." To resounding knocks and calls of "Open in the name of the Law!" the law was finally admitted. The law seized the thirty sacks of liquor which they found in the prominent citizen's house and took it from him. There were no arrests.

"Can't arrest all the chief men in the county," said the officers. "Be a scandal!" So, as the paper said, "they were released after carting the illicit prizes to coast-guard trucks. Doctor, lawyer, merchant, thief, all turned out to help the fishermen and the clam diggers gather in the sacks at various Cape points. The road to Brewster carried a ripe whisky odor, left by passing porters of the salvaged liquor."

Seth Nickerson was a stout, robust man. He measured several yards about. But he seemed, as he loomed out of the fog, far fatter than usual. And sure enough, hidden under his slicker was suspended a fringe of bottles. He was padded with bottles, bulwarked with bottles from stem to stern, the coast guard reported. And he grew thinner by the moment as they hilariously stripped his bottles from him.

In Brewster Centre, the only human being left was the postmaster and his assistant. Like Casabianca, he stuck to his post in the face of magnificent temptation; and what's more, he made his assistant stick, though by force.

Queer, how completely out of their orbit this something for nothing swung the whole Cape. Queer, what a gay lawlessness was afoot. Life ran swiftly in those days. Our town was furrowed up. People's eyes were gleaming. Women bragged in low tones about their husbands and menfolk finding likker.

Our whole town had been turned into a liquor dump, a bootlegger's town, a hijacker's town. We traveled, as the fishermen say, on our beam ends.

[279]

Gradually the excitement died. No longer was the night made uneasy by cars whooping past, full of tight men and girls. No longer were the nights a-rustle with people searching the beach. No longer did the government agents scurry from liquor dump to liquor dump. Young bands of hijackers, who stole and counterstole, went back to work or to loafing around the wharves. The Cape took on its workaday face again, again became thrifty and laborious. The red days were over. The sons of pirates and buccaneers forgot the stirring in their blood.

In the papers and among the citizenry, the whole thing was a huge joke, a gay carnival. It had been a great time for merriment and rejoicing. The old instinct of loot had been unleashed for a while, and, having looted, people felt better. Having drunk their fill free, they went back soberly to work.

CHAPTER THIRTY-THREE

The Eclipse

I

THE eclipse with its end-of-the-world feeling was a fitting climax to the epoch which came to its close in 1932.

Cars poured into Barnstable County in tens of thousands. By noon the Cape tip was so overloaded that the State Police put a halt to any more coming down any farther than Wellfleet, fourteen miles away. Some came from as far as Chicago and Norfolk.

This was the last eclipse the Eastern part of the United States was to see for more than a generation.

We decided our own back yard was the best place from which to watch it.

Every afternoon the rays of the sun filter through the leaves of our big willow tree to form a moving pattern of light and shadow on the roadway beneath it and on the white side of the Freeman house next door. The day of the eclipse was windless and the leaves were still. Each ray of light that reached the roadway repeated a perfect unmoving round of brightness, a thousand little images of the sun, each one exactly like the one by it.

As the moon commenced to cover the sun, the spots of light changed in shape. Finally each circle was only a crescent. The road became a tapestry upon which the new moon reappeared in a formless Persian design repeated a thousand times. This particular pattern had never occurred before and would never happen again.

It was starting to get dark. The robins and orioles and flickers who nested in the big tree flew to their nests and chirped sleepily overhead. Late-evening sounds filled the early afternoon. Out on the harbor the gulls streamed to Pamet River and the Eastern Harbor.

We watched the side of the barn for the shadow bands that precede a total eclipse. Suddenly they appeared. The whole white side of the little building seemed to flow and waver as bands of dark and light swept across its surface from right to left.

The threadlike crescent that was all that then remained of the sun vanished. There was a short moment when all that could be seen of the daystar was a curved row of brilliant dots, Baily's beads. The light of the sun streaming to earth through the valleys of the mountains of the moon.

Now the eclipse was total. For fifty-nine seconds the sun's corona flamed around the jet-black disk that was the moon. Not far away Mercury, the seldom-seen planet, shone faintly. Other stars came out.

The sun was fully covered. The shimmering white light of the corona streamed out to all sides of the jet-black circle that was the moon.

Then it was over. The thin crescent of the sun appeared on the other side of the moon.

The crescents of light re-formed themselves under the tree, facing in the opposite direction.

The sun was lower now and the crescents were longer. As the sky brightened the birds woke up. One robin started his morning chirp in midafternoon. The gulls flew back. They protested noisily, for they had flown far to their nesting grounds and now had to return.

Three long, thin crescents appeared on the side of the Freeman house, glorifying its plain clapboard sides as they were never to be glorified again. The crescents grew quickly.

The curtain was down. The show was over.

[282]

The eclipse came at a period of social disintegration.

The effect of the crash of '29 still reverberated through the country. It had wiped out the money of a number of people in town who played the stock market and engulfed the savings of others.

Ordinary people who lived outside of the circle of speculation had been tightening their belts for some time in Provincetown. The boom days of fishing had stopped with the war, so the first impact of the crash was felt less on the Cape than in some other parts of the country. The disaster of the crumbling of the financial structure crept up on us slowly. But gradually jobs grew scarcer; the depression had caught up with the Cape.

Liquor ashore was a high point in the disintegration that had been going on all over the country, leaving grown men jobless and making loafers and bootleggers of boys.

The Bonus Expeditionary Force had marched on Washington with its thousands of desperate veterans. When they marched on the Capitol, President Hoover retreated into the depths of the White House like a monarch afraid of a revolution, and although General Glassford had the situation well in hand President Hoover called upon the army to disperse the veterans. Four troops of cavalry, four companies of veterans, a machine-gun squadron, and several tanks were used to disperse people who would have left of their own accord. The burning of the Bonus Expeditionary Force's shacks on the Anacostia flats and the use of tear gas on the fleeing veterans, men shot because a President of the United States was afraid, will never be forgotten.

This was the time of Kreuger's colossal swindle and the Kreuger suicide. Foster and Peabody, the Boston bankers, had urged several people in Provincetown to retain their Kreuger stock, so strong a hold had this extraordinary financial crook on the imaginations and faith of the most conservative bankers in this country.

This too was the year of the kidnaping of the Lindbergh baby. Through prohibition, crime had been organized. Cities were dominated by the gangs of such men as Al Capone.

There have been cycles of depressions in the United States, but none which equaled this with its millions of unemployed. A gray cobweb of bread lines and files of tired men standing before any place which might give employment were spread over the land. In some places, as before the Ford factory, men trying to get work were shot down in their rush for employment. "Hoovervilles," the shanty towns built out of tin cans and the pickings of the town dumps, sprang up in the outskirts of towns and cities.

On every street corner of Fifth Avenue in New York, men and women were selling apples. These bright apple baskets were a constant reminder that there was no work for men anywhere. In industrial towns, like Youngstown, the pall of smoke was lifted and people saw the sun for the first time in years. In Provincetown, tons of fish were thrown into the sea from the cold storages to make room for the fresh fish for which there was no market. The market for fish and the price for fish had sunk like a plummet.

America was as rich as ever in actual wealth. Gold was here, the productive plants, raw materials, and the labor force. Nothing had happened to the rich farm land. All the means of prosperity were still here, but the way to use them had fallen apart. The United States had slowed all its productive capacity. Its banks had failed, its financial system cracked, and it was in a fair way of no longer being a going concern. Business which could not function still resisted any new ways of production.

Even the farmers revolted. Their crops rotted in the ground. It did not pay to harvest and transport them, while people hungered in the cities. The whole country was in turmoil. The farmers' depression, like that of New England, had begun long before the crash of 1929. In states like Iowa and Nebraska where people had owned their own farms, they saw them taken by the banks and insurance companies. In Virginia, within a few weeks, thousands of farms were forfeited for nonpayment of taxes. The farmers who for years had tried to work through their local granges, their legislators both state and Federal, took a Farmers' Holiday under the leadership of Milo Reno. They barricaded the roadways and spilled milk that was to be taken into the cities, and for once no one cried, "The reds!" Mortgage sales were stopped, magistrates were threatened. The farmers were closer to 1776 in their revolt than to revolution.

In the industrial centers chimneys were dark and men hung around corners, out of work. Coal towns were dead. Banks which had prospered for over a hundred years in the Middle West folded, and conservative investors who had thought their bank stocks as safe as United States bonds found themselves suddenly debtors as well as losers.

In the White House sat Hoover. Hoover's sands were running out. He had made a brave effort to have a disarmament conference, which had failed dismally. The Smoot-Hawley bill was the outstanding legislation of his regime.

Franklin D. Roosevelt was nominated for President.

CHAPTER THIRTY-FOUR

Bank Holiday and Relief in Provincetown

I

DURING the last months of Hoover's administration, the country's tangled affairs slipped ever faster downhill. Hoover, who had been so quick to give food to hungry people in Europe and who, being a sensitive man, had wept at the spectacle of the starved children of Belgium, felt that the feeding of the unemployed should be left to private charity, as though the Ladies' Aid could handle the Flood.

No President ever stepped into office amidst such economic chaos as did President Roosevelt. The bank holiday came as a relief throughout the country. People took it the way they had some other major disasters, with something like gaiety.

In New York, the bank holiday was spectacular. In Provincetown the banks closed. Then they opened in due time. Nothing earth-shaking happened here, though people agreed that this was a strange world where you had money in the bank and you couldn't get it.

While great financial houses went bankrupt, there were fewer bank failures in Massachusetts than in any state of the Union. The depression came so early to the Cape and deepened so slowly that in one of the first years a Truro summer resident sent a sum of money to the selectmen in Truro asking that it be used for whoever needed it. The selectmen wrote back that they had been looking around for someone to help and though no one had much they seemed to be getting along. But they had at last found a widow who had children sick with measles and if the giver thought it was all right they would hand her the money.

Up to 1932 the Overseer of the Poor looked out for people in distress. There had been so many tragedies at sea and so many women with young children left widowed that Provincetown had evolved a kindly way of looking after its needy. There were almost no rich people in Province-town and few in actual want except through disaster. Fishermen are poor. There is always plenty of pinching and the hidden starvation of not the right kind of food. There are the long bad times when debt stalks around, but people have held their heads up and expected to do for themselves.

For those whom disaster had overwhelmed, the town owned or rented a number of houses which were called "widows' houses," where a widow's family could have a decent place to live, rent free. There was a coal fund and the fund of the Helping Hand to which a Seamen's Fund was joined. Provincetown had its share of the Shaw Fund for seamen's children, which bought boys' clothes and shoes. So the families of the men lost at sea "got along" with the town's aid and when there was a supreme disaster like that of the gale of '17 help came from all around.

By 1933 things were bad here. The bottom had fallen out of the price of fish. Boys and girls who had formerly left town to get work stayed here doing nothing and those who had had jobs came to live at home. But there was still fishing and never the despair here comparable to that of coal towns or industrial towns.

II

Shortly after the inauguration of President Roosevelt the great relief plans rolled up one after another and people got work through them and extra food through the Surplus Commodities Corporation. It is as impossible to visualize all the New Deal accomplished as it is to visualize this country as a whole. Men went to work all over the country. Young men filled the C.C.C. camps. Rural electrification lighted thousands of homes. The T.V.A. furnished a new pattern of living. Great dams made fertile millions of arid acres. Public buildings sprang up throughout the country. Our wasted soil was built up by Soil Conservation. Great housing projects were made. Education widened its doors from nursery schools, on the one hand, to workers and adult education, on the other. Social security changed the lives of old people and cushioned unemployment. The arts projects developed writers and artists and musicians. The theater blossomed for a little while and invented new forms. There was, above all, a new atmosphere, a feeling of responsibility toward preserving our resources—human as well as natural.

Provincetown benefited by all these things. The arts projects saw many fine pictures painted, men and women wrote good books. Provincetown added *The Cape Cod Pilot* by Jeremiah Digges to the American Guide books. The pictures and murals of Provincetown artists became even more widely known.

Many children are well today instead of undernourished, even if all the children who needed food most didn't get it. Many families kept from despair. The morale of many young people was saved.

In physical gains we have an airport, which was costly. We have a new post office. Mosquitoes are under control. Every day there is a gay chatter past my house, a band of babies under the benign care of Rilla Alexander. This is one of our three nursery schools.

We have a Community Center. Like all the innovations in Provincetown since the front street was built, there was opposition. If I could write the story of the ups and downs of the Community Center I would come close to writing another *Middletown*. The story of the Community Center is that of the political history of this moment. There was, of course, the good citizen who didn't want a community center because there had never been one before. And the other who didn't want it because it was Communistic.

"Why is it Communistic?" he was asked.

"Well, just listen to its name. Doesn't that tell you what it is?" he replied.

To make the Center, people of many kinds had to get together. Yankee and foreign, winter and summer people, Catholic and Protestant. By political sleight of hand and great patience, Charles Hapgood, the director, got an organization together that worked.

The Community Center was set up in the abandoned Eastern School House. A little while ago this was an empty, tumble-down building, rapidly falling apart. Repairing and painting and equipment have cost the taxpayers nothing; the money was raised through the community. The children in Provincetown before this had no place to play winters, when the beach is too cold.

After the Center came, every game from dominoes and checkers to basketball and table tennis were played. There was at last a rival to the poolroom. They even had their own pool table.

In one room the boys made ship models and learned to build boats under the direction of one of the best small-boat-builders in the country. In another room the band practiced. There were several bands, from the harmonica band for the little boys up to the swing band.

There is no livelier place in town than the Center evenings. There are dances for enlisted men, classes for defense and first aid. It justifies itself every night of its existence.

[289]

It is yet uncertain if the few hundred dollars can be raised to keep it going.

III

The story of relief in Provincetown has been repeated generally throughout the country. To blame individuals is useless.

In 1932 the Overseer of the Poor was replaced by the Welfare Department, composed of the three selectmen. From that moment politics and welfare were joined as if in holy matrimony.

It is a question which no one can answer why the sum spent on relief has more than doubled since 1931. One would think that the relief load would be less. Yet in 1940 and 1941 more than ever was spent on relief. Nor does this amount include W.P.A. expenditures or those for surplus commodities. The price of fish has not been so high since the First World War. The draft and well-paid work in near-by cities have sucked away the unemployed.

What has happened here is a small mirror of what happens wherever there is something to give away put in the hands of politicians. As soon as there is a link-up between the relief agencies and the political agencies, it would take the purity of Israfil not to use this enormous power.

Whenever people can get something for nothing it is inevitable that those who have political pull, large families of voters, will drink at the fount of plenty. It is easier for the demoralized and discouraged to live on an income, however small, than to work, and it is more secure. An increasing number of people took what they can get free, here as elsewhere. This helps to perpetuate the political machine which dispenses welfare. Welfare and handouts, instead of being matters of emergency, take on the aspect of inalienable rights. The edge which divides those who need help and those who with some effort could help themselves is knife-blade thin.

IV

One of the town officials with whom I have talked stated the general opinion that "the benevolent town fathers are supporting a strong political machine, using relief appropriations to insure their continuance in office."

The town auditor, Benjamin R. Chapman, states in his report for 1937:

"There is a widespread belief that there are a good many chiselers on the relief rolls. In fact it is a powerful factor at the polls."

In the Town Report for 1940, Mr. Chapman again cries aloud:

"There could be approximately a saving of a hundred dollars on each carload of coal if bought directly by the town. Two carloads are used each year. This is the third time I have brought it to your attention. How can we be so dumb?"

"Soon now," cries the *Provincetown Advocate*, "quite a large group of regular welfare recipients will be drawing on their Unemployment Insurance, to which they are entitled because of seasonal employment, but how about avoiding a duplication of drawing State Compensation checks and Welfare slips, all in the same breath?"

There are many who criticize the manner in which the surplus commodities have been distributed. I went into the home of a friend of mine who said, "Looka this. See what I got. I got three pounds of surplus butter, ha-ha!"

I said, "What's a robber baron like you doing with surplus commodities?" My friend was by Provincetown standards well-to-do.

"Oh," he said, "up to the Town Hall they're handing

out things to anybody who stands in with the gang. If I hadn't taken this out someone else would."

Here, as elsewhere, the surplus-commodity food is sometimes thrown away. No one "on surplus commodity" wanted grapefruit, and as I write a consignment of it decorates the town dump. People reject anything but white flour, and there is no one to teach them to use the whole-wheat flour.

One of-the W.P.A. projects was the airfield. There was supposed to be work for any man who owned a horse. A young man who owned a horse was in desperate need of work, but he found that horses belonging to prominent businessmen and well-to-do citizens had already filled the quota. Projects suggested, like the sewage project, were rejected.

Eternal vigilance, however, is the price of purity in public affairs, and who will take the trouble to be eternally vigilant as to what is happening in Town Hall or City Hall? So here as elsewhere people grumble at the officials they themselves have elected.

CHAPTER THIRTY-FIVE

The Changed Town

I

DURING the three years after bank holiday, great social changes occurred throughout the country, which were sharply reflected in Provincetown. I was away a great deal of that time, coming back for a visit in the fall of '36. I returned to find Provincetown had made another of its sudden transformations.

Since Provincetown stopped making salt, it has had only one crop. That crop was fish, when, as Thoreau said, "a village seemed thus, with all its men ploughing the ocean together, as a common field." It had a few cranberries and a few summer visitors.

Now it had another crop—tourists—and so had all New England. New Englanders have slowly, almost imperceptibly, changed from earning their living from farming, manufacturing, and fishing to the business of pleasuring, which now is its second source of income; and how different is the mentality of a town which caters to tourists from one which holds itself, almost belligerently, aloof from "off islanders" while it makes its living from the sea.

Forty thousand people visit the monument in a season. Officer Cabral reported that fifteen hundred cars came into town in two and a half hours one day in late July, 1940. It is like sending a streamlined engine on a single-track, narrow-gauge road. We almost crack under the strain.

The approach to Provincetown over the high moors,

[293]

where there is a view of both bay and sea, had been marred by a congeries of auto camps, some of which had taken their architectural lines from the privy. Almost all had been built with no thought of their relation to the town. A solid line of camps which flowed along Beach Point.

Renting extra rooms to pay the taxes was no new thing in Provincetown, but now large signs saying ROOMS were everywhere. The whole town had become a rooming house.

A stream of tourists choked the streets. Two-way traffic was still allowed on the front street. There was a perpetual tie-up of cars, which stretched as far as the eye could reach, their owners honking impatiently to add to the confusion, while sweating traffic cops tried to untie the snarl.

The New Beach drew people from the whole Cape. With its striped umbrellas and its water games it was almost as popular as Coney Island. Luckily it was on state land, so hot-dog stands and bathing pavilions were forbidden. Of all the beaches that surround Provincetown, it is the only stony beach and the only crowded one, yet here people congregate like sand fleas on a dead fish.

II

During my absence repeal had changed the pattern of living of America. Nowhere is the power of government more clearly shown than in prohibition and repeal. A law is passed prohibiting the sale of liquor, the result of years of agitation by a determined good people. Its unpredictable results changed the aspects of all social life.

As a drop of poison flows through the veins, so this law penetrated through every hamlet in the country. Who could foresee that a law passed by idealists, led by devout women and ministers of the gospel, would breed Al Capones, and wipe out the gains of temperance of a century? Innumerable towns like Provincetown where no liquor had been sold for three generations should begin to drink; that women would get tight and mixed drinking would become general, young boys tote flasks and young girls get "blotto"?

Nor could it be foreseen that with repeal, the social life of the nation would move into bars and taverns. From having drinking parties of illicit liquor in private homes or carefully guarded speakeasies, people rushed to drink in public places. Throughout the country, taverns, bars, night clubs sprang up. The habit of going to cafés for one's entertainment spread through America.

During prohibition, there was one single night club in town called The Ship, run by Inez Hogan, who is known throughout the country for her children's books, which she illustrates herself. The night club was a pleasant meeting place for artists, art students, townspeople, and the actors from the Wharf Theater.

Now it was as if this innocent Ship had spawned like a herring. Such places as the Flagship, the Lobster House, the White Whale and others have become well known through dint of excellent food and pleasant surroundings. Many other night clubs and taverns come and go. Hot-dog stands, hamburg-sandwich joints, restaurants of various prices were as prolific as the taverns.

The town is checkered with small and desperate trades— have your silhouette done, wait for a picture to be painted, get your caricature. There are shops which sell sandals, African masks, etchings, hooked rugs, handmade jewelry, pottery, and the midtown shops which have every sort of gadget for the boat tourists.

Thirty-five years ago Berry had the only antique shop. He had a round sign which read on one side, ANTIQUES. Come September 15, when the boat stopped, Berry turned this sign around. It then read OLD JUNK.

Then the only souvenir of Provincetown which one could buy was a picture postcard of the back view of an enormous woman in a bathing suit which reached her ankles. On her capacious rear were printed the words, IT FLOATS! And in smaller letters underneath, BUILT FOR COMFORT, NOT FOR SPEED. A variation of this tender souvenir is still sold. One might call it the first far-off intimation of the hot breath of honky-tonk which, with the coming of tourists, blows over the town from July 4 to Labor Day.

An industry has sprung up which might be called the knick-knack industry. It too has changed the aspect of the town. The stores all sell these "souvenirs." The newspaper store sells them, the drugstore sells them. There are stores given completely over to them. These are the type of thing that you can buy for a small amount, like a lighthouse stuck into a cork ring, or a painted clamshell—clutterers and dust gatherers that have neither use nor beauty. There are stores where things of taste and beauty are sold, but such stores are swamped by the knick-knackeries.

Provincetown had, for many years, been noted for its interesting stores. The Hook-rug Shop of the Coulton Waughs was famous in its day. There have been many fine antique shops like that of Mrs. Young's, or the unique stores, like the inimitable Peter Hunt Peasant Village. There is a group of fine craftsmen who make jewelry or carve wood, blow glass, embroider and sell interesting wares from the four seas; yet knick-knacks are what first strike the traveler's eye. Even the children sell decorated clamshells along the sides of the streets.

With what nostalgic longing one remembers Duncan Matheson's store in the old schoolhouse which was floated over from Long Point. It was a nautical store full of fishermen's clothes. There, piled up helter-skelter, were all the clothes to keep folk warm and dry fishing. There were hand-knitted wool socks and mittens smuggled by the fishermen from Nova Scotia, flannel shirts, the best that money could buy, substantial fleece-lined union suits. Bright-red union suits bought at Dunc's, now to be seen in the fashionable sports' shops, used to flap their crimson lengths on washlines. There were both yellow and black slickers and so'-

westers, and hip boots of white and red; heavy blue and red sweaters suitable for keeping fishermen warm on an icy day, and for summers—jumpers of sailcloth like those the coast guard wear. Now Duncan Matheson and his store are gone and no gadget emporium can take his place.

III

People on the Cape had not taken the depression lying down. To many the depression came as a spur which created new trades. The things that grew on the Cape and in the back country, and the old crafts of the Cape gave inspiration to many.

Every Cape housewife puts up beach-plum jelly which has an unparalleled flavor. There are blueberries in profusion, wild blackberries and strawberries, "pucker-mouses," wild cherries, juicy pears, and bogs of cranberries run wild.

The richness of the Cape put it in the minds of people to use the jellies and jams that are made from these things to eke out an income. A Cape Cod woman, Anne Standish Clifton, had a famous recipe book from which she made her jellies. Dotted all down the Cape are little Cape Cod houses called jelly houses. This small venture became a big business and the Cape Cod jellies spread all over the land and even as far as England. The Royal Family are customers.

The coast guard are great whittlers. They whittle windmills, they make fine boat models. Someone had an idea of making a business of these homemade toys. All over the Cape and beyond, in every town, there is one yard bright with little painted windmills of all forms, wooden toys, and garden seats. The coast guard no longer whittles them; they are made in factories for mass consumption.

Many famous boat models have been made on the Cape and have found their way into collectors' houses and have been bought by museums.

Bayberry candles of which there were always a few made on the Cape, dipped in the old-fashioned way, now have become another important business. Mrs. Anna Bagley, in Wellfleet, buys tons of these berries every year. It takes seven to ten pounds of bayberries to make one pound of wax. It is a pesky business to melt the wax off, refine it, and dip the long strings time after time into the wax.

Again the Cape has furnished an inspiration which has given work to many people, in a new perfume developed by Marion Blakeman, called "Bayberry Mist," which is sold in her fine store, Personal Appearance.

New industries, the fruit of true imagination, have come into being since the depression. Tiny Worthington first thought of making a vogue of fish-net clothes and household accessories, which has spread over the whole country.

The story of the Cape Cod fish-net industries is a true success story. It includes such things as the finding of a cast web net, handmade and used on the Florida coast and in California, very wide and circular, which made a beautiful skirt. It includes hanging the nets to dry on the rafters of the loft and watching them as they swayed back and forth to test the blending of two or three tones and one new design after another. These fish-net accessories were taken up by the top-ranking fashion designers in shops everywhere. They are lovely and original, yet the fish nets that the old men used on their ships when I first came here are more beautiful than any adaptation ever could be.

IV

Provincetown's greatest asset is its unique situation— its surrounding austere beauty of bay, sea, and dune. The historic town itself with its two long streets of Cape Cod houses is situated on the Bay. All these make it a place to visit and a place to live in. Whatever marred its beauty or its dignity took from it not only something essential to the people who lived there, but robbed those who must now partly make their living from the tourist trade.

A few people have been allowed to damage the beauty of Provincetown. The few rowdy night clubs, the wholesale selling of worthless knick-knacks, make it possible for a leading magazine to come here and brand the place a "honky-tonk." Those few who cater to some unwholesome element for a little money rob themselves as well as the whole town.

CHAPTER THIRTY-SIX

How to Get to Provincetown

I

SINCE Provincetown has become a popular resort it has, until recently, been one of the most difficult places to reach, except by car. A new bus service has been announced by the New England Transportation Company with three daily busses connecting with New York trains and the Providence boat.

It has always been easy enough to get here from Boston, but at the Information booth in the Grand Central Terminal information about Provincetown is swathed in mystery.

The last time I started to Provincetown, on what has practically become an individual piece of exploration, Grand Central Information gave the time for the departure of the Cape Codder fifteen minutes late. When I remarked that this had caused me to miss my train, "So what?" the young man at the Information desk countered jauntily. It was just as well, because had I caught the train I would have wasted four hours at Yarmouth. There was no connection between the Cape Codder and Provincetown at that date.

I asked again at the Information booth if there was any train for Providence with a bus connection.

"No," the young man said coldly, "no connection."

There was a connection from Providence, but the bus was not a New York, New Haven and Hartford bus, and therefore nonexistent to the proud young man at the Information desk.

Getting to Provincetown by land has always been difficult. There was a time when packets ran from Provincetown or Truro to Boston at least three times a week. You had something there.

It was not until the middle of the nineteenth century that anyone thought-of making the journey to Boston in any other way than by water. Shebnah Rich gives a fine description of the packet days:

In about 1830, Captain Rich and his friends determined to build a first-class packet. The result was the schooner *Post-boy*, the finest specimen of naval architecture, and of passenger accommodation, in the Bay waters. Her cabin and furniture were finished in solid mahogany and bird's-eye, and silk draperies. She was the admiration of the travelling public; all that had been promised in a first-class packet, and was often crowded to overflowing with passengers. . . .

Here was sure to be some Marco Polo captain, who had killed elephants in India or seen the Brahma's great white bull. Some Western adventurer, who discoursed of steamboat races, herds of buffalo, and Indians. Here were the home traders, discussing the price of sugar, eggs, and palm-leaf hats. Skippers talked of mackerel and codfish. If the sail flapped idly against the mast, somebody had been becalmed in the Indian Ocean for weeks, without a cat's-paw on the face of the water, or had run down the trade winds from the Windward Islands to the Equator, without starting his topgallant studding-sail brace; or, like the Flying Dutchman, had beaten for weeks off Cape Horn.

The King's Highway was laid out around the sand dunes of the Eastern Harbor, over a track in the sand. For a long time travelers came as far as Wellfleet by stagecoach and then by vessel the rest of the way. Not until later did the stagecoach lurch to Provincetown around the sand hills of the Eastern Harbor. Thoreau gives an engaging account of his ride by stage down the Cape to Truro:

I was struck by the pleasant equality which reigned among the company, and their broad and invulnerable good humor. They were what is called free and easy, and met one another to advantage, as

[301]

men who had, at length, learned how to live. They appeared to know each other when they were strangers; they were so simple and downright. They were well met in an unusual sense; that is, they met as well as they could meet, and did not seem to be troubled with any impediment.

II

By 1873, the railway which had made progressive stages down the Cape finally reached Cape End. Each new step was greeted with bands, cheering crowds, and the engine wreathed with flags. Twice a day an actual passengers' train arrived at Provincetown. It was probably the slowest train in the world and it stopped so often that legend had it that when the train saw a new cranberry shack along the road it halted automatically. Though the trains spent more time in stopping than in going there was one thing about them—they finally got to Provincetown. You could be perfectly sure when you started from New York on the Fall River boat that ultimately you would get to your destination. In 1940 the Cape train stopped at Hyannis.

There is a New York-to-Providence boat which connected with the bus. Try and find out about it in New York without going down to Pier 21. There is a boat that goes from New York to New Bedford three times a week. It was said to have connections with Provincetown, but all these things remained until recently in the realm of rumor.

At best these boats are poor specimens compared with the Fall River Line. Then you left the heat and noise of New York and stepped not into another world but another century. To the last, the Fall River Line kept an air of elegance and the manners of the Victorian era.

A boat runs between New York and Boston through the Canal. Unless the boat is delayed by fog it makes connections with the excursion boat *The Steel Pier*, which goes to Provincetown during the season, but there is often fog in the Canal, so the New York boat is late, the traveler must spend his day in Boston, and arrive in Provincetown by train and bus, haggard and disheveled.

All these difficulties in getting to Provincetown, except during the brief season of the Cape Codder which has a direct bus connection at Yarmouth, are needless. Standing empty at Buzzard's Bay on the Cape Cod Canal is a fine large station. It communicates with the Boston boat. The happy thought had been that the Boston boat would let passengers out at Buzzard's Bay, where a bus would take them down the Cape.

Powerful transportation agencies willed otherwise, and so people groped as though in the dark to find the way to Provincetown. Now at last with the new bus service it will again be possible to get to Provincetown in other than obscure, uncomfortable ways punctuated by long waits in remote hamlets.

CHAPTER THIRTY-SEVEN

The Changed Neighborhood

I

THERE has been an incalculable span of time since I first came to Provincetown in 1906. My neighborhood reflects that change. The core of the neighborhood thirty-five years ago was a blacksmith's shop, a shipyard, and the shop where David Stull made his whale oil.

Now these buildings have been turned into a popular night club, the Flagship, and the famous artists' club, the Beachcombers.

But at the very center there is still a forge. It is as though the fire had refused to go out. William Boogar, Jr., the sculptor, casts his delicate bronze sea gulls where Clarence Snow used to swing his great sledge and put shoes on vessels as well as on horses.

This ganglion of shipyard, art school, and smithy, together with Burch's store, formed a place in which many interests centered and many people came. And it still does in its metamorphosis of today.

On the remnant of Kibbe Cook's old wharf beyond Pigeon's, artists painted when I came. The big "store" past the Cooks' and later Pigeon's then housed Mr. Hawthorne's art classes. In 1907 he had finished building his own studio for criticisms. The little shack in front of Duncan Matheson's house was taken over by Ambrose Webster, the painter, who stretched it out, built a second story for an apartment, and used the lower floor for his art school.

Later, stretched still more, it grew itself a wharf and became the unique building which houses the Flagship. Buried somewhere in it are a few of the old timbers of Dunc's shack.

II

The shipyard was opposite my house. Later it was used for the Atlantic Coast Fisheries to bring up their weir boats in winter. Now Pat of the Flagship has bought it for a parking space.

Two men who seemed old already in the shipyard days, Mr. Atwood and Mr. Pigeon, were perpetually tapping oakum into the seams of boats. That gentle tapping was the music to which my writing was done. I went to work to the sound of the mallets opposite and quit when there was a silence in the shipyard.

All summer Mr. Pigeon and Mr. Atwood worked on boats, scraped their bottoms, calked and painted them. Large boats would be rolled up by a horse and windlass; or all the men loafing in Snow's blacksmith shop would tail up on the windlass and walk round and round, heaving the vessel on rollers up on the beach.

Mr. Pigeon seemed already an old man when we came here so many years ago, and as the years progressed he was only a little grayer and a little frailer. We knew each other very well, although in all the years we talked but little. We would exchange remarks about the weather or the fish or some water-front gossip, such as the deer caught in the fish weir, the great catch of horse mackerel, or that there were blackfish in the harbor.

When I sat down on the beach I had a comfortable sense of companionship. The old men, Mr. Atwood and Mr. Pigeon, were sound and sweet as good apples. Their faces were browned from living on the beach, their skilled hands deft from the care of the boats which they tended. The serenity of their lives and their thoughts showed on their faces. Mr. Atwood went first and Mr. Pigeon worked on for many years alone. But when the noise of his tapping mallet was stilled, something good and comforting, something very essential to this neighborhood, went out of our lives.

III

The passing of the blacksmith shop marked an even-greater change. Clarence Snow, the smith, was a big, red-headed man. He had been selectman and Overseer of the Poor. After he married Ina Small he gave up his smithy and went to Arrow Head Farm. He was one of those men whose death one cannot credit, so full he always seemed of life, with his love of music and his zest for enjoyment. His smithy was one of those informal forums of democracy where the opinion of the nation is formed. It was a neighborhood club where men came to discuss fish and politics.

In front of the smithy was David Stull's whale-oil shop. There was a subtle aroma around those premises as though the ghost of a whale had passed by. David Stull had a stiff leg and walked bent double. He had sparkling, bright-blue eyes and his chin stuck out and there was a mole on it. With his stiff leg and stick, he looked like some fabulous seafaring man. There are still legends told about him and the fortunes he made in ambergris.

He would often come to me with German and French letters to translate, for he sold his oil all over the world. It was made for the finest precision instruments and for the most perfect watches, and it came from blackfish. Blackfish, though small for whale, is large for fish and can be as long as thirty feet. From time to time they attack our coast in a furious feeding rush after small fish or succulent squid. The little escaping squid make a terror-stricken rush for shallow water and after them charges the greedy whale, plowing the water with its great rubbery fins.

They get stranded on the beach and there they die and stink. Wherever there were blackfish David Stull would buy them, for in the top of the blackfish's head is a reservoir of oil which is pure and fine. This reservoir was ladled out to make the oil for precision instruments.

With Hawthorne's classes and Webster's classes held here, this neighborhood recorded the coming of the artists to Provincetown; and the Art Association and the Beachcombers' Club made this part of town the center of the art colony. These buildings watched the whalers go and the artists and summer people come to occupy them.

It would be hard to find a more interesting and diverse neighborhood anywhere. Cater-cornered to my house is the fine house of Commander Donald MacMillan, who has been to the Arctic a score of times and who knows more of the lore of the Arctic creatures than any man living. His many visits and his careful, painstaking work give him a perception and a knowledge of the strange region above the Arctic Circle that more spectacular explorers never attained. His house faces the Bay and the whole top story houses his Arctic library.

I do not know anything that can give one more of a sense of time and eternity than to hear Commander MacMillan tell the story of the flights of birds over thousands of miles of land ways that have long since ceased to exist.

At twelve o'clock the whistles of our cold storage blow and promptly his malemutes, the Eskimo dogs, mingle their Arctic howls with the sirens.

Another Arctic explorer in the neighborhood is Jot Small. Little, compact, full of New England tang, Jot Small might well be carved of a knee of fine hardwood such as is used for the construction of vessels. For a long time he kept a fine shipshape little restaurant a few doors away from here. He is primarily a boatbuilder who has developed a type of boat with a Marconi rig, called the Eskimo boat, which until this summer raced every Sunday. More than a dozen of these little boats raced across the Bay. Alfred Mayo, the great fisherman, another neighbor, frequently won the races in his *Akpah*.

Nearly opposite Jot Small's is Dr. Frederick Hammett's house in whose laboratory in Truro is being studied the mystery of cell growth, with the objective of unlocking the mystery of the wild growth of cancer cells. Never well, small, lively, Fred Hammett accomplishes more than two large healthy men. His brilliant, restless mind plays over the range of interests from international politics to far reaches of science. He has his finger in a dozen pies of the town. People come to him for help and advice on from how to build a house to how to run the Community Center.

Among the nine painters of our neighborhood is Richard Miller, of whom I have spoken. As fastidious an artist in her way as Richard in his is his wife, who has the secret of everlasting youth. As if by magic, she has formed from a gully, a big willow tree, and an old barn a beautiful house and garden as lovely and poetic as any one may find anywhere in the world.

Up the street a way from my house is Peter Hunt's Peasant Village, a fantasy which some people call an antique shop. It is unlike any other shop in the world, for here Peter has loosed on barrel, table, and chair his unbridled decorative fancy. Surely so much gay imagination has never been squandered on furniture and furnishings.

IV

Currents and countercurrents eddy around such outstanding personalities, such mixtures of writers and painters, captains of vesels and great fishermen, scientists and Arctic explorers. Never did a neighborhood make its living in more diverse ways, for besides artists, sculptors, and nightclub proprietors we have two building contractors, a teacher, a chief of police, an iceman, an electric-light man, an express man, and a famous interior decorator. But the majority still make their living directly or indirectly by the sea. There are more fishermen and more coast guards than anything else, though several of our deep-sea fishermen have retired and others in their late years have taken to sea-clamming and lobstering.

In our neighborhood you can see how the town has been taken over by the outsiders. There has been that peculiar shift and ebb which is a terrifying part of American life. There are more newcomers like myself, a steady infiltration of us, coloring and transforming the stream of Provincetown life.

We ourselves are part of the process of change. My brother, Fred Marvin, and I both bought old houses and made our homes here. All over the town the same story is repeated. All over town new people come in steadily. Romeyn Benjamin bought old Ves Ellis' property and Ves Ellis lived on his boat, almost to the day of his death, with his cat, Jerry, who was as expert a fisherman as Ves.

There are, roughly speaking, about sixty-five houses in my immediate neighborhood, from Lovett's Court to the cold storage. Of these, twelve have been built since I came here and several shacks have been made into cottages. To offset the new houses, three houses have been moved away, two by jigger and one by sea.

But of the families living in the neighborhood when we came, only thirteen remain where they were a quarter of a century ago, to nail it down into a semblance of what it was. Beneath the surface, though, Provincetown is stable and follows some long-established pattern. The neighborhood has come up. Ephraim Cook's handsome colonial house two doors from me, which had degenerated into a two-family tenement, is now the Art Association.

There are several restaurants within the little span of

two blocks and you can buy a strange variety of things between the Christian Science Church and St. Mary of the Harbor, both newcomers during the last quarter century.

You may go to church, amuse yourself free of charge at the Community Center, or go to a night club without stirring two blocks either way.

There are some things that have not changed. My other family, the Avellars, are still in their house. The Dutras still live on Bangs Street. Margie Seaver still sails her boat. And my good neighbors, the Higgins, still live next door.

CHAPTER THIRTY-EIGHT

Beam Trawlers and Dorymen

I

THE vessels and fishing boats I see from my window have altered more than the houses of my neighborhood. Ice and power have changed all fishing in the last thirty years. The greatest alteration has been brought about by the beam trawlers, which are destroying the fish in the sea.

A big mechanized vessel moves slowly through a sea of dead fish. The ocean to the horizon is white with their bellies. They boil up at the vessel's bow like a wave as it plows through the young dead scrod. At the sea's bottom is another layer of dead fish. Scrod are young haddock. It takes two years for a haddock to grow. Presently there will be no more. Those which have not had the air pocket punctured stay on the surface, when they are damaged they sink. The dredges of the deep-sea scallopers come up half filled with dead scrod. The sea, top and bottom, is filled with this wasted food in a starving world. From forty to fifty thousand pounds of fish will be thrown overboard from each vessel daily as the big pouch of the moving fish trap is lifted by engine-powered winches and tons of fish are spilled on the deck and sorted.

A fleet of these "otter" trawlers sails from Boston mostly to the George's Banks. They scrape along the bottom and bring up everything that is there, not only the young fish but also tons of "shack," the bottom stuff on which the fish feed. This fish factory drags its heavy dredge on the sea's floor. It is cone-shaped, tapering to the closed cod end.

These trawlers are the reason why fishing is getting poorer every year. When the beam trawlers get to shore with their cargo of 300,000 pounds of fish, the lower layer of fish may be as much as ten days old. It will be iced, of course, but the fish will first have been bruised in the trawl and then crushed by the pressure of the tons of fish above it.

On the Fish Pier in Boston a single jobber may buy the entire catch and sell it in lots to successive bidders. At a given point, he can question the quality of the fish. He can, if he wishes, call the inspector and have part of the cargo condemned as inferior, therefore reselling at a lower price. The fishermen, naturally, get less. Finally, the lower layers are bought by small local dealers. A little retail shop near the fish pier may sell fish that are not as fresh as those from the same vessel hurried by truck to a town in Pennsylvania or Ohio.

This looting of the fishing ground has happened in Europe. The beam trawler has made its way across the Atlantic and it is history that it has destroyed great fishing grounds across the ocean. As early as 1915 the United States Bureau of Fisheries made a special investigation which proved that what had happened in European waters would inevitably happen here. The nets used by these vessels were a three-inch diamond mesh. The Bureau of Fisheries urged that if a larger mesh were used, the scrod could escape. But the corporations had as much interest in conservation as a boy robbing an apple tree. The warning of 1915 was recently repeated by the Bureau of Fisheries.

They recommended, beginning February, 1938, that the cod end—that is, the cone of the great netted pouch—should be four and three-quarter inches instead of three. The sea of dead scrod through which the vessels plow shows the indifference of the companies to the Bureau of Fisheries request. Like the lumber barons urged by the

Forestry Bureau in Washington to enter into a voluntary agreement to preserve the forests, the companies owning the beam trawlers also agreed cheerfully to follow the suggestions—and did nothing. Up to now the lobbyists employed by the fish corporations have been able to stop any legislation which would put teeth in these recommendations.

Meantime the beam trawlers go on plowing up the bottom of the sea and laying it waste. Fish are getting progressively scarcer. More and more the fishermen who use hooks and trawls are finding it hard to compete with the fish factories. More and more fishermen are forced by this competition to become draggers. The fleet of small draggers increases and they destroy the bottom of shallow waters, as the beam trawlers do around George's Banks.

One of our great resources inevitably is being destroyed. As the wealth of our forests has been laid waste, so the fish of the sea are being annihilated.

It was because of competition with the steam trawlers that the great fresh fishermen, so recently the glory of the sea, cut down their masts and put in engines. They now carry foresail and a triangular trysail, used only to steady the vessel. Some of them became draggers.

II

At the other end of the scale from the great beam trawlers are the diminishing dory fishermen and the other small fishermen who fish with hook and trawl. These are the direct descendants of the fishing fleets of a hundred sails that jigged mackerel and hand-lined ground fish which made the waters around Cape Cod so lively a hundred years ago.

The captains of these small vessels are as proud as the captains of the fresh fishermen. Walking along with one of them, we passed a man of substance who makes an ample living and owns his own house. Fishing had been so poor that winter that the captain's wife and boy had collected wood for their stove. He looked with pitying eyes on the other man.

"Too bad, ain't it, that a nice man like him should think he's got to work for wages?" he said. He is his own master and possesses his own boat. It is a converted cabin cruiser and is better fitted than most fishing boats. Come good or bad, he works for himself and he plays the immense gamble with the sea, which, until the days of the mechanized steam trawler, was the essence of fishing. This was why men were willing to undergo incredible risks and perform a toil harder than almost any other profession. It takes a stout fellow to fish. Fish are scarce, death is near. Many times a storm may come up that will wreak havoc with your trawl.

Manny Zora is one of the best fishermen out of Provincetown who owns his boat. He was fishing off Chatham with his cousin, Picana, and a storm came up of such violence that they had to cut the gear. At this, Manny lifted his great hands to heaven and cursed Saint Peter, the saint of fishermen.

His cousin was on his knees praying.

"Saint Peter," he cried, "Saint Peter! It's not I who am cursing. It's he—Manuelo—who is cursing—not I—remember!"

Since then, whenever Manny's boat moves down the harbor in Provincetown, a fisherman in another boat will fall on his knees and gesture to Manny: "It's not I, Saint Peter—it's he, Manuelo!" Picana is not the only man in a small boat who has prayed.

Formerly, when sail was still used, the small fishing boats out of Provincetown which fished beyond the Point were a seaworthy type of boat—the Swampscott dory. Getting around the Point was hard in the winter, so the settlement called Helltown was formed between Wood End and Race Point. Legends grew up around Helltown. People said that

[314]

wreckers lived there—men who put out false lights to lure a vessel to destruction. But as a matter of fact, it was a settlement of huts where the fishermen slept in bunks so that they could, in winter, avoid the long journey around Race Point and get quickly to their fishing grounds. At the end of the nineteenth century, these Swampscott dories were replaced by power.

The first gasoline engine was bought by two Portuguese fishermen in 1901. The story is that Joe Gasoline, who had the initiative and temerity to buy the first engine, and his dorymate were caught out in a stiff gale and the engine sputtered and died. The dorymate dropped to his knees and prayed to God if He'd only make the engine go this time more, he would smash it for good when they got to port. They spun and spun the wheel and nothing happened.

With difficulty, they rowed in around the Point, while the other dories making port passed them derisively, making the ultimate insult of holding out a rope—meaning: do you want a tow? Just as they were nearing the harbor, chuff-chuff went the engine. The spark had caught. The engine started. God had answered the prayer.

They came to anchor and before Joe Gasoline could stop him, his devout dorymate smashed the engine forever and beyond repair. This first gasoline engine was only a forerunner. Within the next few years the whole fleet had power.

III

High up on the dial, the dorymen and small draggers talk to each other over the shore radio.

"You got feesh?" "No feesh is here where I am, no feesh." "You ask Manny he got feesh." "No I ain't got feesh, no feesh where I am today," Manny lies. The fish are coming overboard fast. Each man protects his fishing ground from someone else nosing in. They josh each other, develop their fine, juicy vocabularies, as each tries to find out how luck is going with the rest of the fleet.

In the old days when I sat up late, I would be warned that morning was at hand by the soft slap-slap of rubber boots of fishermen going to work. Then came the noise of a hundred gasoline engines—first one and then another, until they made bedlam along the whole water front. Later there was a second lesser explosion of sound—the weir boats. In those days, if I worked late, some one of my neighbors would say to me, reproachfully:

"Seems like you don't ever go to bed, Mis' Vorse. You work too hard. Seen your light when I went to work." I had the feeling of friends watching over me and caring whether I got my sleep.

CHAPTER THIRTY-NINE

Wonders of the Deep

I

WHALES from time to time still spout in the harbor and heave their great gray sides from the water, big as submarines. Blackfish still follow their prey to the shoals and are left high and dry on the beach. Today no one comes to strip them. They are an embarrassment for all concerned, tons of blubber which only infect the air. Last year there were blackfish in the Bay for weeks. One never went sailing without there being young blackfish plunging and playing around the boat. Some of the captains rigged harpoons and one blackfish was actually speared.

Disquieting are the recurrent stories of the giant squid. The little squid which comes in shoals and is chased up onto the beaches by greedy fish propels itself forward and backward at will and clouds the water with its sepia. In turn, it catches its own prey with the tentacles which have suckers like those of a tiny octopus. The idea that this creature grows to giant size has obsessed the fishermen and they will tell you that a tentacle of a squid, big as a man's thigh and covered with suckers as big as a dinner plate, has been seen, cast up on the shore.

A ten-foot shark is lying under Railroad Wharf as I write, and no one knows what to do with him.

Only last summer a sea turtle weighing hundreds of pounds was on view up at Sklaroff's Wharf—here pronounced Skyloft; while some boys to the westward had a baby seal on exhibition.

[317]

II

Not content with authentic wonders, Provincetown has its legends of sea monsters. One of these accounts, given by the uncle of Benjamin Franklin, declares that in 1719 a sea monster came up in Provincetown Harbor which a whole fleet of shore whalemen failed to capture:

Boston, Sept. 28, 1719. On the 17 Instant there appear'd in Cape-Cod harbour a strange creature, His head like a Lyons, with very large Teeth, Ears hanging down, a large Beard, a long Beard, with curling hair on his head, his Body about 16 foot long, a round buttock, with a short Tayle of a yellowish colour, the Whale boats gave him chase, he was very fierce and gnashed his teeth with great rage when they attackt him, he was shot at 3 times and Wounded, when he rose out of the Water he always faced the boats in that angry manner, the Harpaniers struck at him, but in vaine, for after 5 hours chase, he took him to see again. None of the people ever saw his like befor.

The fanciest sea monster, however, was that which George Washington Ready, the old town crier, testified under his signature to having seen. Hiding behind a plumberry bush in Herring Cove, he saw a creature rising up with a head as big as a two-hundred-gallon cask, a body twelve feet thick, scales as big as the head of a fish barrel, colored red, green, and blue, with six eyes, movable and protruding three feet out from its head, and four rows of ivory teeth. Its eyes were red and green, like port and starboard lights. The sea monster cut off the scrub pines as it undulated over the dunes and, smelling strongly of sulphur, seared the undergrowth. It dove into Pasture Pond, leaving a fathomless hole.

III

There is seldom a time when there are no gulls soaring and sweeping over the Bay. Some of the gulls come from as far as Plymouth for the rich pickings from the Provincetown boats. No one has been able to explain the congregation of gulls I saw once near Peaked Hill Bars. There is a flat behind the high sand hills called the bone yard, because here are the bones of many dead ships, swirled in long ago by Race Run.

Once I found the bone yard carpeted with gull feathers and droppings as if there had been here a great congregation of birds. Soon after, walking across the dunes, I noticed gulls hovering inland. As I came nearer these sentinel gulls must have warned of my approach, for out of the bone yard there erupted hundreds of gulls.

The sun was low in the horizon and it turned their white bellies to rose. They circled in ever-widening arcs, hundreds on hundreds of them, then they divided into two banners, one streaming back to Pamet River and the other over the Bay to Plymouth.

What were they discussing at this convention, the Plymouth gulls and the Pamet River gulls, and why did they meet there at all? No one has been able to tell me why they congregated, nor have I found them there at any other time.

IV

In the Eastern Harbor, there are muskrats. Formerly the trappers were able to get a few muskrat pelts, but though they continued to see the animals' tracks in the sand, they could not catch any.

Old Man Morgan, deprived of revenue from trapping, decided to find out why. He took a bottle of whisky one fall evening and went down and hid behind the willow stumps to watch his traps. It was a full moon and presently a strange procession approached, all the muskrats of Eastern Harbor walking two by two, captained by the grandfather of all muskrats, a sly, gray old fellow, whom he recognized.

[319]

The grandfather went up to the trap and put his thumb to his nose and wiggled his fingers solemnly. He was followed by the young bucks who also thumbed their noses at the trap. Last of all came the mother muskrats with their children, and when the children were too little to know what was expected of them, the mothers lifted their thumbs to their noses for them. After that they all plunged into the harbor and swam away.

"And that," says Old Man Morgan, "is why you can't catch nary a muskrat in Eastern Harbor no more."

One of the strangest stories is that of the penguin. An engineer, a war casualty who was recuperating here, was walking on the outside shore and there he found a great bird mired in oil but still alive. He took it in his arms and brought it home, but his mother, with whom he was living, would have none of it, so he remembered that Alice Palmer is kind to all living creatures and he took the bird to her.

When the oil from the Diesel engines had lapped the shore and her kittens had got black with it she had cleaned them with cornmeal, so she painstakingly scrubbed the bird. It turned out to be white with black flaps instead of wings and a neat, small black head. It wouldn't eat, but drank thirstily. In the morning she heard the plash of its webbed feet on the wooden floor as it walked to and fro, and as she went downstairs there it was, like a Senator, stalking up and down. It stood by the door as if asking to go out.

The tide was brimming full upon the shallow steps that lead from her house to the sea. The bird walked down the steps and with inconceivable rapidity made for the Point, while an angry crown of sea gulls circled it screaming.

I asked Commander MacMillan if this could indeed be a penguin or if there were some other Arctic bird that could answer this description. He said it was the habit of sailors from the South Seas to bring penguins north as mascots and that they sometimes survived the tropics in the refrigerator rooms. So this poor creature must have escaped ship and have been bound for the South Pole when he was mired by Diesel oil and cast up at Peaked Hill Bars.

V

The ponds and inlets on the Cape are the way stations of migratory birds in their mysterious flight from the Arctic regions southward. Wild duck of every kind pause in the hidden ponds to rest and feed. One can see their V-shaped squadrons like tiny airplanes in the sky. Flocks of wild geese cry over our heads as they fly southward. A young couple once lived on the outermost shore and once when their purse was so low that they were at their wits' end for food, as if in answer to an unspoken prayer, came upon a wild goose, still warm, that some hunter had shot, lying near their shack on the ocean side.

Northern gulls stop to rest and feed in the salt marshes and lagoons by Pamet River and toward Eastham and Orleans. Later in the year, when these are gone, come the birds from the Arctic Circle and the tundra—eider duck and coots—dovekies. These are sea birds who never leave the ocean but sit beyond the surf, balancing themselves in the icy water with comfort, for this is to them a Florida.

In the spring there are weeks when, at night on the outside shore, there is a perpetual noise of the wings of birds on their flight north. On the return, they do not stop to feed, but flow, a ceaseless stream, toward their northern home.

Then comes the time when the surface of the sea and Bay in certain places heaves and sways with living creatures—the herring or alewife coming up to find fresh water through the creeks and make their way to the ponds where they spawn. Forever they must return to the same place, and in the young herring there will be the inevitable urge to return from whatever home he goes to in the winter to spawn in the same fresh water where he was hatched.

VI

Dr. Henry Marion Hall is an authority concerning birds that make this coast a stopping place, as his many articles show. He has seen all the birds in their secret hide-outs, and can tell you of the loons near the Truro shore and of the blue heron, of the sandpiper, of which there are fifty-one species, and of the Arctic gull who is only a recent comer.

One time Henry Hall and his grandson found a golden eagle mired in the swamp on the way to the New Beach. The great creature was getting himself deeper in the mire by the effort of his powerful wings to free himself. When they rescued him he did not fight them. They took him home and cleaned him and took him to the back country where he spread his mighty wings and soared down the Cape.

Another time Dr. Hall found the nest of the least tern. Two tiny chicks had hatched and the third egg he took home for his collection. He put it for safekeeping on some cotton in his wife's trinket box. In the night a strange rustling came from the box and a peeping so tiny one could barely hear it. The least tern had hatched out and was returned next day to its family.

This summer a great whale was cast up on the outside shore between Peaked Hill Bars. Now, instead of the town rushing out to mark this prize and drain his oil from him and capture his bone, he lay there unwanted, the grandfather of whales.

He was so old that barnacles had encrusted him and given him the name of "Barnacle Bill," and these were no barnacles as we see them on wharves, but barnacles two inches across. There was a great commotion in Town Hall concerning on whose property he had been cast up. One may imagine someone living in the Middle West or the

Rockies, receiving a letter from the town fathers asking him to remove from his shore a whale!

The air began to smell when the wind blew from the west, as it hadn't since the invasion of the blackfish. But just in time came a storm which lifted Barnacle Bill off the beach and floated him out to sea. Barnacle Bill is a monstrous footnote to our changing days. One of the old captains remarked:

"He'da meant money once to this town, and now he was just so many tons of stink."

CHAPTER FORTY

The Outside Shore

WITH all the changes that have taken place here, there has been one unchangeable thing, the outside shore. There are fifty miles of beach that run between Race Point and Monomoy. Except for the timbers of a vessel here and there, this outside shore is as untouched as when Thoreau made his walk from Highland Light to Race Point, and the beach had not changed before that except for its perpetual shiftings, since the first white man put his foot on Cape Cod.

There is something more remote and beautiful where the sea meets land than anything else of which one may think. You are caught up in this everlasting exchange of sea and land. For a moment you are living in that rhythm of time where a thousand years are as a day. Now, more than ever, the outermost shore has gone back into its everlasting loneliness. A little while ago there were two more lifesaving stations between Race Point and Highland. Now Peaked Hill and High Head have been discontinued.

This outside shore, this long hook of the Cape, is the remaining rampart of an old continent. The never-ending battle of land and sea has been going on for untold centuries. This fringe of land on the Atlantic coast is old land, and since the time when the continents were sundered and there was a sea, the ocean has been eating it away, throwing against the ancient shore one fierce storm after another. Savage and immemorial, the conflict goes on and the sea wins. Each decade the sea has altered and broken down some defense of the narrow land.

The fury of the winter storms comes down on this shore. Out at Race Point the pounding surf will be white as far as you can see. The inhuman clamor of the surf fills the universe. The storm sweeps unbroken across the whole Atlantic and piles up wave on wave against this frail remaining barrier of the continent.

There is something like battle in the unleashed fury of a gale on this desolate coast, and you wonder at the temerity of man that he should ever have dared put out to sea in his frail vessels, as the gale roars on.

Long after the gale is over, when the town is bathed in the winter quiet and the night is ghostly still, five miles away the crashing roar of the surf can still be heard.

There are winters when gale piles on gale and the fury of the sea seems never to stop. At that time the very color of the sand changes and has a gray, deathlike look. The warm radiance of fall and spring and summer is gone. There are no foot tracks of any of the little creatures that traced the sands in warmer weather, or the little slithering prints of insects.

What has changed the most are the seas beyond. These once were full of vessels. The seas were never empty. Today you may sit the whole afternoon long and perhaps see but a half-dozen small fishing vessels or the smudge of a steamer on the horizon.

There was formerly a perpetual traffic between the outside shore and the town. Wrecks came ashore and people would stream over the dunes to them. Always the sea was throwing treasure trove on the shore—cloth and liquor and wood for building, everything could be found a man might need. Beachcombers were ever busy looking on the beach. Today one lone beachcomber patrols the shore for what he may find. You may still pick up strange things. Recently I found part of a carved frame with a bird on top and vine leaves. Mostly one finds things like wooden buoys and perhaps the round doughnut of a life preserver, or a bit of canvas or perhaps a seaman's jacket lost off a vessel.

Behind the pure beauty of this beach rise the sand cliffs. Beyond High Head they tower above the shore. Each portion of the beach has its own quality and character. You may walk from Race Point to High Head and when you have left the Race Point beach with its sparse picnic parties you may not meet a soul, except a few bathers below Peaked Hill.

After High Head the beach rises steeply. The highlands have begun. At Highland Light are the clay mounds, strange formations of clay whose origins no one knows. They tower 125 feet above the beach, streaked with ocher and umber. At Long Nook, most beautiful of beaches, the high sand cliffs are a warm yellow and are reflected in the sea, so you swim in a dazzle of blue and gold. At Cahoon Hollow the sea breaks into bar after bar and inshore into lagoons in which children love to dabble.

There are nine hollows that lead from the sea between High Head and Orleans. At the end of each road is a small, evanescent handful of bathers, children, and dogs and bright umbrellas that are only a fleck upon the immensity of this solitude, coming late and soon gone, leaving the beach untenanted by anything except its own creatures.

The memories of this beach are tragedy, memories of the thousands of vessels which perished along this dangerous coast. Its every step has been littered with dead men. On every foot have been piled up the timber of lost ships and the cargoes they carried.

The stories of these wrecks include stately men-of-war, ships from India, vessels carrying cargoes of liquor, stone vessels carrying granite. Lumber schooners enough have been wrecked off this shore to build all Provincetown; cargoes laden with stock and horses; ships from the China trade. They say that a procession of dead ships off these

[326]

shores would reach from Race Point to Monomoy, if they were placed bow to stern. Men from every country have been drowned here and thousands of others rescued by the often superhuman courage of the coast guard. The fishermen have lost more men and vessels than all the other lost craft put together.

Every now and then the British man-of-war, *Somerset,* which went ashore in 1778, is uncovered again where it lies; as the beach makes and unmakes, the skeleton of the old wreck is silted over or laid bare again. She was wrecked on Peaked Hill Bars and lost two hundred of her five hundred men and officers.

The *Whidaw,* the pirate Bellamy's vessel, was wrecked when the storm of 1717 tore the Cape apart at Orleans and Captain Cyprian Southack rowed a whaleboat from bay to sea over Meadow Creek, Jeremiah's Gutter, Town Cove, and Nauset Harbor. Bellamy was lost and 145 of his men.

Strange wrecks have happened, for which there is no explanation. Near the new Peaked Hill Bars station, there was for years a wreck of a sweet two-masted schooner, about eighty feet long. This vessel had come ashore on a bright moonlight night, and neither the officers nor the crew could explain by what mischance or miscalculation a vessel could have been wrecked on such a night. She sat upon the shore as lightly as a butterfly, as if ready to take off again; and yet the inner injuries were so great that after looking her over it was decided that it would not pay to haul her off.

At first we would go down into the cabin, where the meal had been left set on the table. Gradually a hole was ground in her hull, and at high tide fishes swam in her hold. For years she remained there resting on even keel, more and more abandoned, more and more a wreck; and finally one of the great storms broke her up altogether.

Here is Provincetown's final contrast. A few miles away

from a buzzing town with its froth of summer people and its night clubs and its stream of cars, its trivial little shops, is complete isolation, the majesty of undefiled beach, the sea stretching out with nothing between you and Portugal or Spain.

This arm of land, which holds Provincetown, a dot in the crook of its fist, is surrounded with mystery. The prehistoric struggle still going on between land and sea, the mystery of the birds' migrations and that of the fishes in the sea, make Provincetown only an evanescent speck in time and eternity.

CHAPTER FORTY-ONE

The Hurricane

I

THE hurricane of 1938 came riding up out of the Caribbean, whirling on its axis like a huge, invisible top sucking up water as it came. It was just at the moment when Chamberlain was flying to see Hitler. The news of the hurricane's destruction and the destruction of Czechoslovakia came alternately over the radio. Two great disasters, that of Europe and that of the hurricane, were contrapuntal to one another.

The hurricane struck almost without warning. There had been talk about it for two or three days in the paper. It had reached Hatteras, it had come farther north, it was going to Washington, it was going out to sea. But it didn't turn, and it roared over Long Island and through New England.

Two low-area districts, one from the Atlantic and one from the Great Lakes, formed invisible mountains between which the hurricane roared like water down a canyon.

The hurricane cost more than five hundred lives and tore

down more than fifty thousand homes. Three billion board feet of timber were lying like jackstraws piled house-high. Beautiful old towns like Amherst and Hadley in the path of the storm lost trees that had taken a hundred years to grow. Long Island was prostrate and so was the whole New England coast up to New Bedford and Fairhaven. It turned inland to lose its fury near the Canadian border. It was like the storm of which Governor Bradford had written three centuries before.

The hurricane came to my house with a knocking on the door that precedes disaster. Someone put his head in to shout that my boat, the *Molasses VII*, was going adrift, but she landed on an ebbing tide as lightly as a leaf and Joe rolled her up out of harm's way.

The storm blew up fast. A branch of the willow tree crashed. Then very quietly and with dignity the silver maple behind the barn toppled over into Mrs. Rose's yard. Shingles were flying from Mr. Higgins' house like a pack of cards. The new octagonal shingles were flapping in the wind.

One part of the ridgepole of our house was loose and made a drumming noise like thunder over the orange room. Joe got up and nailed it fast. There is an exhilaration which is a well-known psychological effect of a hurricane. Joe and Ellen rushed through the storm with delight and used this ecstasy climbing all over the roof to see if everything was tight.

From Miss Freeman's porch I watched four boats go adrift. Margaret Seaver's boat sank at the mooring and Charlie Mayo's and Joe Oliver's boats were adrift.

II

When evening came the lights were off and telephone wires were down. We were isolated from the world. We lighted candles, but the wind blowing through the sides of

[330]

the house blew out the candles, and we had to hang heavy blankets over the doors to keep them alight, and even then they blew horizontal.

Word went out that afternoon that the sea had covered Provincetown and that the Cape was swamped; but we were just outside the course of the hurricane's fury. Moreover, our tides are different from the tides toward Buzzard's Bay and New Bedford and Providence, where the gale hit at high tide and hurled boats far inland. The water rose so fast in Providence that people drowned in taxicabs near the station. No wonder they thought we were done for. Whole seaside communities like Horse's Neck near New Bedford were wiped out so completely that there was no sign anywhere even of wreckage of the fine houses.

It was the Provincetowners away from home who suffered most. One woman was on her way back on a bus from New Bedford just about to go over the bridge near Fairhaven, when a wave lifted a three-masted schooner onto the bridge, and the bus, which had only entered the bridge, backed gingerly off. So she went to the New Bedford Hotel to spend the night. Just as she got in, she heard the loudspeaker announce that the Cape didn't exist, that it had been swept away, that nothing had been heard from it for hours.

One Provincetown man who was in Worcester, waiting for a plane to Springfield, learned that there was a hurricane sweeping through and started for home. Plate-glass windows exploded almost in his face as he went through towns. Trees fell a second after he passed. Someone showed him a little-traveled and safer road, and through all his journey he had believed that Provincetown was perhaps gone. When he at last saw Provincetown, he wept.

Connection to the Cape was finally made by England's wirelessing the big station on the Truro coast. Word came back to America via England that the Cape was still there. The first contact with the outside world was made by a radio ham, Ted Chase, lighthousekeeper of Long Point. Another radio ham who did great service was W. Everett Briggs of Brockton, who cleared messages for the State Police over his short-wave set. Those of us who lived here got hundreds of anxious telegrams from our friends and relatives.

III

Norman and Anna Matson drove down to Watch Hill, where Anna's mother has a cottage. Very little had happened to their house but two rows of cottages that had cut them off from the sea did not exist any more. There was no sign or trace of where these houses had stood a few days before, and the Walling house was swathed in blankets, draperies, curtains—even towels, sofa cushions, and pillows blown from houses in front of it. There stood their house undamaged but muffled up like a strange old lady.

The piled-up waters hurled great vessels inland and left them among trees or dropped them in a meadow a long distance from the shore.

I went to Providence to meet a friend about ten days after the storm. People had begun immediately clearing away the rubbish and cutting away the uprooted trees, but the roadside was littered with trees not yet hauled away. Along the water front, buildings and pavilions slumped together like enormous trash heaps. In one field, far from any house, rested a red-lacquered breakfast set. There the table stood with four chairs around it. A wave had lifted them and carefully and with precision arranged them.

The trip from New York to Providence usually takes about four hours. This had taken seven and one half. After ten days, communication had not yet been established. In Providence there was still no electric light. Our civilization built on radio and wires had proved a frail and transitory thing.

We went into a café near the station. The marks of the water were almost to the ceiling. The waiter told us that when the guests escaped up a stairway he swam back to get a couple of bottles of whisky to warm up the drenched people.

The water had risen to the railway station far above the plaza below, where a torrent had roared through the under-cut. One friend of mine was marooned in the Providence station for a day, keeping her feet dry by putting them on her luggage as the water crawled across the floor.

IV

The hurricane was mixed up in a strange way with all the things that were happening in Europe. Over the radio had first come the details of the storm's incredible havoc, then had come the news that Chamberlain had flown to Germany.

We lived by the radio in those times. At one moment we would hear the mounting death toll from New England. The details of the destruction came slowly. There was the dramatic moment when we sat waiting for war. Two commentators with elegant English accents explained what was going on in the House of Commons. Then Chamberlain's voice warned how close war was, followed by the message from Hitler.

Chamberlain's voice, "Peace in our time, gentlemen," rang out triumphantly. Immediately after came the increasing flood of disaster, of the hurricane.

There was the account of the meeting of the Four Powers, Czechoslovakia absent. And all of us who had any historic knowledge knew that was the end of Czechoslovakia. For what did Hitler care about the Sudetenland? In the voluminous protest made by Germany against the Versailles Treaty never once was the Sudetenland mentioned.

There was the day we listened to Hitler's speech. His guttural German came over clearly. This was the speech in which he said he had no more territorial aspirations. The two disasters—certain war and the great, irrational disaster of the hurricane—made a strange checkerboard of our days.

Who were there except such people as Chamberlain and Daladier who could imagine that with the national defenses of Czechoslovakia in his hands, Hitler would stop there and would not go on and take the rest of Czechoslovakia. Who could imagine that he would care more for Karlsbad than for the Skoda works?

V

The hurricane left a fire hazard behind that had an explosive quality similar to that which wiped out such vast parts of the Oregon forests in two hours and a half a few years before. Such a fire in New England would mean the wiping out of towns and villages. The hurricane area contained millions of people, and these people were caught in the deadliest firetrap that ever threatened a crowded community—a menace far beyond that of the hurricane itself.

A fast-moving and appalling conflagration was only too possible, sweeping over miles of country at breakneck speed, incapable of being stopped by any human power. The wood roads and lanes were choked and blocked by the tangled debris of the hurricane. The day after the hurricane it took two hours for a man to penetrate a mile inside the Harvard Forest and most of the time he was ten or fifteen feet above the ground, climbing over the fallen timber. The beautiful forest had been reduced to kindling. Some twenty-five thousand farmers had had their timber blown down, which often represented the accumulation of a lifetime. Only swift government action could save them from bankruptcy.

The Federal and state officials didn't realize that the real crisis was not the hurricane itself, but the threat of an unparalleled fire disaster. It was due to swift, persistent action by Ward Shepard, then Director of the Harvard Forest Service of Harvard University, that the people of New England at last woke up to the danger.

As a result, Governor Hurley sent to President Roosevelt a plan to stop the fire danger. This plan's first job was saving people from destruction. Timber must be taken out of the woods by the next May. The government when necessary should buy the logs or lumber and feed it to the market over a period of years to prevent disrupting the entire lumber industry of the nation.

The Federal government acted at once. F. A. Silcox, chief of the United States Forest Service, was appointed by the President as co-ordinator for the whole forest-protection problem for New England. He skimmed the cream of the forest service—hard-hitting, hard-boiled men drawn from the national forests—from Oregon, Washington, California, the Rocky Mountains, the Great Lakes, and the Appalachians.

Thousands of W.P.A. workers were set to work removing fire debris near farms, villages, and cities. Patrolmen by the hundreds were put on the roads to warn people against the danger of setting fires by throwing away burning cigarettes or making bonfires. Hundreds of C.C.C. boys were immediately moved into the area for fire fighting, for opening roads, and for re-establishing and strengthening the whole fire-protection system of lookout towers, telephone lines, and debris firework.

The complete story of this great Paul Bunyan job has yet to be told.

CHAPTER FORTY-TWO

A Provincetown Winter

I

THE hurricane blew in a cold winter. Ever since Munich there was the feeling of uncertainty which the shadow of war brings. Even people who were not politically minded knew that the taking of the Sudetenland did not mean "peace in our time." People turned their radios to news more than ever.

On the other hand, people tried to shut out what was happening. Whenever war is near, life assumes a desperate gaiety. Jazz ushered in the World War, and dancing madness swept the country from 1912 on.

In the years before the present war, the jitterbugs danced frantically. Boogie-woogie became a cult. Popular band leaders were mobbed.

That winter I stayed in Provincetown with Nea Colton for company. I felt snug within my house. During the summer the road which people had made through my yard was closed. That road was the story of a weak-minded woman who liked to stay at peace with her neighbors. It was my own particular Munich—my own private appeasement. The weakness of a woman who can see two sides to a question. Wilbur Steele said to me once, "Margaret wouldn't have seen two sides to that road. She'd have known she was right and the only one who was right and she'd have closed it up tight."

And so would anyone with character. There had been

a lane leading to the barn and we had kept it closed and used it for ourselves coming in from the back street. The first time the gates were taken down was when I was in Europe as Overseas Woman in the Red Cross. I put up new gates which disappeared in the night. So little by little people began going through my yard, until there was a stream of cars and trucks.

Every car that went through told me I was a woman with a soft mind. Now the place had been put through the Land Court, agreements with neighbors had been made, and there was again a fence with a stout gate at the back. The fence had been made three times—by Bert, by Joe O'Brien, and by young Joe in turn. Now I had a fence that would last me.

There were double windows downstairs. The house was "chinked up" and we were cozy and protected in that especial way one is in the country, where you watch every hour of the day and part of life is the endless changes of the weather of the Bay.

My daughter Mary Ellen and her husband Jack Beauchamp and the baby were in and out. They had bought a house at the other end of town. There was a fine sort of feeling to see one's children having their own homes and being part of Provincetown. That winter I was especially conscious of the town and how long I had been here. Boys who had played in the yard as babies were now coming to dinner with their wives. I was conscious, too, how little part I had taken in the activities of the town. It was my fault, I realized, that I still had only the status of a summer person. At first there had been so little time, and now that there was more time it was too late.

Our home was full of young people, and part of the winter a refugee sheltered with us who was writing a learned book on Leonardo da Vinci but who could hardly empty a scuttle of ashes, so handless was the poor creature. Being asked to put the kettle on threw him in a panic. But it seemed natural to have extra people around.

Once the summer people are gone the town takes up its own life again. People see more of each other. Out-of-town guests, both the paying and the nonpaying kind, take all a body's time in the weeks of summer.

Among the various clubs and church societies and the high-school children there are continual parties and suppers and get-togethers. The Beachcombers have their weekly supper. That winter the Community Center, under Charles Hapgood's able guidance, was coming into full bloom.

At the Center, near us, at three o'clock a crowd of children from grown boys to little bits of girls were waiting in front of the door of what had been the Eastern School House. The older boys were the strong, fierce-looking boys of a seaport town, who formerly would have gone to work young. Now there was no work for them, nothing to do but hang around poolrooms and get into mischief on the water front.

Now there was always something going on for them at the Center or at Town Hall. The town was filled to the brim with activity.

II

Yet underneath the affairs of the town and the warm, neighborly life in our house, coming into it over the radio every day, was the news from Europe—an ominous background which made the pleasant life we had more significant because it was so fragile.

Certain events stand out, like the town meeting which was hastily called to discuss a burning question: should women wear shorts on the streets of Provincetown? The conservative element led by the Catholic Daughters of America had become scandalized by the scanty garments worn on the public streets by men as well as women, and

[338]

an article had been put through at an earlier town meeting barring shorts and similar indecencies on Provincetown streets.

This resolution resounded throughout the country. Papers in distant parts editorialized to the effect: "Provincetown isn't going to allow shorts! Ha, ha, no shorts in Provincetown of all places! We all know that that town is a den of darkness and sin and yet they won't have shorts!"

Editors in New Mexico talked about King Canute and his bout with the sea and mentioned that the rising tide of shorts could not be quelled by any one village. Other editorials took a sterner view. In a way it was natural, they commented, that the old home of the Pilgrims and the cradle of the Blue Laws should pass sumptuary laws which had always been impossible to enforce.

The last straw was when the Hawaiian papers noted the fact that on the strands of Provincetown shorts were to be banned. Hawaii was shocked by prudish Provincetown. Provincetown hadn't been in the papers so often since President Theodore Roosevelt laid the cornerstone of the Pilgrim Monument.

It was a snowy night but the Town Hall was filled as never before. On the one hand were the matrons who stood for dignity and decency. On the other side were the businessmen of town and those who had come as a matter of principle, muttering things like, "My sister wears shorts and there ain't any quieter girl in town. This resolution is as good as saying her character ain't what it oughta be."

In an atmosphere of tenseness the resolution was read. Dr. Blank arose to his feet. What he said amounted to this: This was a port where sailors came. Sailors of the United States were brought into bad ways and bad thoughts by the dreadful spectacles presented before their eyes. These clean young men came ashore and what did they see? He told what they saw. It was evident that he spoke

[339]

from a full heart and that he had spent a long time organizing his material.

Dr. Hiebert defended the navy. As for venereal disease, he protested, statistics showed that the navy had less disease than the average of the country.

But here the Health Officer, Mr. Flores, jumped to his feet.

"What I want to know is," he said, "are we here to talk about venereal diseases or are we here to talk about women wearing shorts?"

The simple honest view prevailed: first, that men had never yet stopped a fashion by making laws; second, that it would be bad for business. The question was not voted from the floor but by personal ballot.

Shorts won.

III

The high point of the winter was the Fishermen's Ball. The Fishermen's Association had been formed the year before to oppose a law which had been slipped into the legislature by the Atlantic Coast Fisheries. This prevented dragging in the shallow waters of Massachusetts Bay. The big draggers go far out to sea, as far as George's Banks, but the small draggers which make up many of the Provincetown fishermen drag in shallow waters.

Meantime the weirmen and the small-dory fishermen supported the proposed law, which contended that dragging in shallow water disturbed the bottom where the fishes spawned and where the fry fed.

The inshore draggers contended that as long as the big beam trawlers were permitted to operate, why should the small men be put out of business and hundreds of fishermen lose their means of livelihood. The Fishermen's Association acted just in time to keep their right to use the waters.

[340]

The ball in the winter of '39 was on a blizzard night, but that kept no one home. Here was real Provincetown. There were not more than a dozen summer people. You couldn't buy a ticket to the Fishermen's Ball. It was strictly by invitation, and invitations were much sought after. It was a fine, gay party with one of the best bands from Boston and with interesting fish-net decorations.

Here you could again see the face of the town. It was a reassuring face. After all, Provincetown still was a fishing town, still earned its living from the sea, and the spectacular summer crowds were no more important than a few strings of confetti. These were the people who had made Provincetown and who kept its heart beating.

IV

In March, 1939, Hitler marched on Czechoslovakia, as every thoughtful person knew he would. In Provincetown, no one missed a news broadcast. The British and the French had knocked out the keystone to the defenses which could put a limit to Hitler's plans of conquest. He seized Memel. At Easter, Mussolini marched into Albania. Then the situation in Danzig became acute.

It was impossible to stay home, and I sailed for Europe to do a series of articles on the crisis countries. I made a special study of German penetration of the Balkans. They were ripe fruit, ready to fall into Hitler's hands. I was checking my figures in Geneva when the announcement came of the Russo-German pact.

Before war actually comes, no one really believes in it, except those who plan it. Like death, war always comes as a surprise. The German people didn't believe in war. They believed their *Führer* would go on with his bloodless victories. Maybe he also believed that he could dominate all Europe without fighting, as he dominated it economically.

After war was declared, there was a long time of inaction in France. The railways were congested with troops. The censorship was in chaos. I was in a fever of anxiety to be home to write about Fascism which now clearly menaced this hemisphere. Once home I had again the nightmare feeling which I had had in 1915 of not being able to communicate with those around me. It was like calling fire in a burning house without making people hear.

Everyone was talking hemisphere isolation. The Neutrality Act was in force. "Let's Keep Out of It" was the slogan. Syndicates and magazines didn't want articles on Germany's plans. They had correspondents who might be asked to leave if something unfavorable to Germany were published. No one would believe that Hitler already had Mussolini in his pocket. It took a louder and more important voice than mine to get a hearing.

We, in Provincetown, slumbered like the rest of America through the fall of '39 and the winter of 1940, until the invasion of the Low Countries. The fall of France and Dunkirk aroused us from our lethargy, but did not give us, or America, a living awareness of danger.

CHAPTER FORTY-THREE

Fish on Shore

I

WAR was on the way, even though we closed our eyes to it. The defense program swung into action slowly at first, with many mistakes and delay. The sensitive barometer that is Provincetown showed war was near. In wartime the price of fish goes up, the distribution widens.

Fish are important. America's meat was going to Europe. Fish will more and more replace meat. Already, in 1940, the demand for fish was greater each month and the price of fish rose with its demand. Our fishing fleet was therefore becoming essential to this country; how important is shown by the fact that the considerable number of the big beam trawlers which were commandeered by the government were most of them returned by the summer of 1941. In the last war our fish were considered important enough by Germany for her to send over submarines to destroy the Nova Scotia fishing fleet.

Refrigeration, bringing fresh fish to market iced, began as long ago as 1858. This developed the great fresh fishermen and the cold storages. Then came the quick-freezing process and the filleting and packaging of fish.

Filleted and packaged fish, because they are easier to keep fresh, easier to ship, are going to develop further markets. Since 1936 more packaged and quick-frozen fish have left Boston markets than any other fresh fish. Large filleting plants ashore are a new source of employment, and throughout the Middle West and even to Oklahoma the fish sandwich and a plate of fish and chips elbow the hot dog at the roadside stand. The quick-freezing process has been in use in the New England fishing towns for fifty years. The idea of frosted vegetables and meats came from the frozen fish.

II

How the fish market has widened can be realized by watching a huge trailer truck, its roof even with those of the story-and-a-half Cape Cod houses it passes, roll slowly down Provincetown's narrow Commercial Street and back up to the platform of the Consolidated Cold Storage Plant. Men as warmly dressed as Eskimos bring box after box of frozen fish fillets from the interior of the sixty-foot concrete icebox and load them on the truck. A fog like mist envelops the boxes as they cross the low, short platform, for their temperature is −6° F. In all, ten tons of whiting go inside the truck. Then it pulls out. Destination—Oklahoma City.

Though the load might gain 30° F. during its sixty-hour journey, it would arrive at the end of its 1800-mile trip still well below freezing point.

The best, freshest-caught fish come from Cape Cod—Hyannis, Chatham, and Provincetown. Provincetown is close to a fine fishing ground. A fish that was swimming Thursday afternoon can be served for breakfast in New York on Friday morning. New York's own fishing fleet can't get fish to the market quicker. A fish trapped in a weir in Provincetown at six in the morning may be on the Boston market by noon. Speed is necessary. The haul must be fresh when it gets to market. Only enough ice is loaded into box or barrel to keep the fish at low temperature until reaching market. The loss of an hour might mean the loss of the fish. If a truck is late, every gas station will be combed for it. If a truck breaks down, the driver must immediately transfer his load to another truck, even though it would only take half an hour more to repair the truck than to change over the load of fish. Fish must keep rolling.

In swift vans, on whose sides are painted a map of Cape Cod and the company's name, the fillets start their journey. Fish will stay in prime condition for a week or more, but must hurry to its destination. "You can't hang a wild haddock like you hang a wild goose."

III

The first trap boats come in at half-past eight. Then the shipping sheds are abuzz to get the fish out. Mackerel and butterfish are packed in barrels and ice is shoveled in on top. Enough water goes in each barrel to cover the fish. Water keeps the barrel at an even 32° temperature through the trip and also acts as a shock absorber. Fish trucks don't slow down for bumps, and the semifloating state keeps the fish from bruising.

Fish run in schools with occasional strays of other fish. There are strange lots which come in. Sometimes enough of the big skate are caught to cut off and ship their wide fins, which reappear in French restaurants as *raie au beurre noire*.

From the twelfth to the sixteenth of September, 1941, the shipping sheds had the look of a carpenter shop crossed with a slaughterhouse. There had been a record run of horse mackerel—that is, tuna. Nine hundred of these huge fighting fish, averaging seventy-five pounds apiece dressed, were caught in one day. The huge heads and fins are sawed off by hand, the spine and neck and tail chopped off with an ax. If a fish is too big for the four-foot boxes, the overlapping tail end is sawed off and the pieces tucked into what were the fish's innards. So for nearly a week the Provincetown crews on pier ends dressed and boxed hundreds of tuna; then the tuna vanished to the occasional one that appears among the mackerel, herring, and whiting.

By ten-thirty or eleven, the fish from the weirs are rolling down the Cape or are already in the freezers. The packing sheds are quiet until the draggers and dories start to come in around four o'clock. They bring in ground fish: cod, haddock, pollack, and various flatfish. Now and again there are a few redfish and hake, and rarely a sturgeon, but in the spring and the fall they catch whiting. The fish the draggers bring in have already been dressed and sorted for kind and size. The fish are iced almost from the moment they are caught. The boxes are lowered below deck. The hold of the dragger is always cool. When they get to the pier, nothing remains to be done but unload the boat, weigh the boxes—from 135 to 150 pounds to the box—shovel cracked ice into each box, and nail the lid. The box is stood on its end to show it is ready to go. The fish broker goes around with his stapling machine and clips the consignee's card onto the pine lid of the boxes, and then the loaded truck pulls out for New York.

The morning's catch is in and away. The crew of the shipping shed gather in a little room off to one side. They remove their heavy rubber boots and change to more comfortable clothes. The men relax until the first dragger shows up. They spin yarns; play practical jokes on one another. One stretches out on a wooden bench and has a snooze. On a shelf in one corner of the little room a radio is tuned to a station that gives market and weather reports twice a day. The men listen. "The dragger *Mary D.*—so much cod —so much haddock—so many redfish" and so on down the list for each boat unloading at Boston. Then come reports from other fishing towns. Portland, so much. New Bedford, so much. "Provincetown, for October 11th, 12th, and 13th: 1000 pounds cod, 2000 pollack, 12,000 whiting, 9000 dabs, 3000 bass."

"Who caught those?" one man asks. "Some come through here but not that many."

"Got 'em in traps up t' th' west'ard. Landed a lot of 'em in North T'uro," another answers.

The radio goes on: "500 pounds of butters, 15,000 mackerel."

Later the prices on the Boston market come in. The average price for all fish is quoted around six cents a pound. Here the men can remember the days nine years ago when it cost money to go fishing—when the price of fish was less than half what it is now and it sometimes cost more money than a catch was worth to bring it in. Being a fisherman was a luxury. Now the shipper foreman, a noted pessimist, smiles slightly.

He says: "With those prices, looks 's if the fishermen are goin' to make some money—if they catch the fish."

IV

Boston is the center of the fresh-fish industry. From its wharves over four hundred million pounds of fish are distributed every year. The price of fish at the pier in Boston decides the price of fish for the New England seaboard as surely as the price of steel throughout the United States is based on quotations from Pittsburgh.

The catching of fish is only a fraction of the fishing industry. The fishing industry has become big business. Besides fishing there are processing, canning, wholesale jobbing, retailing, and national distribution. The small draggers and dorymen that I can see at anchor from my window are little cogs in an industry controlled by mass capital which reaches into Wall Street.

Fishing is a rich industry. It has advantages above all others. You do not have to plant the fish or feed them. The ocean has never been parceled off, and the least fisherman can go out fishing where he chooses. If the risk is bigger than in most industries, insurance cuts the risks, though insurance is too high for the little fellow.

For a long time the big firms or corporations have owned all of the fishing industry except getting fish from the sea. During the last twenty years the corporations have also gone into the fishing business. I have already shown that they own the weir boats, weirs, and cold storages. Today they operate the beam trawlers as well.

When during the last World War fishing became an important part of national economy, the government made a thorough investigation of the industry.

Their conclusions about the business of the Fish Exchange on the Boston Fish Pier were that:

Unconscionable profits have been made by the relatively small group of men who have been able to control the conduct of the business of the Exchange.

With the fishing grounds nearest to our shores, with the largest fishing fleet on the Atlantic Coast, and with the most modern and complete facilities for the receipt and distribution of fish at the Fish Pier, the cost of fish to the retailer should be less than in any other state, but the statistics show that fish are delivered to the retailers at less cost in tweny-two states in different sections of the country where the expense of handling and transportation is presumably greater. The obvious conclusion is that charges of excessive profits from the producers to the retailer are sustained.

Of these excessive profits "from the producer to the retailer," the committee found that the largest share

. . . went into the pockets of the large wholesale dealers who operated on the Exchange, and more particularly those who owned and operated steam trawlers and made a double profit.

Another fact brought to light was that the wholesalers by stock ownership had control not only of the Fish Pier but of the Fish Exchange and

. . . were practicing certain abuses in the conduct of these facilities, largely at the expense of the fisherman and partly at the expense of the general public. They practiced collusive buying, restricted the market and forced big lot sales, which together with a number of specific charges all reduced the fishermen's small profit.

Translated from report jargon this means that in Massachusetts, the core of the Atlantic fisheries, the cost price to the retailers is higher than in any other state in the Union except the strange companions of Nebraska, Colorado, Maine, and New Jersey, the two last also fishing states. The nearer to the sea you are, the more you pay for fish!

Boston housewives have paid fifteen cents a pound for cod when the same cod in Toronto cost eleven cents, after paying a duty of a cent a pound.

The big fellows who control the price of fish have it fixed so, if they lose on the catch of a vessel, they can make up in wholesaling and processing. A corporation which owns fishing vessels can sell to itself at low prices; so if the crew is working on shares, the fisherman will get a smaller portion. The corporation can then turn around and charge the retailer.

V

A generation ago during the First World War, when the government made an investigation of the fishing industry, the marketing and distribution of fish were controlled by a number of big men. Today it is controlled by a smaller number of corporations. This is why the N.R.A., when it made a study of the fishing industry, couldn't get full figures and found this business cloaked with New England reticence.

They discovered, however, that this rich New England industry pays its fishermen less than those of any part of the United States, including the red-snapper Negro fishermen in the South, otherwise the lowest paid of all fishermen. The larger the vessel, the less will be the fisherman's share. It's the big beam trawlers who pay their men least.

Fishermen on the Atlantic coast have largely fished on shares. In a small fishing boat employing from two to four men the fisherman gets his fair share. The fisherman's share diminishes almost to a vanishing point when he is employed by a corporation, though he is still under the illusion that he is in partnership as he would be dory fishing.

Here is the operating statement of the steamer *Foam* on a 17-day beam-trawling trip, dated April 29, 1934: The deductions made from the crew's share are first the salaries, such as those of mate, fireman, engineers, and expenses such as those of the radio and the fathometer. Left for the crew's share, $1248.46. After that the crew's expenses were deducted, fuel, oil, ice, provisions, and so forth. At the end of the seventeen-day trip the crew's individual shares were $22.73.

The fishing industry, vessel competing against vessel, with the tradition of the race for market only a short span of years away, makes the fishermen highly competitive and individualistic. But there is today a current of unrest among Atlantic-coast fishermen. The old men may have a fatalistic idea that they can't do a thing about the setting of fish prices on the Boston Fish Pier and that they have to sell their fish through a broker.

The young men are talking among themselves about co-operation. What's the matter with the fishing industry? They ask: why do we get so little for our fish? Why do fish cost so much? Though the grumbling is less at the moment because of the high price of fish, it will go on.

CHAPTER FORTY-FOUR

The Beach,
Garbage and Cesspools

I

IN THESE war-shadowed years, the cleaning of the beach offered a comic relief. When the first settlers came to Provincetown a folkway was established for the disposal of garbage and slops. They were thrown on the beach.

We strayed far from our founding fathers in other ways, but Provincetown showed its reverence for them by following faithfully in their footsteps when it came to swill and slops.

Until recently if a man had an old mattress he wanted to get rid of he dragged it down to the brimming tide and expected the sea to do its duty. Sometimes he set fire to it first so it smelled a little.

This year, 1941, due to the efforts of Irving Rogers, the Public Health Officer, the silver sands are at last emerging from among the trash. The *Provincetown Advocate* vividly pictures the Augean task confronting him:

Already stretches of the shore which surpassed the backyards of slum districts in slovenliness are beginning to betray the fact that there was white seashore sand under the old logs, sticks, tin cans, broken toilet bowls, discarded rubber tires, ends of rope, odd shoes, rubber boots, dead fish, bottles whole and bottles broken, rubber hose, worn out girdles, old brooms, rusted oil drums, wrecks of chairs—in fact just about anything and everything that this so-called civilization could devise to discard.

It was found, however, that much of the refuse along the shore was either too heavy or too firmly embedded in the sand to be moved by the beach-cleanup squad. But the limited budget of the department did not permit the hiring of horses to drag the heavier objects to places where they could be hauled away.

Gathering trash was not enough. Some of the boilers, engine parts, and water-logged spiling were so deeply embedded that it took a crew of men with a truck to extract them from their place. A private Beach Clean-up Fund was raised, sponsored by Town Auditor Benjamin Chapman. The Silva Trucking Company co-operated, giving especially low rates. When the accounting was taken the sea had given up her dead to the extent of 113 loads of unnamable junk and much water-logged spiling.

Ever since I have been here, nearly thirty-five years, people have grumbled about the state of the beach.

Our own beach was especially rich. From various stores floated entrails and rotten cabbages, melons and other decayed vegetables. It was a poor day when there was not some large bone being worried by dogs, while a bit of offal and fat flip-flopped with the tide. The cold storage to the eastward threw its surplus fish overboard and there was often a bright fringe of dead fish along the water front or floating peacefully in the sea.

In the early days three old men used to patrol up and down and bury the dead fish. There were days when all one would need to do to have a nourishing fish chowder would be to scoop up a bucket of water and boil it.

The beach has much improved since the cleanup. Still there is work to be done. Although from our beach were taken loads of ironwork, bedsprings, and other objects enough to furnish the contents of a town dump, there remain on the risin' the rusted contents of what looks like a ship chandler's shop. There are rocks enough from the jetty to stock the rock gardens of Provincetown.

The other day a halibut head flopped back and forth in

the water as large as the trunk of a murdered woman. This obscene object idled down the tide toward the Malicoats'.

II

Not that things have not improved since I first came here. In those days there were many more wharves than at present and on many a wharf a pig was kept. Along the water front a fine rich odor assailed your nostrils and you would hear a rich grunting above your head.

One time Chocolate Silva, a neighbor's boy, got hold of his father's caulking tools, caulked up the pigpen tight, and then ran the hose in it until the pig was adrift, splashing in the pen and screaming horribly. Chocolate caught it good for that—most as good as the time when he took a can of green copper paint from Mr. Avellar and painted his father's gasoline engine with it. He was a fine, inventive boy.

Pigs have long since vanished from the water front and from around town generally, though of course their disappearance has made the garbage situation much more tense.

Formerly, a little boy with a bucket appeared every evening and remarked simply, "Swill!"

He said that to a guest of mine, a gentleman of quite elegant pretensions, who replied indignantly, "Swill yourself!"

Now there is no such easy solution to the daily recurring garbage question. Just as one can say there are no snakes in Ireland you can say there is no garbage disposal in Provincetown. You can get your garbage taken away for from two to three dollars a month. There is no more lordly creature than the garbage man. He comes or he doesn't come and when he doesn't come for a while you can get him only by groveling.

Garbage must remain strictly edible. City dwellers who class trash and garbage as one find their garbage pails overflowing.

The collector remarks simply, when he has found the garbage not up to the standard craved by his animals, "Do you think my pigs eat butts an' paper?"

There are long, arid periods when you bury the garbage in the yard, but if that is done too often, though it may enrich the soil, it also draws fierce wharf rats who can be seen in the moonlight, big as skunks, sporting above the odoriferous burying ground.

Though it is forbidden, many a person still slinks down, under cover of darkness, to the beach with his garbage pail and buries the garbage on the beach as his ancestors did before him. Others, with a large seagoing gesture, dump the garbage on the ocean's face. Next morning there will again be a fringe of squeezed oranges, lemon rinds, and wilted cabbage leaves on the beach.

There was a terrible summer when two different garbage cultures met in our house. My sister belonged to the garbage-burning school. She tried to teach a Provincetown girl how to burn the garbage. Mary belonged to the burying school and though she admired and loved my sister, this unnatural way of getting rid of refuse by fire went against her nature. So she struck a compromise by wrapping it up in paper bags and secreting it in all the many little hideaways in the house as a squirrel hides nuts. For weeks after she left I was always coming on it.

Thus ever do the weak defeat the strong.

III

Here in Provincetown sewers and cesspools you can see the slow-grinding process of one civilization superceding another. This never happens painlessly like a duck swimming. Old customs go reluctantly. The old people see themselves passing with the old ways. It's not in Provincetown alone by any means that one encounters this situation. The richest man in Marfa, Texas, opposed this rich little town's appropriating money for flush toilets in the schools.

"Privies," said the stalwart descendant of Jesse James, "was good enough for my grandad, an' they're good enough for my grandson!"

There is always a dislocation in a vital change of folkways. The day of the great liberation for women came when water was laid on in the kitchen and people no longer had to go to pumps or bring water from distant wells. This great change had already been accomplished in Provincetown when we came. But Provincetown was still in the privy and cold-water-faucet era. Since then, it has slowly been making the painful change to the plumbing era. When Provincetown sewers first led to the beaches, only sink water entered the Bay.

During the war when the price of fish was high you would seldom go down the street without seeing a jigger with bathroom fixtures on it. The secret desire of each woman's heart was a bathroom. Bathrooms were put in all over town before the idea of a sewer system had entered into the public consciousness. Many people on the Bay side had their sink water go into the Bay, those on the back streets had cesspools, and there are many who follow the time-hallowed ways, disease or no disease.

Wild memories cluster around the cesspool. I remember going for Mr. Engels, a man of worth and of a salty flavor. Like all plumbers in Provincetown he was hard to catch. It is, and always has been, next to impossible to catch a Provincetown plumber. Mr. Engels was more elusive than most. I have seen him on his bicycle, rushing away from me crying,

"Keep away from me, widder, I'm a married man!" when I was trying to lure him to my house to plumb.

I went to his shop to see why Hot Times had not come to clean the cesspool.

"You won't get him," said Mr. Engels. "He's gone on

a 'time.' Tell you how I know. He come in here. Sez, 'Got a file?'

" 'What you want with a file?'

"Sez, 'My back teeth's too high. Want to file 'em down.'

"Seen right off he's stewed. Always files down his back teeth, Hot Times, when he's stewed."

Mr. Engels bent down. A button fell off.

"More work for your wife," I observed.

"Wife, shucks!" he returned. "Ain't a woman on earth fit to trust with a button. Charley," he called, "where's them tweezers?" Swiftly Mr. Engels got a slender piece of copper wire, deftly passed it through his overall button. "There," he said, "that's the way to sew on a button. Give me a copper wire and tweezers when it comes to buttons. Women, pah! So you see you'll have to wait to get your cesspool done till Hot Times gets finished filin' his back teeth down."

Cesspools have had to wait in Provincetown. Then deep in the night the "honey wagon" would draw up. Lights would wave and the night echoed Three-Finger Baker cursing everything that could be found in cesspools.

Now the old honey wagon is no more. It has gone the way of Hendy's skunk farm. Mr. Silva comes along now with a fine wagon that works on a suction principle. He does not have to come in the dark of the night when the fewest number of people will have to smell the cesspool being cleaned. His new sanitary cleaner can be used at any time of day.

IV

All plumbing in Provincetown breaks. Pipes in Provincetown become rusted and rotted out because of the iron and salt in the water, so of all workmen, plumbers of Provincetown are the most sought after. They are also invariably men of character and of interesting personalities. They have the air of those who are standing on top of the world.

Washers drip, ball cocks won't work, cesspools fill, pipes become so stopped with rust that only a needle could go through them, as the faint trickle from the faucet proclaims. So the plumbers are never idle.

Indeed, when you go to the plumber your position is that of a commoner petitioning royalty. If approached with appeals to his better nature, he arrives at last, applauded by his cringing minions. He works. surrounded by an aura of gratitude.

All the trouble with the cesspools, all the trouble with the sewers in the Bay, could have been put an end to within the last few years. The P.W.A. would have made a sewage system one of its projects if Provincetown would raise the sum of $2500 for a survey and blueprint and pay twenty-five per cent of the cost, but the town fathers, balanced precariously between two cultures—the culture of the back-house and Bay sewer, and the culture of the plumbing era—dexterously side-stepped the costly and embarrassing affair.

Trash on the beach, the absence of garbage disposal, the town dump, home of a thousand rats—"You can see the rats from the dump, walking down Bradford as far as Vine Street," says Blaney—all make a magnificent monument to our public spirit, to our local government, and to our town fathers.

CHAPTER FORTY-FIVE

Summer Folks

I

PROVINCETOWN in summer, during the season, and life during the rest of the year are so different as to be fantastic. The tourists who come bringing with them their transient way of living often see only each other and do not even get a glimpse of Provincetown.

Provincetown has this difference from most resorts. The majority have been built for pleasure, catering to people whose business is in the city or to a holiday crowd. Provincetown has become a resort through what it has to offer and, underneath the summer rumpus, keeps its character, conditioned by the hard work of the sea which made it and still sustains it. It needs to, for from the Fourth of July to Labor Day, Provincetown is swamped, run over, by tourists and vacationers. Crowds pour into town like herring up herring creek. Our little streets are choked with their cars. Daily the boat spouts its hundreds upon us.

There are so many people, so many cars, so many stores and restaurants and night clubs which cater to tourists, that people passing through think of Provincetown only as a resort. Some days the churning froth of summer people for a time obliterates the outlines of the town. You can't see the town for the crowds which surge up and down the street. The tooting of their horns drowns out the normal noises of the town—the solemn warning of the fog bell, the sounds of the vessels going out to sea.

The fishermen loafing around the bank and the New York

store, or on the wharves after their work, seem only a bit of local color. The rest of the Provincetown people actually disappear within the crowds and become as if invisible. To add to the unreality, a phony town crier in a Pilgrim costume clangs his bell perpetually up and down the street.

Around dinnertime there is a crowd in each restaurant, eating like locusts; clamshells fly like dead leaves in a wind, chowders pour down gullets, tables are littered with the carapace of the lobster. Countless steaks and fish are going down voracious maws. The very pies get sold out.

There are times that the summer froth becomes so dense it seems like some monstrous growth climbing up over the little white houses, and one wishes that an equally monstrous hose could be taken to it, making the place clean again.

Something like this automatically happens directly after Labor Day, for though September is the most beautiful month of the year, the crowds then depart, urged as though by a common impulse like the migrating lemming, though, unfortunately, not throwing themselves into the sea as does that small rodent.

II

A few years ago there was a convention in Washington of the Country Women of the World. This is an international organization. To it came thousands of farmers' wives of America. One of their most interesting discussions was "What Are We Going to Do About Our Summer People?" For with the coming of cars, this is a universal problem.

They discussed the tourist, who leaves the obscene remains of his lunch upon the beach, who picnics in peoples' front yards, breaks off branches of apple and pear trees, lights forest fires with his careless camping; who drives up in a station wagon or a small truck, backs it up to a sand flat, and fills it with clams.

The trail of the tourist since cars became general has

defiled the countryside with cans and debris and garbage from the mountaintops to the desert and from sea to sea. Such people can be dealt with by education and public opinion. They are not our most serious problem. Nor are the overnight tourists who come often after dark and leave in the early morning, who fill the overnight camps and the rooming houses.

A more serious one, since they give a false impression of the town, are the visitors who hire small shacks, a converted fishhouse or barn or studio, so called because a north light has been put into a garage or a former henhouse, who come for anything from a week to a month for a good Bohemian time. Many are onhangers of the arts, who believe that the only firm foundation of painting is plenty of alcohol.

Among these are children of desperation who come here without a nickel, hoping to get jobs, others cadging their way through a summer. They are no unique phenomenon seen only in Provincetown. The same sort surge down to Miami and land in Key West. California has them and so does any place that has a little theater or an art colony. The loafers and cadgers are only the chaff around the many serious students, writers, and actors, at whom so many tourists come to goggle.

This minority has given Provincetown the reputation of having more "quaint" characters than any other resort, as though the town were a strange-bird sanctuary, toward which the irregular moved as birds migrate. But this is not the case. The odd and the queer are conspicuous. Like the American tourist abroad in the old days, the extravagant few stand out. The majority who come to enjoy the sea or to work seriously are unnoticed.

III

The problem that the Country Women of the World discussed most seriously was not the young whoopee-maker or the predatory tourist. It was the migration of city people into the country. While there has been a steady tide of migration of young people to the city, there has also been a flow of the city people to the country. This migration grows each year. Barnstable County, which means Cape Cod, has had a greater increase in population than any other county in Massachusetts. Now all over America, anywhere within a radius of a couple of hundred miles of any city, the old houses are being bought up by city people.

There has always been a cleavage between the summer people and Provincetown people. Recently an old Provincetown friend of mine said to me, "We've gotten to think of you as one of us." But it had taken me thirty-five years to be so accepted.

Cape people have always looked down on those who were off Cape, just as in the islands of Nantucket and Martha's Vineyard off islanders are at a disadvantage. You may live in Provincetown summer and winter, send your children to school here, and even come from Cape people elsewhere, and you still remain "summer folk." There are many off Cape people who are not considered pariahs and of whom the town is even proud. They were proud of Hawthorne and Frederick Waugh and many of the other painters. There is this feeling of strangeness which at its best is a feeling of difference which has not been bridged.

Mr. William Young, formerly President of the First National Bank and one of the founders of the Art Association, tried, through the Art Association, to knit together the newcomers and the townspeople.

In the old days any suggestion made by summer folk was resented. I well remember the indignation of one old Provincetowner when a summer person who had lived here a matter of only twenty years insisted that there was such a thing as mosquito control, that the pest of mosquitoes, at that time like one of the plagues of Egypt, could be got rid of.

"I've been able to stand mosquitoes, and my father and

my grandfather and my great-grandfather could, and I guess you summer folks can stand 'em too," quoth the native sourly.

IV

The Cape, and Provincetown especially, has been fortunate in its type of summer resident. There have been few people with much money, almost none who are ostentatious, and almost without exception, they have been kind to the old houses which they have bought.

Each of these old houses and every garden added to Provincetown maintains its charm and adds to its wealth. The summer people have brought so much to the town that it is impossible to list all of their contributions.

Outstanding are the Hawthornes, both father and son, for Joe Hawthorne has for years had a series of beautiful concerts given Sunday nights in the Art Association for a nominal sum.

At the other end of the town, the Frederick Waughs, the Coulton Waughs, and the Clymers have woven themselves into the town's fabric with houses and gardens and have added to the town's reputation with their paintings. The generosity of Frederick Waugh helped build St. Mary's of the Harbor, which is one of the loveliest of little churches, and it was designed by Provincetown artists and decorated by them.

Paul Smith's Bookshop is a feature of Provincetown, and his never-failing hospitality has made his house a center for young people. Through him, the ping-pong tournaments were made possible during the winter months.

The Tennis Club is the work of summer people. The *Provincetown Advocate*, so ably edited by Mr. Paul Lambert, speaks with an authentic voice of Provincetown. Yet Mr. Lambert is comparatively a recent resident. Many of the most unique stores and some of the most charming hotels are run by people "from away." The fabric between the summer people, the off islanders, and the Provincetown people is too closely woven to be pulled apart without disturbing the whole design of the town.

The Provincetown theaters have long been built and run by people in the summer colony. After the Wharf Theater fell into the sea, Heinrich Pfeiffer, a well-known Provincetown artist, gave his moving-picture theater known as the Artists' Theater. For some years he had given superior films that could not be seen elsewhere. Now The New England Repertory Company, a theater which gives interesting plays and whose first thought is not box office, has made a great addition to the town.

One could go on indefinitely with the list of off-Cape people who have brought gifts to Provincetown. Yet when all due credit has been given, some of the blame for the cleavage between the townspeople and the newcomer can be placed at the door of the off-Cape people who formed a group apart from the town's affairs.

So many of the writers and painters were content in each other's company that they made little effort to form closer relationships with Provincetown people, except with their near neighbors. Few vote or attend town meeting, join the Board of Trade, or the Town Criers. Townspeople complain that the resident colony, while remaining aloof from town affairs, has been prolific in criticism, doing little to remedy the conditions which they criticize.

The people from the cities who come to bring their children up in the country, or to buy country houses for their old age, bring with them different manners and morals. They are further separated from the townspeople by the fact that they do not make their living through the town and so are independent of public opinion.

The problem we have in Provincetown is repeated throughout the country. How make a synthesis that will be a happy solution for all of us—newcomers and old residents.

V

In the old days Eastham settled Wellfleet and Truro, and Truro settled Provincetown. Now there has been a reverse process going on. Many of the writers and artists who first settled in Provincetown have moved out and gone to Truro and Wellfleet and there succeeded in making a better community adjustment.

In Wellfleet especially there is a heartier attitude toward off islanders. Instead of the summer people remaining outsiders, Wellfleet has taken in its new residents. There has been a happy amalgamation between the newcomers and the people of the town. The two cultures have become a mixture that is warm and fruitful and creative.

When you buy a house the friends give a surprise party to the new settler, bringing small household gifts. Speedily the newcomer is asked to be a member of the Board of Trade. The community takes in its new people with friendship.

In 1940, Wellfleet got up its first Fair. Here were assembled all its resources, both of its new people and of its inhabitants who had lived here from generation to generation. All the natural wealth of Wellfleet was spread out— books and pictures, scallop and oyster and clam, together with flowers and vegetables, proud roosters and able hens. Here were notable books of the writers of Wellfleet. There were pictures by local artists, and there was a fine exhibition of local arts and crafts. Here was a display of beautiful quilts, and there a clam-chowder competition.

There was something unusual in this little Fair, something very lovely and very good, people working together for a common purpose. Life becomes barren and it has no meaning when people don't work together and worship together, and here in the little Fair that community spirit had sprung up again. Though the Fair was the work of many people, Frank Shay's leadership and enthusiasm helped make it the memorable thing it was.

The scene has changed in Wellfleet through the coming together of the new people and the old. Lately Wellfleet invited a speaker, well known for his views to the extreme left. Almost everyone disagreed with him, but it was a truly democratic gesture of the right of free speech. It was also a statement of the community that in wartime democracy is menaced by spy hunters and witch hunters and it is important to recognize this menace and to support more than ever our civil liberties.

The two forces, the Wellfleet newcomers and the people who had lived there from early days, showed what their co-operation could do. They saved the fine old Town Hall, raised enough money to repair it, and now it is being used. Salvaging this fine building could not have been done without this co-operation.

We have lived through generations where people have lost their habit of doing things together. The old records of Provincetown, Wellfleet, and Truro tell of a common creative effort, a flow of life, where people worked and played and worshiped together.

Take pieces of stone and wood and iron, and by themselves they are nothing at all, but you can put them together so you can form a home. Just so a town which has lost its community spirit is only a collection of houses. When the people who work in the sea or farm the land or put up houses are living apart from the people who create in another fashion, everyone is robbed.

Most of the people who come to live on the lower Cape have come because they love this country. They have come, many of them, to make their homes permanent, summer and winter. With many of them there is an involvement with this piece of land that is peculiar and deep. The Cape is not just pleasant country for vacationing, but the place beyond all others where they wish to live.

People who come with such a feeling, and after a wider world experience than the people to whose town they move, have something to contribute to the community life.

CHAPTER FORTY-SIX

A World Ends

I

THERE was a sense of unreality in the things we were doing in the summer of 1941. We were getting ready for something in which we couldn't quite believe.

In the summer of 1940 the churches and the women's clubs were sewing for the British. We were doing works of mercy for stricken people far away. We reflected the country. People throughout the United States were against even the thought of war, as if they believed they could vote against a hurricane. Let Europe have its wars and let's keep out of them. But, of course, let's help the sufferers.

Provincetown reflected, too, the general disbelief that Hitler meant to dominate the world. The people in Provincetown, while they raised money for aid to Britain and made clothes for stricken England, felt safe.

The summer of 1941, incredible as it seemed, people were working to defend themselves from an actual enemy. First-aid and defense classes were being held. The sign, FIRE WARDEN, appeared on houses. Sirens rang for a practice air-raid alarm. It seemed ridiculous until one remembered seeing German cities and Russian cities rehearsing for air raids in 1933.

The Cape newspapers were full of items like "CLUBS TO TRAIN BIRDS FOR DEFENSE. The Barnstable Homing Pigeon Club has offered the Barnstable Civilian Defense

Committee the facilities of its lofts and will raise and train birds for use in defense."

There are headlines from Cape papers such as: CHEMICAL OFFICER GIVES TALK; BOY SCOUTS TO COLLECT IN BREWSTER, which goes on to say "The drive for old aluminum for national defense will be conducted in Brewster by the Boy Scout troop"; BLACK-OUT IN HYANNIS SUCCESS; PROVINCETOWN TO REHEARSE EVACUATION OF WOMEN AND CHILDREN BY SEA. Most people thought these unceasing activities were silly or had the unreality of nightmare.

The iron wall of naval vessels out in the harbor was no dream. History was being made again in Provincetown Harbor. From this harbor, we believed, streamed the patrol of submarines and destroyers which guarded the warship where the President met Churchill.

Some identified Massachusetts Bay with Churchill's description of the place of meeting, "a nearly land-locked bay in American waters." The submarines and destroyers, the battleships and cruisers, may have had nothing to do with that historic meeting, but in Provincetown everyone felt that the vessels in the harbor were part of the patrol as they came in and then disappeared.

Many people thought they had seen the President's yacht in the harbor, resting here after making contact with the battleship that was to carry him to the meeting. For the people here, it was so. We were part of this dramatic and fateful encounter. Yet that belief, that identification with the meeting, which might change the whole destiny of our country, seemed unreal, too.

II

There were certain pictures that stand out. The bright New Beach covered with brown vacationers, sailors on shore leave, drifting up and down to see what prospects there were for amusement. Out in the Bay before us maneuvers were going on, the practice of dive bombers, the huge things sweeping down with their incredible noise. This was real as death, but no one believed yet in death. Nor could anyone watch the frightening and beautiful spectacle with skepticism. There it was. We were still living this side of war, but how narrow a margin divided us from it.

All this life of night clubs and beach parties and the summer crowd—these all belonged to the world we were now living in; but the dive bombers and the vessels in the harbor belonged to war. They were preparing for war, they were almost in it, and we would soon be at war, all of us.

Provincetown windows had been shaken time out of mind by the reverberations of naval-target practice. It's nothing new to have windows rattle and to hear a distant sound of artillery hour after hour. Target practice this time was like a war drum when day after day the windows rattled and the houses shook.

The streets were lined with sailors drifting up and down, looking for anything to do, hoping to find a girl, puzzled with Provincetown. "In other places," an officer's wife explained, "the night clubs always tell the enlisted men the place is full, so when they're allowed in, they don't understand and think they're in a dive." In all the Provincetown night clubs but one, enlisted men and officers sat side by side, the sailors from the submarines grousing:

"The crews of every vessel have their wives down here, but we got to get back at night. Why? I've been in the navy fourteen years and I can't get leave to see my wife."

"Huh," said another, "they got an idea it's bad for us to fraternize with civilians. Somebody got an idea that it's going to spoil our morale to fraternize with civilians. Hell!"

"Look around here. There's some guys from destroyers, and there's one from a cruiser. They got shore leave. They're going to see their wives. Look at me, I got to be back in the dinghy at midnight. It gripes you."

What it was you couldn't put your finger on, but something new had happened in the submarine service, some kind of reorganization that kept the old-timers cussing. All sailors ashore crab, but the submarine men crabbed the most. Their mother ship, a grim piece of machinery, sat in the harbor and beside her, in a neat row, the submarines.

You picked up odd pieces of talk. A bunch of sailors ashore in a restaurant, and one of them saying,

"We're the reds!" as one of them gets up and does a burlesque of a Union Square speech. They had a big joke among themselves. It goes on and on and all the other boys listen to them. Then suddenly, from a table where two quiet boys are sitting, comes,

"Agnes Smedley, she was a Communist, wasn't she?"

Some of the boys were as educated as the old Wobblies. They'd read everything. On the other hand, there were a great many who hadn't bothered to read at all. There were boys from the South, from Missouri and Arkansas—sweet, young, and tough. One boy said soberly:

"The *Alabama* she's full of rebels!" He meant Southerners. He came from the John Brown country where the abolitionist question had been so bitter that Southerners are still "rebels" there.

The townspeople were swamped with sailors. The Civilian Defense hastened to give dances. But the sailors groused about the dances too. One dance for the officers had too few girls and too much liquor; the other dances had girls enough but no liquor at all.

They sat in restaurants, grumbling:

"They roll up the sidewalks at ten o'clock. This is a hell of a town to be ashore in."

"Why don't you go to the dance then?"

"Hell, I was to the dance. I danced with a girl older'n God's aunt."

"Well, you can't be in China all the time."

"Hell, no, but you don't need to be in a graveyard neither."

[369]

A few of the sailors enjoyed themselves with the summer people. Fifteen people—eight sailors and seven boys and girls—crowded into a roadster which careened down the street toward the beach.

III

There was more of everything than ever before—more people, packed restaurants, signs on menus, "No more lobster, no more pie," the places eaten out; everybody buying gadgets; traffic blocked on the front street and the back street.

Underneath was a long town of austere Cape Cod houses, and people thinking, "Are we really going to war?" A minority getting ready for an enemy. The incredible nightmare of war an inescapable undercurrent. Most people saying the defense program's a racket. People here, as in other parts of the country, trying to wake up people who are asleep. As elsewhere those fully aware are few in number.

Commander Turnbull is the head of the Civilian Defense. He works day and night as though the Germans were at the door. He, with other army and navy men, has too vivid a memory of what happened in the last war. The submarine at Orleans wasn't a show for them. It was a clear-cut demonstration of our vulnerability. The town is districted off, they know exactly the number of houses in it. Each district has a fire warden.

The ambulance corps has just finished its instruction with Jack Connell. He has turned out a group of experienced women ambulance drivers. The first-aid classes have been meeting with Mr. Perry and Dr. Winslow. Up in Dennis they have just had an all-out rehearsal for an air raid.

Yet it was all shadowboxing. It didn't seem real. There are plenty of people among the solid Provincetown folk who wouldn't accept war as possible. They either wouldn't talk about the war at all or they'd burst into invective about this darn foolishness. From the eastward to the westward were people who were still for "keeping out of war" and who think all this bell ringing and defense work a waste of effort.

True, the boys had been drafted. As usual, more than the average number of Provincetown boys have enlisted without waiting for the draft. Camp Edwards spills its men on leave over the town. The navy swamps it. Well, that's happened before. It doesn't serve to awaken people to danger. There are refugee children here and there to remind one there's a war.

There was a great pother up and down the Cape in collecting money for the flying gift ambulance, the Cape Codder. Its sirens honk up and down perpetually. Many of the relief activities had taken on a social nature. But the unity that everybody talked about hadn't come. It existed mostly on paper and in oratory.

Who was going to awaken the sleepers? No eloquent voices had yet been heard here. There had been no personal appeal to the people. All the speeches on democracy are so many words to most listeners. The master word that would quicken men's hearts had not been spoken. They were not yet willing to die for liberty because they couldn't imagine that anyone could take liberty from them. They listened on the radio to the eternal debates between isolationist and interventionist and became confused.

So Provincetown reflected America. The majority were not isolationists—they were not interested enough to be isolationists. They did not believe in danger. There was no flame and there was no unity. Only the intensity of war's pressure can bring the passion needed to meet this hour.

The President's speech came at the end of summer, and the fishermen and the townspeople discussed it soberly. They realized for a moment that America was nearer to the crisis. Still most people believed that this Civilian Defense was the hooey.

In the fishermen's bar the fishermen seldom listen to the radio now. They used to tune in eagerly when England was attacked. Now the principal front was in Russia, and the war seemed remote.

Yet in spite of all skepticism, everyone felt this summer that we were living in a world that was ending. The life that went on here seemed as unsubstantial as a soap bubble. It might explode any minute. Since everyone felt this, there was something frantic about the summer's gaiety. People acted as they did during prohibition, when they drank as though each drink were the last. People acted as though this were the last summer when we would have as much of everything—all the gasoline and all the food and all the good times.

What's going to happen to us now? If we follow the course of history, each war has meant depression for Provincetown, the people all move away. If there isn't gas, the night clubs will fold up. All the churning of the summer people will stop.

Provincetown may be ready for one of its quick, incredible changes that we have seen so often, where all the activities of the town alter and then vanish completely. The night club and tourist days may go. We may become a naval base and so another town. But the fishermen will still be going out and the weirs will still be bringing in their millions of pounds of fish. For Provincetown as for the whole country our future is a vast question mark.

The one certainty is that Provincetown is in history's path as it has always been.

"MAYFLOWER" ENTERING ye HARBOUR
Sept. 16
1620

GREAT WHA
DA
18

modern "gasoliner"

here are great dunes

RACE POINT LIGHT

P R O V I N C E T O W N

Cape Cod heroes: the Coast Guard

THE HARBOUR

LONG POINT LIGHT

WOOD END LIGHT

"ROSE DOROTHEA"
OF
PROVINCETOWN
SIR THOMAS LIPTON
CUP -- 1907

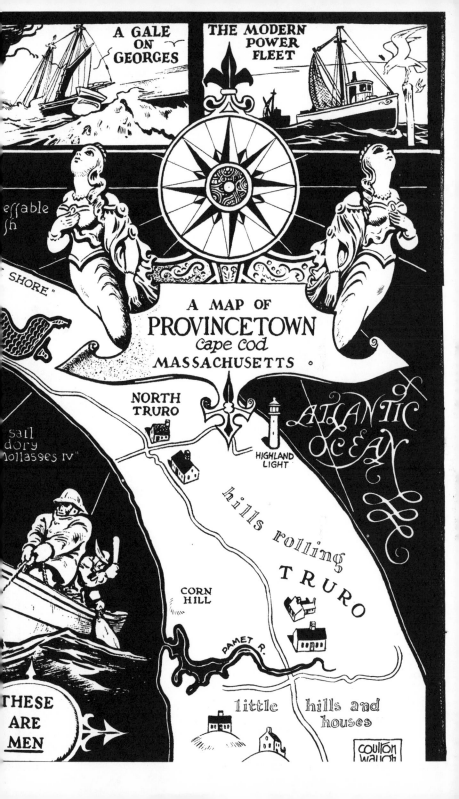